CONTEMPORARY ISSUES IN THE EARLY YEARS

FIFTH EDITION

CONTEMPORARY ISSUES IN THE EARLY YEARS

edited by

GILLIAN PUGH AND BERNADETTE DUFFY

Los Angeles | London | New Delhi
Singapore | Washington DC

First edition published 1992
Second edition published 1996
Third edition published 2001
Fourth edition published 2006
Fifth edition published 2010

SAGE Publications Ltd
1 Oliver's Yard
55 City Road
London EC1Y 1SP

SAGE Publications Inc.
2455 Teller Road
Thousand Oaks, California 91320

SAGE Publications India Pvt Ltd
B 1/I 1 Mohan Cooperative Industrial Area
Mathura Road
New Delhi 110 044

SAGE Publications Asia-Pacific Pte Ltd
33 Pekin Street #02-01
Far East Square
Singapore 048763

Library of Congress Control Number: 2009923277

A catalogue record for this book is available from the British Library

ISBN 978-1-84787-592-1
ISBN 978-1-84787-593-8 (pbk)

Typeset by C&M Digitals Pvt Ltd, Chennai, India
Printed in Great Britain by CPI Antony Rowe, Chippenham, Wiltshire
Printed on paper from sustainable resources

CONTENTS

BIOGRAPHICAL DETAILS OF CONTRIBUTORS

Carol Aubrey is Professor of Early Childhood and Director of Research at the Institute of Education, University of Warwick. She trained as a primary school teacher and educational psychologist and spent a number of years in primary teacher education, with a particular focus on the early years, first at University College Cardiff and then at the University of Durham. Her research interests lie in the policy-to-practice context of early childhood education and care, including multi-agency working, leadership, early learning and development, with an interest in mathematics development and inclusion/special educational needs. She is editor for the *Journal of Early Childhood Research*.

Jacqueline Barnes is Professor of Psychology at the Institute for the Study of Children, Families and Social Issues, Birkbeck, University of London. She has been conducting research pertaining to early years services for 25 years. Most recently she was a co-director of the National Evaluation of Sure Start, director of the 'Right from the Start' evaluation of Home-Start offered in pregnancy and director of the formative evaluation of implementing the Family–Nurse Partnership programme in England.

Kate Billingham is the Project Director for the Family–Nurse Partnership Programme and the Child Health Promotion Programme in the Department of Health. She is a trained paediatric nurse and health visitor. She has held a number of posts in public health and was the Deputy Chief Nursing Officer at the Department of Health prior to becoming the Project Director for the Family–Nurse Partnership programme. She is a visiting Professor at Kings College London and Fellow of the Queens Nursing Institute and the Faculty of Public Health.

Caron Carter is a Senior Lecturer in Early Childhood at Sheffield Hallam University. Prior to her current post, she was an early years teacher and then a deputy headteacher in a nursery and infant school. She is currently studying for a PhD focusing on children's friendships. Her other interests include children's participation and children's literacy.

Tricia David is Emeritus Professor of Education at Canterbury Christ Church University and Honorary Emeritus Professor of Early Childhood Education at the University of Sheffield. She has been involved in the field of Early Childhood Education and research for almost 40 years and considers herself blessed to have worked with international colleagues for much of that time, including participation as rapporteur for the Netherlands in the Organization for Economic Cooperation (OECD) study of Early Childhood Education and Care in 20 countries.

Lucy Draper originally qualified as a teacher and has since worked in a variety of early years settings, as an early years training officer and as a counsellor and group worker with parents. Until recently, she was the Head of Coram Parents Centre, which offers a wide range of parent support and education to families from the King's Cross area of London. She is also involved in the training and supervision of practitioners who work with parents.

Bernadette Duffy originally trained as a teacher and has worked in a wide range of settings over the past 30 years. She is Head of the Thomas Coram Children's Centre in Camden which offers fully integrated care and education for young children in partnership with their parents and local community. Bernadette contributed to the development of the Early Years Foundation Stage framework and is the author of *Supporting Creativity and Imagination in the Early Years* published by the Open University Press. She is National Chair of the British Association for Early Childhood Education and a member of the Department for Children, Schools and Families (DCSF) National Council for Educational Excellence. She was made an OBE in 2005.

Kathy Goouch is Senior Lecturer at Canterbury Christ Church University. She enjoys teaching, researching and writing about babies, young children and their carers and teachers. Her research work particularly focuses on adult–child interactions in play and her doctoral thesis explores teachers' narratives in and about play.

David Hawker has been Director General for Children, Education, Lifelong Learning and Skills for the Welsh Assembly Government since August 2008. Prior to that he was Deputy Chief Executive for Westminster City Council, and previously spent eight years (1999–2007) in Brighton and Hove, first as Director of Education and then as Director of Children's Services. In Brighton and Hove he led the establishment of one of the country's first fully integrated Children's Trusts, and was for a number of years at the forefront of Children's Services reforms in England. He served for two years as national chair of the Association of Directors of Education and Children's Services, before its absorption into the Association of Directors of Children's Services in 2007. He worked originally as a modern languages teacher and his career has covered a number of local authority and central government roles, as well as two examination boards. Internationally he has worked with the British Council and the World Bank on a number of educational reform programmes in Russia, and currently sits on the General Education Board of the Open Society Institute, which sponsors education development programmes around the world. In 2007 he was elected a professor of the College of Teachers.

Gill Haynes   is a consultant in children's services and strategic management. She was the Chief Executive of the National Childminding Association (1993–2005), working closely with government to help deliver high quality, accessible and affordable childcare and early education. Her background includes over 20 years' experience in local government, both as an officer and a councillor, and she is formerly Vice Chair of the Children's Workforce Development Council for England.

Dr Caroline Jones   began her career as a teacher of young children and has since worked in a range of roles with children, parents and professionals. She has been a tutor for over 15 years at the Institute of Education, University of Warwick, where she led the development of the Early Years Foundation Degree. She has contributed to a range of Open University programmes and written chapters on a range of issues including multi-agency working and workforce development. She is author of *Supporting Inclusion in the Early Years*, published by the Open University Press, and co-author with L. Pound of *Leadership and Management in the Early Years: From Principles to Practice*, published by MGraw-Hill. Caroline, a former office for Standards in Education (Ofsted) registered nursery inspector, is Director of a group of early years and childcare settings based on school sites in the Midlands which she established in 1989. She is currently working as an independent educational consultant across the UK and abroad.

Y. Penny Lancaster   is an independent 'young children's participation' advisor and trainer. She was formerly the Director of the successful Coram Family's Listening to Young Children project, which won the Best Education, and Training Project in the 2005 Charity Awards. For the past five years, Penny has delivered a range of Listening to Young Children training courses across the UK to more than 6,000 early years practitioners. She is continuing to deliver this training, but is also now providing an advisory and mentoring service to local authorities in young children's participation. She is also undertaking a new piece of research in young children's participation focusing on 5 to 7 year olds' perspectives of engaging in decision-making in the classroom. Penny is a qualified primary school teacher (New Zealand) and is currently working towards completing her PhD.

Cathy Nutbrown is Professor of Education and Director for Research at the School of Education, University of Sheffield. Her interests are in arts-based learning, inclusive practices, children's rights and the histories of early childhood education. She is author of some 50 publications including *Working with Babies and Children: From Birth to Three* (Sage, 2008); *Early Childhood Education: History, Philosophy and Experience* (Sage, 2008); *Inclusion in the Early Years* (Sage, 2006); and *Threads of Thinking: Young Children Learning and the Role of Education* (Sage, 2006).

Sue Owen is currently Director of the Well-being Department at the National Children's Bureau and was previously Director of the Early Childhood Unit there. In the past she has held a number of posts in the early childhood field including Early Years lead officer for Humberside County Council, Information Officer for the National Childminding Association, Playgroup Adviser for Manchester City Council, and Deputy Director of the Early Years National Training Organisation. Sue's latest book is *Authentic Relationships in Group Care for Infants and Toddlers – RIE Principles into Practice* (co-edited with Stephanie Petrie). Her doctoral dissertation was on the development of professionalism in childminding.

Sacha Powell is a Principal Research Fellow in Education at Canterbury Christ Church University. She works on a wide range of research, evaluation and development projects, several of which have involved collaborations with colleagues in China.

Dame Gillian Pugh retired in 2005 as Chief Executive of the leading children's charity, Coram. She worked previously at the National Children's Bureau where she established and directed the Early Childhood Unit. Gillian has advised governments in the UK and overseas on policy for children and families over the past 30 years and has published widely. She is currently chair of the National Children's Bureau, chair of the Advisory Committee for the Cambridge Primary Review, an adviser to the House of Commons Select Committee for Children's Schools and Families, a visiting professor at the Institute of Education, on the Board of the Training and Development Agency for Schools, a member of the Children's Workforce Development Council and President of the National Childminding Assocation.

Fiona Roberts studied psychology and works as a senior research assistant at the Department of Education, University of Oxford. She is a member of the Families, Early Learning and Literacy research group. Fiona is involved in various early years research projects, including an evaluation of a parenting programme, SPOKES, which aims to help parents support their children's literacy at home. She leads the literacy assessments in the SPOKES reading project.

Mary Robinson   is a senior educational psychologist in the London Borough of Redbridge and is also Assistant Programme Director on the Doctorate in Educational and Child Psychology programme at the University of East London. Prior to her current post, she led the early years team within the educational psychology service in the London Borough of Newham, where she gained experience of the key issues involved in including young children within mainstream education. Mary has a keen interest in fostering collaborative and dynamic assessment of pre-school children with additional needs.

Caron Rudge   has been head of Golden Lane Children's Centre (previously known as Fortune Park Children's Centre) for 13 years, prior to which she headed three early years settings in Islington and Haringey. Fortune Park has been repeatedly used as a source of reference in developing effective learning environments for children up to 3 years of age as well as its extensive work on consulting with and listening to young children and families. Caron is a mother of three children who lives in north London.

Iram Siraj-Blatchford   is Professor of Early Childhood Education at the Institute of Education, University of London. Her recent research projects have included: Evaluation of the Foundation Phase across Wales, and she is principal investigator of the major DCSF 16-year study on Effective Pre-school, Primary and Secondary Education (EPPSE 3–16) project (1997–2013) and of the Effective Pedagogy in the Early Years project. She is working on longitudinal studies as a principal investigator in a number of countries, including Australia and Ireland. She has always been particularly interested in undertaking research which aims to combat disadvantage and to give children and families from these backgrounds a head start. She is a specialist early years adviser to governments and ministers in the UK, where she is conducting reviews of research on child outcomes for the Centre for Effectiveness and Outcomes and advises governments overseas. Iram is the President of the British Association for Early Childhood Education and visiting professor at a number of universities, including Melbourne University and Beijing Normal University. She has published widely.

Kathy Sylva   is Professor of Educational Psychology at the University of Oxford, Department of Education. She is one of the leaders of the DCSF research on Effective Pre-school, Primary and Secondary Education (EPPSE) and on the evaluations of the Graduate Leader Fund and the Early Learning Partnership Project. A dominant theme throughout her work has been the impact of education and care not only on 'academic knowledge' but on children's problem-solving, social skills and dispositions to learn. A related theme in her research is the impact of early interventions on combating social disadvantage and exclusion. She was specialist Adviser to the House of Commons Select Committee on Education in 2000–01 and again in 2005–08. She was awarded an OBE in 2008 for services to children and families.

Helen Wheeler is the Senior Development Officer for Parents, Early Years and Learning (PEAL) based within the Early Childhood Unit at the National Children's Bureau. Helen has many years' experience as a teacher in both infant and nursery schools, most recently working as part of an early years ethnic minority achievement team in the London Borough of Ealing. She has also worked as a home-school tutor, writing courses for and supporting parents educating their children at home.

INTRODUCTION
Bernadette Duffy

Early years practitioners are living in interesting times. From being seen as an optional extra, early years services are now perceived as crucial to achieving many of the government's and wider society's aims. Eliminating child poverty is a key objective and is widely supported and by all major political parties. Early years services are seen as having a vital role in this by improving outcomes for all children, especially the most disadvantaged, and by increasing parental employment and improving parenting. Each of these is important and a challenge to do well – can we really do it all and, if so, where will the resources come from, or are we in danger of spreading our current resources too thinly?

There is no doubt that parental employment does bring children out of poverty. But if that becomes the main rationale for early years services we will introduce practices that increase flexibility to meet work patterns, which may be at the expense of the continuity and consistency that children need. Services for children must reflect family needs and be sufficiently flexible to meet them, but the needs of the child have to take priority. There is also no doubt that high-quality early education leads to improved outcomes for children, especially those who are disadvantaged. However, if we focus on short-term gains and prioritize narrow literacy goals we could be sacrificing long-term achievement. We want services to be of high quality and know that well qualified and well paid staff are key to this. But we also want services to be affordable to parents without requiring ever more public investment.

This dilemma about the priority for early years services is expressed in the lack of agreement about how they are described, which despite the introduction of the *Early Years Foundation Stage* (DfES, 2007) is yet to be resolved. Are early years services about 'childcare', a term which for many is synonymous with putting parents' work before children's needs; or are they about 'early education', a term which can be understood as an early start to formal schooling?

We have made great progress in improving the quality and expanding the quantity of early years services, but are we now be in danger of losing a clear vision and focus on the young child and their needs?

In this, the fifth edition of *Contemporary Issues in the Early Years*, we seek to reflect the achievements and progress that has been made in the early years but also the dilemmas that have arisen and the challenges that need to be addressed. At a time of change and debate about early years services it is even more important that we address the major themes in this book. How can we work together to better meet the needs of young children and their families? How do we ensure that all children have equality of opportunity? How do we use what we know from research and practice to create children's services that truly put the child at the centre?

This book is divided into three sections. Part 1 looks at policy and research, Part 2 addresses putting policy and research into practice and Part 3 explores workforce issues.

The first five chapters focus on policy and research. The *Every Child Matters* (DfES, 2004) agenda is now an accepted part of children's services and Gillian Pugh's and David Hawker's chapters reflect this. In Chapter 1 Gillian charts the development of early years services and reviews the main developments in national policy in recent years. She provides us with a clear understanding of how we have got to where we are, the success we have achieved and the challenges that lie ahead. In Chapter 2 David describes developments in Children's Trust thinking since 2006 and shares one local authority's approach to the development of children's services and children's centres. Chapter 3 looks at the world picture. Tricia David, Sacha Powell and Kathy Goouch provide a valuable insight into the ways early years services are viewed in China and New Zealand, and identify the lessons we can learn from other countries.

Kathy Sylva and Fiona Roberts's chapter looks at quality in early childhood education and the impact of research on policy and practice. They draw on the findings from the Effective Provision of Pre-School and Primary Education Project and present the evidence for long-term effects. The implications of the recent changes to the inspection of early years services are analysed by Caroline Jones in Chapter 5. She describes the new inspection frameworks and asks if they are likely to achieve their aim to improve the quality of provision for children.

In the second part of the book are eight chapters focusing on practice and showing how policies and research are being implemented by practitioners. Penny Lancaster writes the first chapter in this section. She defines what it means to listen to young children within the context of *Every Child Matters*, explores our view of childhood and, drawing on work by Kirklees Early Years Service, shows how practitioners can enable young children to articulate their feelings, experiences and ideas. Chapter 7 is written by Bernadette Duffy and looks at what we mean by the term 'curriculum'. She describes the development, introduction and responses to the Early Years Foundation Stage framework, and, drawing on research and practice, identifies possible areas for curriculum development. In Chapter 8 Cathy Nutbrown and Caron Carter explore the issue of assessment. They discuss the different forms of assessment and the purposes it can be put to. Cathy and Caron highlight the value and visions that need to underpin respectful assessments of young children and describe ways in which early childhood educators can use assessment to understand young children's capabilities and learning. Caron Rudge, in Chapter 9, ensures that the practitioner's voice is heard and shares the development of one children's centre, with all its joys and challenges. She ends by identifying the factors that make a successful children's centre.

Health is increasingly seen as part of early years services rather than as a separate service. In Chapter 10 Kate Billingham and Jacqueline Barnes look at the key role of health in early years services. They provide an overview of health in the early years and identify the issues that need to be addressed when health and other partners work together to promote children's health and well-being.

Diversity, inclusion and learning are the important themes for Iram Siraj-Blatchford's chapter (11) and in it she looks at practitioners' understanding of children's multiple identities. Iram challenges the hidden assumptions which disadvantage children on the grounds of ethnic background, gender or socio-economic class. Mary Robinson picks up these themes in Chapter 12 in relation to children with special needs. She outlines the landmark events for special needs in early years services and argues that there is a growing view that meeting children's special needs is an indivisible part of the children's services agenda. Recent developments and emerging practice in meeting special needs within inclusive settings are also addressed. Many of the authors have included references to the key role of parents as part of their chapter. In Chapter 13 Lucy Draper and Helen Wheeler expand on this theme, drawing on their experiences at the Thomas Coram Centre and with the PEAL project. They explore the ways that parents and practitioners can work together for the benefit of children, parents and practitioners sharing examples of good practice from settings across the country.

Part 3 explores workforce issues. Sue Owen and Gill Haynes discuss the workforce reforms that are currently under way and the professionalization of the early years workforce. They describe the debates about National Vocational Qualifications (NVQs) and the roles of Early Years Professionals and teachers. Sue and Gill end by clearly identifying the changes needed if early years work is to become a career which is valued and recognized by society. Finally, in Chapter 15, Carol Aubrey draws on many years experience of leading and working in multi-agency teams and explores the nature of leaderships and strategies to support leaders.

Most of the contributors to this book are nationally or internationally known for their contribution to the early years debate. All have been actively involved in the research, development of policies and improvements in practice that this book discusses. All share a commitment to the well-being of young children and their families, which comes across strongly in each of their chapters.

The Children's Plan's (DCSF, 2007) stated goal is to make England the best place in the world for children and young people to grow up in. The aim is to put children and young people at the heart of everything the government does. If we are to achieve this we must focus on each child, and their well-being and development has to be the priority. Our task is to ensure that each child is treated as a unique individual who has positive relationships with parents and carers in an enabling environment that promotes their learning and development. We hope this book will support practitioners to play their part in creating such environments.

References

Department for Children, Schools and Families (DCSF) (2007) *The Children's Plan: Building Brighter Futures.* Norwich: TSO.

Department for Education and Skills (DfES) (2004) *Every Child Matters: Change for Children.* Nottingham: DfES Publications.

Department for Education and Skills (DfES) (2007) *Early Years Foundation Stage.* Nottingham: DfES.

PART 1

POLICY AND RESEARCH

CHAPTER 1

THE POLICY AGENDA FOR EARLY CHILDHOOD SERVICES

Gillian Pugh

Chapter Contents

- A brief history
- *Every Child Matters:* a national policy for children and young people
- An integrated strategy for young children and their parents?
- Availability, affordability and sustainability of early years services
- Joined-up services: Sure Start children's centres
- Quality in service provision
- Support for parents – or parents as supporters?
- Staff training and qualifications
- Some challenges

While the nineteenth century was distinguished by the introduction of primary education for all and the twentieth century by the introduction of secondary education for all, so the early part of the twenty-first century should be marked by the introduction of pre-school provision for the under fives and childcare available to all. (Rt Hon. Gordon Brown MP, Chancellor of the Exchequer, 2004 Comprehensive Spending Review)

The past decade has seen considerable developments in the availability and organization of early childhood services. This chapter considers these changes within the context of the broader *Every Child Matters* agenda for children's services and raises a number of issues that are considered further in the chapters that follow.

A brief history

Since the establishment of the first nursery school by Robert Owen, in Scotland in 1816, the development of early education in the UK was until recently remarkably slow by comparison to much of mainland Europe. In 1870, publicly funded education became compulsory at the age of 5 years, but from the earliest days children as young as 2 years were admitted to primary schools. During the course of the twentieth century, successive governments supported the principle of free nursery education but seldom found the resources to fund it. Even with the gradual establishment of nursery schools and, during the 1914–18 war, some public day-care centres, the predominant form of early education in the UK was for 130 years state primary schools. The lack of appropriate provision within the education system led to two parallel developments during the second half of the twentieth century: on the one hand, the emergence during the 1960s through the voluntary sector of the playgroup movement; and, on the other, the growth of full day care to meet the needs of working parents, initially through childminding and, since the 1990s, through the private sector of day nurseries.

This legacy is important in understanding the state of early childhood services at the beginning of the twenty-first century. The second edition of this book, published in 1996, described services in the UK as discretionary, with low levels of public funding compared with mainland Europe, with a heavy reliance on the private and voluntary sectors, with diversity of provision but little choice for parents, lacking in co-ordination between providers from different agencies, and with different services having different aims and purposes, and being used by different client groups – working parents, children 'in need' and parents able to use part-time nurseries (Pugh, 1996).

The levels of concern expressed here were reflected in a number of prestigious national reports published during the 1990s, notably the Rumbold Report *Starting with Quality* (DES, 1990), largely ignored by the government at the time, but very widely used subsequently as the basis for best practice in early years settings. During the 1980s and early 1990s there was a lack of political conviction that young children mattered and a view that children were the private responsibility of their parents. But there were also unclear and conflicting messages about what was required – should an early years policy be most concerned about preparing children for school, or with day care for working parents? Should it provide stimulation for a developing brain, or equal opportunities for women? Was it about cost savings for employers, able to retain staff when they became parents, or about reducing the benefit bill for single parents, enabling them to return to the workforce? Or was prevention the main driver – whether of developmental delay in children or juvenile crime?

The establishment in 1993 of the Early Childhood Education Forum (now known as the Early Childhood Forum) bringing together all the national agencies in the field to speak with a united voice, was one response to the lack of clarity over what a policy for early childhood services should look like. As the Forum gathered strength, with a membership of 45 national organizations by 1998, and as report after report called for an expansion in services and for better co-ordination, the government took action. In 1995 additional funding for the education of 4-year-olds was announced but, controversially, the funding was to be made available to parents through vouchers which could be redeemed in private, voluntary or local authority nurseries. A pilot scheme was rolled out amid mounting criticism, but full implementation was stopped by the election of a Labour government in 1997. Twelve years later the expansion of services for our youngest children has been considerable, and this chapter assesses the extent to which the vision of what was called for during the 1990s has been realized.

Every Child Matters: a national policy for children and young people

The publication in 2003 of the Green Paper *Every Child Matters* (DfES, 2003b) was described by Prime Minister Tony Blair at its launch as the most significant development for children in over 30 years. Although much of the expansion of early childhood services was already under way by 2003, I will briefly describe the bigger picture at this point so that we can see where services for younger children fit into the whole. The Green Paper was initially planned as a response to the report by Lord Laming on the circumstances surrounding the death of Victoria Climbié in 2002. The government remit was to focus on children at risk but, after discussion with many working in the field, the report took prevention as its starting point and accepted the view that to support all children better through well co-ordinated mainstream services was more likely to benefit those in need and at risk than a separate child protection service. Based on a review of relevant research and widespread consultation with professionals and young people, the five key themes of *Every Child Matters* were:

- strong foundations in the early years
- a stronger focus on parenting and families
- earlier interventions and effective protection
- better accountability and integration locally, regionally and nationally
- reform of the workforce.

The overall aim of the Green Paper and the subsequent 2004 Children Act was to improve outcomes for all children and narrow the gap between those who do well and those who do not, through reconfiguring services around children and families. The focus was on entitlements for children through five main (and many subsidiary) outcomes:

- Being healthy – enjoying good physical and mental health and living a healthy lifestyle.
- Staying safe – being protected from harm and neglect.
- Enjoying and achieving – getting the most out of life and developing the skills for adulthood.
- Making a positive contribution – being involved with the community and society and not engaging in antisocial or offending behaviour.
- Economic well-being – not being prevented by economic disadvantage from achieving their full potential in life.

The long-term vision that emerged through the Children Act and the implementation paper *Every Child Matters: Change for Children* (DfES, 2004) was:

- the development of integrated education, health and social care, through children's centres, extended schools and improved services for young people
- better support for parents
- services provided by better qualified staff
- targeted services planned and delivered within a universal context.

At central government level, responsibility for most services for children, young people and families was brought within a single directorate at the Department for Education and Skills (DfES) under the direction of a Minister for Children. The exceptions were children's health, which remained with the Department of Health, although a parallel National Service Framework for children's health was developed (DH and DfES, 2004), and youth justice which remained with the Home Office. *The Children's Plan*, published at the end of 2007 (DCSF, 2007), reinforced the messages of *Every Child Matters*, renamed the DfES the Department for Children, Schools and Families and created a 'dual key' responsibility at ministerial level for health and youth justice. In local areas, the existing directors for social services and education have all been replaced by a director for children's services, and an integrated mechanism for planning and delivering services – a Children's Trust – has been established, although there is still considerable variation in how these are operating. Chapter 2 explores the implications of these changes in one local authority and examines integration in the delivery of services. There is also a common assessment framework, an integrated workforce strategy and a common core of training (see Chapter 14), an integrated inspection framework (see Chapter 5) and a new curriculum framework (see Chapter 7). It is a huge and ambitious agenda.

An integrated strategy for young children and their parents?

Throughout three Labour administrations there has been a commitment from both Prime Ministers and Chancellors to eliminating child poverty by 2020. It is this commitment that has driven the increase of childcare as a means of enabling women to return to work and thus increase family income, together with the substantial body of research which has underpinned the importance of high-quality early learning. Research studies include new thinking about the contribution of early learning to the development of the brain, revisiting long-established studies on early attachments between children and their parents and carers (see, for example, Gerhardt, 2004), and the longitudinal EPPE study (Sylva et al., 2004, and Chapter 4), as well as research into parenting and parental involvement (see Chapter 13).

The combination of the anti-poverty agenda driving the increases in 'day care', and the research into child development and children's learning driving the 'education' agenda has led to an increase in provision but also to tensions between increasing the quantity of provision while ensuring that high quality is maintained.

The policy agenda since 1997 has been considerable:

- The initial National Childcare Strategy (DfEE, 1998), which included an expansion of nursery education and childcare from birth to 14, together with the establishment of Sure Start local programmes and early excellence centres, and a programme of neighbourhood nurseries.
- The 10-year childcare strategy, *Choice for Parents, the Best Start for Children* (HMT, 2004) which aimed to increase the accessibility of good quality affordable childcare and other support for parents. It included extending paid maternity leave (nine months from April 2007 and 12 months by 2010); increasing the hours of free nursery education from 12.5 to 15 per week; reforming childcare regulation and inspection; reforming the career and training structure of the early years workforce; and improving the childcare part of the Working Tax Credit to help low- and middle-income families with childcare costs.
- The 2006 Childcare Act. This not only brings together earlier provision in order to create some 3,000 children's centres, but also places a duty on local authorities to secure sufficient childcare for working parents, and to ensure services are integrated. Local authorities are also required to improve outcomes for children and to narrow the gap between those who do well and those who do not.
- The establishment of the Early Years Foundation Stage, introduced in 2008 to create a framework from birth to the end of reception year (DfES, 2007).
- A national qualifications and training framework for the early years.

- An integrated inspection service for all early years services within Ofsted.
- A recognition that services must meet the needs of parents as well as children. As *The Children's Plan* states 'government does not bring up children – parents do – so government needs to do more to back parents and families' (DCSF, 2007: 5).

The following sections look at some of these developments in more detail.

Availability, affordability and sustainability of early years services

From lagging well behind our European neighbours in the early 1990s, a recent OECD report finds that the UK is now the highest spender on pre-primary services in Europe (OECD, 2008). Figures from the National Audit Office (NAO, 2004) showed that the 10-year childcare strategy (HMT, 2004) was on course to quadruple expenditure between 1997 and 2008 from £1.1 billion to £4.4 billion. Nursery education – currently available for 12.5 hours a week in term time, but increasing to 15 hours by 2010 and 20 hours in due course – is free and is now accessed by 92 per cent of 3-year-olds and 97 per cent of 4-year-olds (DCSF, 2008a). Attendance at day-care provision for 2-year-olds has now increased to 18 per cent.

The public funding for these places is available to nursery and primary schools in the statutory sector, as well as to private and voluntary sector nurseries so long as they meet nationally approved standards. Currently one-third of childcare and early years places are in maintained schools, and two-thirds in the private and voluntary sectors; of just under 2.5 million places in childcare and early years, some 1.6 million are in the private and voluntary sector and 870,000 in nursery and primary schools.

Despite this very considerable additional expenditure, parents still make the major financial contribution to the cost of services, particularly before and after the free nursery education, during holidays, and all provision for children under 3. Affordability remains a key problem, with families spending on average 11 per cent of their income on childcare, and lone parents and low-income families spending even higher proportions (16 per cent and 20 per cent respectively) (Hoxhallari et al., 2007). Working Tax Credit (WTC), introduced in 1998 as childcare tax credit, was intended to assist low-income families with up to 70 per cent of their childcare costs. However, the take-up has been low and, even for those who do claim, the amount received still does not cover the actual cost of a place, despite increases in funding. The Treasury is currently reviewing the support that is available for childcare via WTC and considering what is an appropriate balance between funding supply (the services) and demand (the parents). The precarious nature of the funding and of parents' ability to pay creates challenges for nurseries in the private and voluntary sectors, and in 2007 over half the full day-care providers within children's centres made a loss (DCSF, 2008b).

Joined-up services: Sure Start children's centres

It is clear from the official figures quoted above that government still sees a separation between childcare (mainly in the private and voluntary sector) and early education or early years (mainly in the maintained sector). There are, however, continuing attempts to create provision that integrates care and education – a task that would be eased if a satisfactory term could be found to describe this 'educare' provision. An early example was the targeted community-based Sure Start programme, originally established in 1998 with £540 million to fund 250 local programmes covering 150,000 children. The government official responsible for the programme described Sure Start as:

> a radical cross-departmental strategy to raise the physical, social, emotional and intellectual status of young children through improved services. It is targeted at children under four and their families in areas of high need. It is part of the Government's policy to prevent social exclusion and aims to improve the life chances of younger children through better access to early education and play, health services for children and parents, family support and advice on nurturing. It will be locally led and locally delivered, but will be based on evidence from the UK and elsewhere on 'what works' in terms of improving life chances for children and their parents. (Glass, 1999: 257)

A substantial evaluation programme was commissioned, and even before the ink was dry on the contract the scheme was expanded to 520 communities. Sure Start local programmes were enormously popular with local parents and, although the first major evaluation report showed – not surprisingly – modest outcomes (NESS, 2005), three years later the programme was found to be improving the life chances of children in poor families in a number of key areas (NESS, 2008). It will be difficult to continue to evaluate the original concept, however, as the goalposts were moved yet again, with further expansion of the Sure Start concept but through the establishment of children's centres rather than through separate Sure Start schemes (HMT, 2004). While there was a welcome for the expansion of the concept, there was some concern that the same level of funding would be spread over a wider area much more thinly; the House of Commons Education Select Committee (2005), for example, criticized the government for making significant changes before the evidence was available.

The concept of children's centres, as referred to above, is not a new one, and indeed goes back to the vision of Robert Owen in the early 1880s and the work of the McMillan sisters in the early 1900s. The first combined nursery centre in more recent times opened in 1971, and since then there have been many calls for these integrated centres to become the model for early years provision (see Makins, 1997; Pugh, 1994). The government's 'early excellence centre' programme was launched in 1997 to encourage the development of centres that would provide integrated care and education for children, a range of support services for parents, and access to adult education and training. Most of the centres that were awarded early excellence status were not new centres, but were able to add to their existing provision and take on a training and dissemination role. Preliminary evaluation of the first 60 such centres, which include Thomas Coram (see Chapters 7 and 13) and Fortune Park (see Chapter 9) suggested substantial benefits for children, families and the wider community through the bringing together of a range of services that met families' needs without the stigma attached to specialist provision (Bertram et al., 2002).

In 2003 the government changed direction again, perhaps concerned at the cost of early excellence centres, and announced a children's centres programme, building on early excellence centres, neighbourhood nurseries and local Sure Start schemes, through a promise of a centre in the 20 per cent most disadvantaged communities. Children's centres are less generously funded than early excellence centres, but they do have an additional emphasis on health, being required to provide a base for midwives, health visitors, and speech and language therapists (see Chapter 10), as well as information and support for parents, training and support for childcare workers and strong links with Job Centre Plus. The 10-year childcare strategy went further and promised 2,500 children's centres by 2008 and 3,500 by 2010 (HMT, 2004) and the programme is already ahead of schedule with almost 3,000 children's centres open by the end of 2008.

Quality in service provision

Despite the arguments in the Rumbold Report (DES, 1990) of the importance of the context of learning and the process of learning – the way in which children acquire the disposition to learn – there were widespread concerns at the end of the 1990s that the National Curriculum and the national literacy and numeracy strategies were leading to pressure to formalize education at the earliest opportunity. It was therefore with some enthusiasm that working parties of early years experts developed both the *Curriculum Guidance for the Foundation Stage* (DfEE/QCA, 2000) for children aged 3 to 5, and *Birth to Three Matters* (DfES, 2003a), a framework for all practitioners working with children under 3. Both of these documents were based upon clear and unambiguous statements of the principles which should underpin both learning and teaching, and these principles have subsequently informed the single *Early Years Foundation Stage* (EYFS) Framework, which became statutory in all early years settings in September 2008 (DfES, 2007). The EYFS creates, for the first time, a statutory commitment to play-based developmentally appropriate care and education for children between birth and 5 years of age, together with a regulatory framework aimed at raising quality in all settings and among all providers. It recognizes the central contribution that parents make to their children's development, and specifies the integration of childcare, education and – where possible – health services. Perhaps most importantly it is based on four key principles: every child as a competent learner from birth; the importance of loving and secure relationships with parents and/or a key person; the role of the environment in supporting and extending children's development and learning; and children develop and learn in different ways and at different rates and all areas of learning and development are equally important and interconnected (DfES, 2007: 9).

The Childcare Act 2006 provides for the three EYFS elements – the knowledge, skills and understanding which young children should have acquired by the end of the academic year in which they reach the age of 5 (the early learning goals), the educational programmes, and the assessment arrangements. The six areas of learning are broad based and interdependent and are to be delivered through 'planned, purposeful play, with a balance of adult-let and child-initiated activities'. This is described further in Chapter 7.

The EPPE research noted above, commissioned by government to inform its policy-making, has played a key role in ensuring that, despite the requirement to expand provision as quickly as possible, the needs of children are not lost. Key findings have been that the best quality has been found in settings in the maintained sector which integrate care and education, and there is high correlation between well-qualified staff and better outcomes for children, with quality indicators including warm interactive relationships and a good proportion of trained teachers on the staff (Sylva et al., 2004; see also Chapter 4). These findings have been reinforced by the Millennium Cohort Study (Mathers et al., 2007) and by the evaluation of the Neighbourhood Nursery Initiative (Smith et al., 2007). They are also reflected in the most recent Ofsted report, which found that while 98 per cent of early education settings were satisfactory or better (with 65 per cent good or outstanding) this was compared to only 65 per cent of day-care settings (Ofsted, 2008).

Support for parents – or parents as supporters?

A recognition of the need for greater support for parents has featured strongly in recent government policy, from the Green Paper *Supporting Families* (Home Office, 1998), through the establishment of Sure Start programmes, and *Every Child Matters* to *The Children's Plan*. Acknowledgement of the importance of the relationships between parents and their children, and a recognition that bringing up children is a challenging and sometimes difficult task for which help should be universally available before things start to go wrong (see Pugh et al., 1994), is finally leading to the establishment of a wider range of services, from informal through to the more structured parenting programmes (see Chapter 13). However, the current emphasis on improving outcomes for children has also reinforced the concept of parents as their children's first educators. Pulling together a wide body of research, Desforges and Abouchaar (2003) confirm the view that parental involvement in schools and early years settings, and above all the educational environment of the home, have a positive effect on children's achievement and adjustment. At its best this is building on partnerships between parents and professionals that have been central to good early years provision for many years, as for example in the PEAL project described in Chapter 13. But there is a danger that an instrumentalist view of parents as the key to better behaved and more highly achieving children can also lead to undue pressure on parents at a time when they are also under pressure to return to paid employment.

Staff training and qualifications

As the EPPE research notes, the qualifications of the staff are a critical ingredient in securing good outcomes for children, and yet the early years sector has always suffered from low levels of qualified staff and of pay. The government workforce strategy (DfES, 2005) and the Children's Workforce Development Council (CWDC) quite rightly see the early years as a high priority and have set a target of one graduate in every group setting by 2015 (two in disadvantaged areas) and by establishing the new Early Years Professional (EYP) status. Although the qualifications levels of early years practitioners are improving, there are still only 65 per cent of childcare staff and 79 per cent of early years staff in maintained schools with at least a level 3 qualification, and only 11 per cent of the workforce are qualified at level 6 (graduate level) or above (DCSF, 2008b). Staff across the sector are still seen as having low status, and even within the teaching profession early years teachers are seen as of lower status than secondary school teachers.

There is an urgent need for a graduate workforce, with a range of qualifications and experience, and with teachers playing a key role in curriculum leadership. The new graduate-level Early Years Professional status, being rolled out by the CWDC, has been welcomed by some, although there is concern that funding is at present only available for EYPs to work in the private and voluntary sectors. There is also continuing lack of clarity over how the new EYP relates to qualified teachers, both in terms of their roles and in relation to differentials in pay, and it is difficult to see the rationale for two graduate-level practitioners rather than one. The current training of early childhood teachers is also of concern, for it is not well suited to the multi-agency role of children's centres, nor does it encompass the development and learning needs of children under 3. There are thus considerable challenges in equipping the early years workforce with the skills required to deliver the services that are needed, and the new qualifications and career structure that the workforce strategy envisages will require considerable additional expenditure if it is to deliver a high-quality workforce (for further discussion see Chapter 14).

Some challenges

The achievements since 1997 are remarkable, and there is much to applaud in both the expansion of services and the attempts to improve quality across all sectors. But a number of challenges remain.

The first is one of sustainability and affordability, and of whether sufficient public funding can be secured to realize the very ambitious programme outlined in the 10-year childcare strategy. It is already evident that, with the exception of the 15 hours a week of 'nursery education' for 3- and 4-year-olds, the move towards a universal entitlement for integrated care and education for all children is heavily dependent on parental purchasing power and on their subsidizing a service that is provided largely through the voluntary and private sectors. The Childcare Act required additional services but provided no additional funding, and the promise of a children's centre in every community could mean a 'virtual' centre in many areas, with little provision beyond what is currently available.

The challenges of recruiting, training and remunerating a workforce fit for the early years services of the future are also considerable, both in terms of front-line staff but equally importantly for the leaders, the heads of services and centres who will have to drive the agenda forward. There is also the issue of pay. As a recent report points out, while there is now a clearer framework for early years qualifications and greater opportunities for training, the workforce will not attract or retain high-calibre staff unless they can earn comparable wages to the other professionals they are working alongside (Daycare Trust and TUC, 2008).

The second challenge is to ask where early years services fit within the overall pattern of provision for children, and particularly how they relate to schools – what could be described as the 'L-shaped dilemma'. As the horizontal at the foot of the L (all services for children under 5) becomes greater in number and better integrated, and the extent of the funding and staffing challenge becomes more apparent, the question arises as to whether early years services are the first part of the education system (the upright of the L, going from 0 to 19) or part of a completely different system. Although most 3- and 4-year-olds are actually in nursery or reception classes of primary schools, the government describes early years settings as either 'childcare' or 'early years provision'. The Children's Workforce Development Council is responsible for the overall strategy for recruitment, retention and training of early years workers who are not teachers, while the Training and Development Agency is responsible for teachers, including early years teachers. If the Early Years Foundation Stage is to be really effective, I would argue that it should be revised to cover the years from birth (or whenever a child starts in out-of-home care) to 6 years, including both reception and Year 1 in primary school, and that this should be seen as the first stage of the education system.

This proposal does not, however, assume that the current emphasis on preparing children for school is appropriate. A far more important question, in my view, is to ask whether schools are ready for children. We need to pay more attention to how children learn, and the role of schools overall in promoting learning, if early education is to be effective. We also need to recognize how much of what is best in the early years is also the foundation stone for the *Every Child Matters* agenda – a curriculum which places emphasis on personal, social and emotional as well as cognitive development, and children's centres in which well-trained staff from different professional backgrounds work well together and in which parents are closely involved.

Is it possible to devise a policy that meet the needs of both parents and children? Many parents currently feel torn by the dual messages coming out of government – return to work in order to earn your way out of poverty, on the one hand, but parenting is the most important role that you will play and your child's future depends on the quality of your relationship, on the other. Balancing work and family life is a challenge for parents of children of all ages, but is particularly acute for parents of young children.

As the 10-year childcare strategy continues to roll out, it will be important to ensure that quality of service provision is maintained as the quantity increases, that children's needs remain paramount, and that parents really do feel that they have choice.

 Points for discussion

- How do you think Children's Trusts are going to be able to increase the availability of day care without additional public funding?
- What further measures would improve the integration of care and education in early years settings?
- Has government struck the right balance between parents being encouraged to return to work and caring for their young children?

 Further reading

These five publications provide the policy context within which services for young children and families have been developed in England since the turn of the century.

Department for Children, Schools and Families (2007) *The Children's Plan: Building Brighter Futures*. Norwich: TSO.

Department for Education and Skills (2003) *Every Child Matters*. Norwich: TSO.

Department for Education and Skills (2004) *Every Child Matters: Change for Children*. Nottingham: DfES Publications.

Department for Education and Skills (2007) *Early Years Foundation Stage: Setting the Standards for Learning, Development and Care for Children from Birth to Five*. Nottingham: DfES publications.

HM Treasury (2004) *Choice for Parents, the Best Start for Children: A Ten Year Strategy for Childcare*. London: TSO.

References

Bertram, T., Pascal, C., Bokhari, S., Gasper, M. and Holtermann, S. (2002) *Early Excellence Centre Pilot Programme*. DfES Research Brief RB 361. London: HMSO.

Daycare Trust and Trades Union Congress (TUC) (2008) *Raising the Bar: What Next for the Early Childhood Education and Care Workforce?* London: Daycare Trust.

Department for Children, Schools and Families (DCSF) (2007) *The Children's Plan: Building Brighter Futures*. Norwich: TSO.

Department for Children, Schools and Families (DCSF) (2008a) *Provision for Children Under Five Years of Age in England: January 2008.* Statistical First Release. London: DCSF.

Department for Children, Schools and Families (DCSF) (2008b) *Childcare and Early Years Providers Survey 2007.* London: DCSF.

Department for Education and Employment (DfEE) (1998) *Meeting the Childcare Challenge.* London: HMSO.

Department for Education and Employment/Qualifications and Curriculum Authority (DfEE/QCA) (2000) *Curriculum Guidance for the Foundation Stage.* London: Qualifications and Curriculum Authority.

Department for Education and Skills (DfES) (2003a) *Birth to Three Matters.* London: HMSO.

Department for Education and Skills (DfES) (2003b) *Every Child Matters.* Norwich: TSO.

Department for Education and Skills (DfES) (2004) *Every Child Matters: Change for Children.* Nottingham: DfES Publications.

Department for Education and Skills (DfES) (2005) *Children's Workforce Strategy.* Nottingham: DfES Publications.

Department for Education and Skills (DfES) (2007) *Early Years Foundation Stage.* Nottingham: DfES.

Department of Education and Science (DES) (1990) *Starting with Quality: Report of the Committee of Enquiry into the Quality of Education Experience Offered to Three and Four Year Olds.* Rumbold Report. London: HMSO.

Department of Health (DH) and Department for Education and Skills (DfES) (2004) *National Service Framework for Children, Young People and Maternity Services.* London: DH Publications.

Desforges, C. and Abouchaar, A. (2003) *The Impact of Parent Involvement, Parent Support and Family Education on Pupil Achievement and Adjustment: A Literature Review.* Research Report 433. London: DfES Publications.

Gerhardt, S. (2004) *Why Love Matters: How Affection Shapes a Baby's Brain.* London: Brunner-Routledge

Glass, N. (1999) 'Sure Start: the development of an early intervention programme for young children in the UK', *Children & Society*, 13(4): 257–65.

Her Majesty's Treasury (HMT) (2004) *Choice for Parents, the Best Start for Children: A Ten Year Strategy for Childcare.* London: TSO.

Home Office (1998) *Supporting Families.* London: Home Office.

House of Commons Education Select Committee (2005) *Every Child Matters: 9th Report of Session 2004–5.* London: TSO.

Hoxhallari, L., Connolly, A. and Lyon, N. (2007) *Families with Children in Britain: Findings from the the 2005 Families and Children Study (FACS).* DWP Research Report 424. London: DWP.

Makins, V. (1997) *Not Just a Nursery: Multi-agency Early Years Centres in Action.* London: National Children's Bureau.

Mathers, S., Sylva, K. and Joshi, H. (2007) *Quality of Childcare Settings in the Millenium Cohort Study.* DCSF SSU/2007/FR/025. London: DCSF.

National Audit Office (2004) *Early Years: Progress in Developing High Quality Childcare and Early Education Accessible to All.* London: HMSO.

NESS (2005) *Early Impacts of Sure Start Local Programmes on Children and Families.* Report 013. London: DfES.

NESS (2008) *The Impact of Sure Start Local Programmes on Three Year Olds and Their Families.* Report 027. Nottingham: DfES.

Office for Standards in Education (Ofsted) (2008) *Early Years: Leading to Excellence. Review of Childcare and Early Education Provision 2005–2008.* London: Ofsted.

Organization for Economic Cooperation and Development (OECD) (2008) *Education at a Glance.* Paris: OECD.

Pugh, G. (1994) 'Born to learn', *Times Educational Supplement,* 11 November.

Pugh, G. (ed.) (1996) *Contemporary Issues in the Early Years.* 2nd edn. London: Paul Chapman Publishing.

Pugh, G., De'Ath, E. and Smith, C. (1994) *Confident Parents, Confident Children.* London: National Children's Bureau.

Smith, T., Smith, G., Coxon, K. and Sigala, M. (2007) *National Evaluation of the Neighbourhood Nurseries Initiative.* DCSF SSU/2007/FR 024. London: DCSF.

Sylva, K., Melhuish, E., Sammons, P., Siraj-Blatchford, I. and Taggart, B. (2004) *The Final Report: Effective Pre-School Education.* Technical Paper 12. London: Institute of Education and DfES.

CHAPTER 2

CHILDREN'S TRUSTS AND EARLY YEARS SERVICES – INTEGRATION IN ACTION

David Hawker

Chapter Contents

- Developments in Children's Trust thinking since 2006
- How Brighton and Hove has consolidated and moved on
- A model for integrated children's centres that works
- Key challenges updated

The previous edition of this book described the state of play as it was in 2006 for Children's Trusts nationally in England, and locally in Brighton and Hove (Hawker, 2006). Developments since then have been significant, and this chapter presents another snapshot of the same picture, three years on.

At national level, the three most important influences on the development of Children's Trusts since 2006 have been the establishment of the new Whitehall Department for Children, Schools and Families in June 2007, the publication of the first national Children's Plan for England in November 2007 (DCSF, 2007a), and the issuing of revised statutory guidance on the Duty to Co-operate (including proposed new legislation) in November 2008 (DCSF, 2008).

Government thinking therefore now assumes that the integrated children's services model foreshadowed in *Every Child Matters* (DfES, 2003) and the 2004

Children Act, is in place (or close to being in place) in every local authority in England. Moreover, local areas are now assumed to be working towards the fully integrated inter-agency working on the ground, as set out in the 2005 DfES guidance on the 'Children's Trust in action' (DfES, 2005). By and large this is true, even though implementation is acknowledged to have been somewhat patchy to date (Audit Commission, 2008; DCSF, 2007a).

Overall, the picture is still very mixed, and in that sense the jury is still out over what a fully integrated Children's Trust will look like in the future. However, in local developments like Brighton and Hove, and in the national lead being taken with increasing confidence by the DCSF, we are starting to see a clear model emerge which is now recognizably consistent, despite every area being slightly different because of different local circumstances.

The key thing is that a local Children's Trust, when successfully implemented, provides the best possible environment for fully integrated early years provision. As I shall describe in this chapter, the decisions taken by Brighton and Hove in setting up its Children's Trust have had a profound impact on the way early years provision is organized there, and this in turn has important implications for national policy.

The Children and Young People's Trust in Brighton and Hove since 2005

The origins of Brighton and Hove's Children and Young People's Trust lie in a decision taken in early 2002 to create a children's services department bringing together education with children's social care in one of the first such ventures in the country. When the opportunity to become a Children's Trust pathfinder arose the following year, Brighton and Hove was well placed to respond, on the basis of a vision for a seamless service covering health, education, social care, childcare and youth. The pathfinder Children's Trust deliberately took a whole-system approach, and recognized early on that organizational merger was the best way forward locally to achieve the cultural changes required to create this seamless service. The Children's Trust pathfinder in Brighton and Hove became one of a small minority taking this approach. The first two years were spent building consensus around this new model, developing a commissioning strategy and responding to a large number of related government initiatives, including the development of children's centres, integrated youth support services, a comprehensive childhood and adolescent mental health service, extended schools, play, childcare and community focused services, all in the context of a developing Children's Trust governance structure. By late 2005 the consensus locally was sufficiently strong for the local authority and the local National Health Service (NHS) to take the next step and set up the Children and Young People's Trust as a single organizational entity under the Director of Children's Services. The story of this development is told in more detail in the 2006 edition of this book (Hawker, 2006).

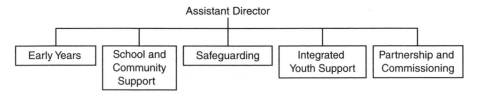

Figure 2.1   Brighton and Hove area team structure

My own role as Director of Children's Services in Brighton and Hove came to an end in late 2007. By then we had completed an ambitious structural and cultural change programme which brought together 1,000 local authority and 200 NHS staff into a single organization, and simultaneously redesigned the service into three area-based, multidisciplinary teams. The results of the change in terms of service benefits were already starting to show by that stage, and by mid-2008 (after I left) the evidence for these benefits had become both quantifiable and sustained in terms of some of the key performance indicators.

Each of the three area-based teams is led by an assistant director, and comprises four sub-teams: Early Years; School and Community Support; Safeguarding; and Integrated Youth Support, together with a smaller team responsible for commissioning and partnership building (Figure 2.1). The leadership of the sub-teams corresponds to their respective principal functions, with health visitors taking the lead in the early years teams, educational psychologists in the school and community support teams, social workers in the safeguarding teams, and youth workers in the integrated young people's teams. In each of the three geographical areas, the team leaders work together with the partnership and commissioning manager, and with the various front line service providers (including schools) to provide overall leadership to the area.

The key to making the structure work was to ensure that all service provision was either managed or brokered through the area teams (so that there was no 'alternative reality'), and that the professional supervision and clinical governance arrangements were sound (so that all the professional groups involved felt safe and supported in their work). Needless to say, there were plenty of voices arguing that their particular profession needed special treatment, or was too small to be disaggregated into area teams. Nearly all of this was recognized as special pleading. It was not dismissed out of hand – there were serious debates about the issues – but finally, virtually all the professional groups accepted the logic of the new arrangements from a service perspective, and were reassured by the safeguards being put in place for their professional practice. The upshot was a significant gain in collegiality, without any loss of professional identity. In terms of marrying together the NHS culture with the local government culture, the old arguments became largely redundant in the face of the new reality of children's services.

Thus it was that the structural change in Brighton and Hove, which started controversially as the local authority's response to *Every Child Matters* (at a time when the received wisdom was that structural change was not the answer), became the principal driver for the cultural change which has resulted in the transformation of the old services into a fully fledged Children's Trust.

In late 2006, as the organizational changes were starting to take effect, the service leaders in Brighton and Hove realized that they needed some very clear benchmarks against which their success (or otherwise) needed to be measured. Three 'super indicators' were chosen to measure the success of the new service – numbers of children in the care system, numbers of pupils excluded from school, and numbers of young people not in education, training or employment. By mid-2008 the area had seen a significant and sustained downward trend in all three figures (see Table 2.1). The key factor was that the area teams adopted a high-level casework approach, in which every family is known in detail by all of them, so there is much more opportunity to work together to meet needs, plan more strategically and achieve better coherence with the various front line agencies. Pressure on the social care teams, which had previously been intense, reduced markedly, and engagement by schools increased dramatically. In terms of workforce development, the new model of professional supervision, which works in a multidisciplinary context across all the sectors, and the new clinical and service governance arrangements which underpin professional practice, have enabled all the statutory functions to be fulfilled safely within a fully integrated structure.

Table 2.1   Trends in Brighton and Hove

	2006	2007	2008
Looked after children	403	393	372
Young people not in education, employment or training	10.85%	9.24%	8%
Fixed term exclusions	–	2,470	2,220

Brighton and Hove has very consciously adopted a 'whole system' approach to developing the new service, with the result that it is in line with the mainstreamed model envisaged by the revised DCSF guidance (DCSF, 2008). It is a fully integrated structure which operates under both local authority and NHS governance; it fully includes youth justice and schools in its governance and organizational arrangements, and it has the mechanisms at both city and locality level for involving third-sector providers, as well as parents, children and young people, in the decision-making processes. There is no longer a local authority children's department as such – there is only a Children's Trust, renamed the Children and Young People's Trust after consultation with young people in 2006.

The evidence so far is that, while being far from plain sailing in terms of implementation, this whole-system model really does work in practice and can produce better outcomes for children.

The Brighton and Hove early years model

The decision to go down a full integration route was taken partly in response to a large-scale consultation with parents over early years services (see Hawker, 2006). It was clearly illogical to advocate for a seamless experience for families and children without redesigning the service on that basis. The new service was built up from first principles, consciously designed around the needs of children, and deliberately breaking down the silos of health, social support, education and childcare which characterized the previous organizational structures. No apology was made for engaging in this wholesale structural change, because it was firmly believed that the cultural shifts which *Every Child Matters* demanded, particularly in terms of joint working between local authorities and the NHS, could only be achieved if there was an imperative to do so via structural change. But the decision to do so could be tracked back directly to what parents and children themselves said about the kind of services they wanted, and to an analysis of their experiences under the pre-existing 'partnership' model.

Inevitably it also had profound implications for the design of those early years services. Three decisions stand out as having been particularly crucial.

First, it was recognized that health visitors were the predominant universal service for children aged from birth to 3 and their families, so early years services needed to be built around their role. This meant moving them from the general practitioner (GP) practices where most of them had been based, into the children's centres, as managers and co-ordinators as well as practitioners. It also meant merging their management structures with the management structures of the children's centres.

Second, the targeting of children's centres in the most deprived areas was felt to be an imperfect response to a situation where 60 per cent of deprived families lived outside the most deprived areas. Hence, what was needed was a service with universal reach and access to targeted provision based on need rather than locality. This determined the way in which children's centres were planned across the city.

Third, the whole system philosophy which underpinned the Brighton and Hove model as a whole meant that, while the early years sector involves a relatively large number of providers, as it does everywhere, the management and leadership of the children's centres themselves, and the commissioning and co-ordination of services, lies within the Children's Trust organizational structure and is not contracted out to partner organizations. Third-sector organizations are involved in providing some of the services, but the core offer is all under the unitary management structure of the Children and Young People's

Trust. This decision deliberately and effectively removed any excuse there might have been for problems with the integration, co-ordination or targeting of services.

Brighton and Hove's response to the 2006 Childcare Act

The children's centres model which emerged from this process allowed Brighton and Hove to respond to the requirements of the 2006 Childcare Act with typical robustness. The 'Early Years Outcomes Duty' set out in sections 1–4 in the Act places a duty on English local authorities working with their NHS and Jobcentre Plus partners, to improve the five *Every Child Matters* outcomes of all young children in their area and to reduce inequalities between them through integrated early childhood services. The aim of the Act was to ensure that children's centres are seen as an important and permanent feature of children's services – not just another time limited initiative.

Brighton and Hove had already designed its early years provision based around geographical clusters, on a 'hub and gateway' model, and by April 2008 all 14 children's centres planned for Phases 1 and 2 of the programme were in place. In developing Phase 3 centres the local area took the view that, as they had effectively already achieved universal coverage of the area, there was a need for additional gateway centres in only three of the more isolated neighbourhoods, and even these would be built within the existing infrastructure rather than separate from it. Children's centres throughout the city are thus viewed not as separate entities but as venues for a city-wide universal early years service.

Then, in order to channel as much of the resource as possible into the front line, the decision was taken not to comply with the government's recommended management structure, which was felt to be too top heavy, but to have a single management team responsible for several centres. A typical early years team management structure is shown at Figure 2.2.

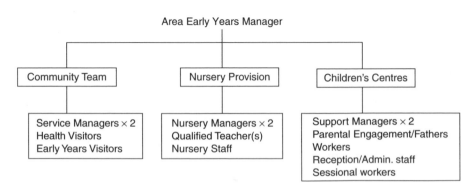

Figure 2.2   Brighton and Hove early years area team structure

Similarly, in terms of governance, a decision was made to create only six advisory boards across the city – one for each cluster rather than one for each centre. The local area has always been acutely conscious of the need to manage its affairs efficiently, which in an integrated service can sometimes be less than straightforward.

The net effect is an organizational structure able to deliver a tightly focused and well co-ordinated service, which is designed to be sustainable after the first flush of enthusiasm (and investment) has passed. Brighton and Hove has been very careful not to overreach itself by being too ambitious in its children's centres, and has been helped in this by some salutary experiences over the difficulty of providing sustainable childcare in the poorer areas of the city in Phase 1 children's centres. To date, none of the nursery provision in these areas has proved to be financially viable without some subsidy, even when it is successful, oversubscribed and socially mixed. So, in order to sustain the long-term provision, some ongoing subsidy has to be factored into the planning. Accordingly, the policy on children's centres has been deliberately cautious in terms of management, governance and other overheads, so that the services can be provided as efficiently as possible. In the less deprived areas the city has a vibrant private sector market for childcare which has expanded over the past few years. Because of this a decision was taken not to create any new childcare places in Phase 2 or Phase 3 children's centres. Instead the centres work with existing providers.

The results are undeniably impressive. The system is set up so that health visitors see every baby born, and make sure that there is a family health plan in place for every family, thus fulfilling the requirement of the child health promotion programme. The health visitors have assumed management responsibility for the home-visiting service (formerly called 'Playlink') which was part of the original social care provision, and are therefore able to target this service to those families where it is most needed, while reserving their own intensive involvement for families at greatest risk. This system ensures that every family is known to their local children's centre, and that both the universal offer and the targeted support can be effectively deployed. The fact that the children's centre clusters are based around the same organizational boundaries, and are managed by the same operational head, as the other sub-teams in the system means that the liaison can be kept strong as children move up the age range through the school and teenage years, and across to family support, parenting support and social care.

The Phase 1 children's centre nurseries, although not sustainable without ongoing subsidy, have ensured that children in the poorest areas can access high-quality childcare. The high quality of the provision has also attracted a socially mixed clientele from both within and outside the area.

So, for example, the Roundabout Nursery on the Whitehawk Estate – one of the poorest estates in the city – is staffed by a high proportion of trained nursery teachers, with an experienced manager and the support of a full multidisciplinary team from the children's centre of which it is a part. A nursery class with low take-up was taken out of the school and expanded to provide flexible, full day care for children from birth to 4. In three years the nursery has transformed into a thriving, oversubscribed nursery which is successful in attracting children from the more affluent areas of the city as well as providing free places to children under 3 identified as being most in need by local health visitors. The nursery is starting to feed the neighbouring primary school with local children with a significantly higher level of social and academic development than had previously been the case. The upshot is a social system which is starting to renew itself via its early years provision, and bodes well for the future of the local area.

The five key challenges revisited

In the 2006 edition of *Contemporary Issues in the Early Years*, I listed five issues which I felt were of particular concern to the national programme at that stage. In revisiting these issues for the current edition, it is clear that none of them has gone away, but that more progress has been made in some than in others.

Building a wider partnership

The new organizational structure in Brighton and Hove has created a more robust framework for building local partnership working than the previous city-wide, but fragmented, structures. The primary schools have settled well into their extended services clusters, and are relating well to the area teams, although their relationships with the children's centres need to be developed further. The GPs have, by and large, taken the move of health visitors well, although their active involvement in the planning and case management arrangements is still not well developed. Both Brighton and Hove and other areas are hoping that the forthcoming Child Health Strategy, and in particular the inclusion of children in the NHS Operating Framework (DH, 2007), will provide sufficient incentives for GPs to engage with their local Children's Trust over time.

One area where partnership working within children's trusts continues to present a challenge is in the commissioning of services. There are significant differences in the way the NHS and local government understand these processes, which have, if anything, increased since the inception of the NHS 'World Class Commissioning' programme. To seek to build more common understanding, the Faculty of Public Health, in conjunction with the Association of Directors of Children's Services and others, produced a joint statement on joint commissioning in children's services in early 2008. This emphasized the whole system approach, and used a four-stage commissioning model adapted by Westminster Primary Care Trust (PCT) and Westminster City Council from the original DCSF Planning and Commissioning Guidance (HMG, 2006). The significant point about this joint statement was to demonstrate that it should be possible to operate a single commissioning strategy within a children's trust, despite the different historical and cultural starting points.

The DCSF shared the concern that commissioning at local level was at a relatively early stage, and in response set up a commissioning support programme in late 2008. The aim of the programme was to identify and disseminate good practice in commissioning in local children's trusts, in order to take the whole system forward.

Looking more broadly, in most local areas, partnership working has started to move from talk to action, and there has been some progress in implementing joint commissioning arrangements. Many local areas now have joint commissioning posts between the council and the PCT. In Brighton and Hove it was realized that this joint approach needed to go much further, by embracing integrated management as well as integrated front line delivery, and that the model was just as relevant for other areas of the Children's Trust's activity as it was for health-related matters. The partnership could only succeed if it meant something in terms of mainstream expenditure. The whole point of Children's Trusts is that they bind the partners into a commitment to joint action, and a shared agenda.

The government's Job Centre Plus service is highlighted as a key partner in the outcomes guidance, and is now included in the list of organizations covered by the duty to co-operate in the new draft legislation. Its role includes the planning and delivery of services to help reduce child poverty by tackling worklessness and supporting parents back to work. However, local experience is that Job Centre Plus services often struggle to find the capacity needed to engage fully with the work of their local children's centres.

Nationally, the picture is still very mixed, with many areas less than enthusiastic to embark on the kind of thoroughgoing change which Brighton and Hove has undergone. Sometimes this is due to the wider partnership not being fully signed up to the agenda, but one suspects that more often it is because the local authority itself is not yet convinced of it. There is clearly some way to go in securing the system change which the Children's Trust guidance envisages.

Developing new, more integrated ways of working

The Brighton and Hove system is predicated on a fully integrated service model, where staff working in the service have adopted new roles in relation to one another, and to their clients. In fact the reality is more complex. For the most part, the staff groups have adapted very well indeed to their changed roles, and have viewed the integrated service as supportive, rather than undermining, of their professionalism. But a number of staff groups have had to change their mode of working quite significantly. Some staff were slotted into roles in the children's centres for which they were not necessarily suited, and this has required some effort in terms of retraining and on-site supervision.

In the greater scheme of things, these issues may not seem over-significant, but the nature of change is such that it is often precisely this kind of apparently minor problem which can prevent a new system from operating successfully. So there is a real onus on Directors of Children's Services in every area to pay attention to the detail of the change management processes involved in setting up their local Children's Trust.

Developing a new service model

The basic argument about geographical coverage has been won in Brighton and Hove, as it will have been in most places where there is a commitment to equality of access to services. But there continues to be some tension between the twin principles of offering a universal service while at the same time targeting it to the most disadvantaged. There is still a long way to go, in Brighton and Hove as elsewhere, to construct a service which faithfully reflects the government's espoused principle of progressive universalism (see HMT, 2004). There is no doubt that the intention, and the fundamental service design, which drives the Brighton and Hove Children and Young People's Trust, has the potential for delivering this objective, but the reality has some distance to catch up.

Balancing local autonomy with central specification

Undoubtedly, the Brighton and Hove model has become more centralized in the past three years, with the implementation of a universal service specification and a unitary organizational framework. Since 2005 the city's local Sure Start and New Deal for Communities projects, both of which operated more or less autonomously and had their own management boards, have been absorbed into the city-wide early years programme, and their management boards have lost their autonomy. They have become, in effect, local steering groups for a city-wide service.

The question is whether this is a good or a bad thing. Those who would like to 'let a thousand flowers bloom' would regret the passing of such autonomy. But in the past year or so there has been a distinct shift away from such think-ing at national level, with the creation of the new Centre of Excellence and Outcomes in Children's Services, and a recognition that the sector needs to start weeding out ineffective approaches to service delivery, in order to concen-trate more on what works. So the thousand flowers blooming era is probably past. At local level, it no longer seems desirable for each locality to develop a completely different offer, depending on what its local population wants. The new orthodoxy is to have a relatively firm specification for the core offer, in order to provide a clear entitlement to all families in a local area, and then allow some minor variations in terms of the balance and mode of services offered according to local circumstances and needs. So, the role of local boards-turned-steering groups becomes much more advisory, with community governance far less to the fore than under the previous local Sure Start model.

The risk is that this may discourage local people from taking ownership of their local children's centre, and for the centre to become just another local office of the state. The key to this not happening of course lies with the quality and approachability of the local staff, backed up by a responsive and un-controlling central administration. The onus is on the local Children's Trust to be inclusive in the way it conducts its business, so that local people feel they are being listened to, even if their role in the formal decision-making processes is reduced. Ultimately, of course, the main factor determining local satisfaction is the quality and accessibility of the services themselves, and not the particular form of governance adopted.

Sustainability of childcare provision

The final issue, of sustainability for childcare providers, has if anything become more intense.

There have been significant developments in the way that early education is funded. The clear message from government that free early education really should be free for parents with no strings attached drew strong reaction from many private providers across the south-east of England in particular, who argued that they could not afford to offer the entitlement at the rates paid by local authorities. It is clear that the national extension of the free childcare entitlement from 12.5 hours to 15 hours per week will only be accepted by these providers if the extra hours are funded at a realistic rate.

So there is an issue concerning the total amount of funding available in the system. There is also an issue of equity across the different sectors, in terms of the funding formula for this provision, which has been heightened since the decision was made to include all such funding in the Dedicated Schools Grant.

The government has asked English local authorities (LAs) to complete an analysis of the costs of their local providers in order to introduce a common funding formula and counting systems across all settings by 2010 (DCSF, 2007b). In developing the new formula LAs will have to balance funding led by costs (for example, to reflect the high property costs of some private day nurseries) with funding to improve outcomes (for example, to reflect deprivation).

Furthermore, childcare costs have risen consistently over the last few years without being fully reflected in the childcare element of the Working Tax Credit. Providers have to balance attracting and retaining well-qualified staff with ensuring that fees remain affordable for parents.

This tension is particularly acute in council-run children's centre nurseries where the combination of well-qualified staff on council pay and conditions makes it impossible for nurseries to be sustainable if fees are kept at affordable levels. Brighton and Hove, in common with other local authorities, is currently using government grants to subsidize these nurseries, in order to ensure they remain affordable. The issue is how long, and to what level, this subsidy will continue. The social benefits are clear, but the ongoing investment needed to sustain it will require continued political will at both local and national level. Whether this will be forthcoming will be one of the big tests of social policy in the decade to come.

Points for discussion

- To what extent is the revised statutory guidance and proposed legislation concerning Children's Trusts likely to support the development of fully integrated early years services based on children's centres in your area?

- What lessons does the Brighton and Hove experience of health visitor-led early years services have for your area?

- To what extent is the 'hub and satellite' model of children's centre provision helpful in planning to meet the needs of the communities in which you work?

- What strategies do you have, or can you put in place, to address the five key challenges set out in this chapter?

 Further reading

Department for Children, Schools and Families (2007) *The Children's Plan: Building Brighter Futures*. London: The Stationery Office.

Department for Children, Schools and Families (2008) *Children's Trusts: Statutory Guidance on Inter-agency Cooperation to Improve Well-being of Children, Young People and their Families*. London: DCSF.

Also, you should look out the Children and Young People's plan published by your local authority.

References

Audit Commission (2008) *Are We There Yet? Improving Governance and Resource Management in Children's Trusts*. London: Audit Commission.

Department for Children, Schools and Families (DCSF) (2007a) *The Children's Plan: Building Brighter Futures*. London: The Stationery Office.

Department for Children, Schools and Families (DCSF) (2007b) *School and Early Years Funding Arrangements 2008 0 11. Explanatory Note for Local Authorities, November 2007*. London: DCSF.

Department for Children, Schools and Families (DCSF) (2008) *Children's Trusts: Statutory Guidance on Inter-agency Cooperation to Improve Well-being of Children, Young People and Their Families*. London: DCSF.

Department for Education and Skills (DfES) (2003) *Every Child Matters*. Green Paper. London: The Stationery Office.

Department for Education and Skills (DfES) (2005) *Statutory Guidance on Inter-agency Cooperation to Improve Wellbeing of Children: Children's Trusts*. London: DfES.

Department of Health (DH) (2007) *NHS in England: Operating Framework for 2007–2008*. London: Department of Health.

Hawker, D. (2006) Joined up working – the development of children's services', in G. Pugh and B. Duffy (eds), *Contemporary Issues in the Early Years*. 4th edn. London: Sage.

Her Majesty's Government (HMG) (2006) *Joint Planning and Commissioning Framework for Children, Young People and Maternity Services*. London: DfES and DH.

Her Majesty's Treasury (HMT) (2004) *Choice for Parents, the Best Start for Children: A Ten Year Strategy for Childcare*. London: Stationery Office.

CHAPTER 3

THE WORLD PICTURE
Tricia David, Sacha Powell and Kathy Goouch

Chapter Contents

- What is early childhood for?
- Learning from other countries 1: early childhood education and care in China
- Learning from other countries 2: early childhood education and care in New Zealand
- So what can we learn about early childhood education and care from other countries?

Multiple caring is not new and many cultures have adopted this approach to child rearing for centuries, as pointed out in the last edition of *Contemporary Issues in the Early Years* (David, 2006). In some societies, as they have changed, becoming industrialized and more recently 'information' societies, the need for care other than by parents and family members at or near the home has increased. Additionally, research, especially in psychology and neuroscience, has recognized the amazing capabilities of babies and very young children and their capacity for learning, emphasizing the need for synthesis in care and early childhood education. Government ministers began to recognize that early childhood should be considered the first phase in 'lifelong learning', of equal importance to any other. Education Ministers whose countries were members of the Organization for Economic Cooperation and Development initiated a thematic review, *Starting Strong* (OECD, 2001; 2006), to provide information about early childhood education and care (ECEC) provision. After surveying services in 20 countries, the OECD identified eight key elements characterizing successful ECEC policy:

- a systemic and integrated approach to ECEC policy
- a strong and equal partnership with the education system
- a universal approach to access, with particular attention to children in need of special support
- substantial public investment allocated to services and infrastructure
- a participatory approach to quality improvement and assurance
- appropriate training and working conditions available for all staff
- systematic attention to data collection and monitoring
- a stable framework and long-term agenda for research and evaluation (OECD, 2006: 3–4).

These key elements can be used while exploring the ECEC policies of any government. Twenty years ago the United Kingdom's responses to all the above elements would have been negative, so one must analyse not only developments but also *why* developments have occurred.

What is early childhood for?

In order to understand ECEC policy and practice, it is necessary first to explore the shared understandings of members of that society. Rosenthal (2003) has suggested that what is thought appropriate for young children depends on the role assigned to early childhood in a particular society. She argues that in societies where the community is seen as more important than each individual the needs of that community will take precedence and adults, seen as superior to children, will pass on rules and knowledge and group members' *interdependence* is stressed. In individualistic societies, in contrast, children are regarded as of equal importance to adults. Their ideas, thoughts and independence are encouraged. While the intention of a national policy may be the development of a particular kind of society, ranging from highly community oriented to highly individualistic, the ways in which policies are enacted in practice will vary owing to the assumptions and traditions of local cultures and staff in different contexts (see David, 2006).

Further, national family policy, especially policies relating to parental employment, also impinge on ECEC provision. In countries with high rates of female employment outside the home, or aspirations to encourage mothers of young children to remain in or to re-enter the workforce, care provision may be heavily emphasized.

What the OECD review highlighted is the way in which some countries have been slow to foster the integration of education and care and that a lack of attention to the learning needs of young children – and concomitantly the education, training, qualifications and status of staff – has consequences for the whole society. Bennett (2003) and Neuman (2005), the two researchers most heavily involved in the thematic review (OECD, 2006) have each concluded that the care–education divide often persists, because true integration is a complex process. However, the survey also concludes that dominance by a 'pre-primary' (or 'readiness-for-school') curriculum in the early childhood phase, rather than a 'social pedagogic' approach (a broad preparation for life, the foundation of lifelong learning, as in the Nordic and Central European countries), is 'poorly suited to the psychology and natural learning strategies of young children' (OECD, 2006: 13).

In this chapter we will approach central issues concerning developments in ECEC by providing examples illustrating the ways in which differences in provision can highlight differences in histories, values and assumptions related to the dominant cultures prevailing in those countries. We will also attempt to explain what we can learn from these differences.

The themes it can be helpful to address in exploring 'the world picture' are:

1 *Policy issues*. What do different societies provide as education and/or care services for young children and why does provision take this/these forms? What are the aims of the provision? Which government department is responsible for policy at national level? Are policies for young children dealt with in isolation or are they linked to family policy and education policy? Do the policies imply that babies and young children are seen as strong, capable people/citizens who have agency?
2 *Practice issues*. What understandings about how young children learn are held in different societies? What are the origins of these understandings? What implications for staff education and conditions of service have been recognized and acted upon? Can influences from other countries/cultures be detected? Is play accented and, if play approaches are emphasized, how are play and learning interpreted?

We close the chapter by highlighting certain issues which continue to be relevant, noting the limitations of attempting to cover 'the world picture' in one chapter (a whole book would probably prove too short!), and raise further questions concerning the links between responsibility to the world and to early childhood.

Learning from other countries 1: early childhood education and care in China

China's recent political history and economic development have significantly influenced the nature and extent of provision for the education and care of young children across the country. As such, the current picture of ECEC is one of abundant change and marked disparity.

Out-of-home provision for the education and care of young children has existed since the beginning of the twentieth century and seen three main phases of development, the most recent being since the late 1980s. Traditionally there has been a clear division between care for babies and children under 3, and education for children aged between 3 and 6 years. There is also a distinction between the more formal provision (run by local education bureaus, employers or private companies) and less formal provision that may be organized by local communities.

Formal provision for babies and very young children has traditionally been childcare, under the remit of the Ministry of Health. It is commonly offered in settings called *tuo'ersuo* (nurseries). However, responses to research evidence (particularly in the field of neuroscience) and to parental demand for 'systematic' education by trained professionals are leading to changes. Some nurseries are now increasing their scope to include early education and the responsibility for their guidance falls to Education Commissions. Although scope is widening in some cases, Corter et al. (2006) cite research that shows a decline in enrolments in nurseries from 26.3 per cent in 1990 to 12.7 per cent in 2002, said to be because of the reduction in child population and cost saving by some providers.

Settings for children aged 3 to 5 or 6 years vary in the nature and extent of provision (full-time, part-time, boarding, mobile, community, and so on) but have a clear educational role and responsibility, falling under the remit of the Chinese Ministry of Education and local Education Commissions. These settings are often grouped under the title *you'eryuan* (kindergartens), with pre-primary classes for 5- or 6-year olds.[1] Once again, there is some shared responsibility with the Ministry of Health. Corter et al. (2006) report discrepant figures on enrolment rates and declining numbers of kindergartens but that kindergarten rolls must have increased.

Access to ECEC in different regions across China's geographically vast and diverse nation is variable. The most extensive provision is in the economically well-developed eastern coastal areas. In rural areas, the predominant form of early childhood education provision (accounting for over half and often the only provision available) has tended to be the one-year pre-primary classes, some of which are affiliated to primary (first) schools (*xiao xue*) (Zhao and Hu, 2008). Thus despite government efforts to develop ECEC, rural families are still relatively underprivileged (Kilburn and Datar, 2002; Zhao and Hu, 2008).

According to Zhao and Hu (2008), the Chinese Government aims to increase enrolments, having published *Recommendations of Early Childhood Education Reform and Development* in 2003, requiring one year of ECEC for 80 per cent of rural children and three years of ECEC for 50 per cent of rural children by 2007. However, the UNESCO Institute for Statistics (UNESCO, 2008) indicates that this goal had not been achieved and one of the barriers is insufficient funding. The level of funding the government provides for ECEC and the costs to many families are widely criticized (for example, *China News*, 2006; *China Today*, 2001; Renmin Ribao, 2007; *Shanghai Evening Post*, 2006; Wang, 2003).

Corter et al. (2006) have also pointed out that discrepancies in fees leads to differences in the quality of provision and means that low-income families may be less able to access the better quality kindergartens. In 1999, 1 per cent of total education expenditure was allocated to ECEC compared with 34 per cent for primary education (UNESCO, 2008), and between 1992 and 2002 an average of 1.3 per cent per annum of government expenditure went on ECEC (Zhu, 2002), despite national recognition for the importance of early years provision.

In 2001, the China National Statistics Bureau reported that one in three parents in Beijing, Shanghai and Guangzhou was spending roughly one-third of their income on their children's education, including ECEC (*China Today*, 2001). The Ministry of Education is developing regulations to standardize the pricing for ECEC provision and to ensure one year's free nursery[2] provision (Xinhua News Agency, 2008).

Since the late 1980s, China's ECEC has been subject to central government-led reforms intended to extend, regularize and refocus provision. In the 20 years since the publication of the *Regulations on Kindergarten Education Practice* (National Education Commission of the PRC, 1989), the government has sought to promote a balance of child-initiated, play-based learning and teacher-directed 'instruction'. While the latter had been the more traditional approach to education in general, including early childhood education, the former presented a new pedagogical approach introduced as a result of China's outward-looking 'Open Door' policies of the 1980s onwards. Liu Yan and colleagues at Beijing Normal[3] University studied the effects of the new ECEC policies and noted that they demanded changes to 'a long-standing practice of focusing on group lessons at the expense of play and the predominance of the transmission model of teaching over children's active involvement in learning in kindergarten settings' (Liu et al., 2005: 3).

Guidance on kindergarten practice since 1989 shows three interesting new features. The first is the importance of locally relevant and meaningful content of ECEC programmes, which has led to greater devolution of planning. The other two are an emphasis on play as the foundation for kindergarten activities and children's individuality and difference with reference to developmentally appropriate practice[4] (Powell, 2002). Liu et al.'s study of the effects of the reforms (2005) used children's perspectives of play as their main source of evidence. They noted that children tended to view kindergarten activities as play (*'wan'*) only if there was no adult presence or intervention; and the children reported that they most valued the teacher-led 'group lessons'. The authors comment that children's perspectives have undoubtedly been influenced by teachers' remarks about the importance and value of the group lessons and suggest that their findings present challenges for teachers to participate in, support and extend children's play.

There have been efforts to increase the numbers of qualified staff and the levels of qualifications within the early childhood education sector. Despite these efforts and the inclusion of new conceptual approaches to ECEC in early childhood studies programmes, Zhu and Jie (2008) have suggested that the progressive ideas embedded within curriculum reform have perplexed many working in ECEC settings. Their professional identities are often embedded within teacher-led paradigms stemming from previous teaching traditions. Many now have difficulty implementing approaches that are both meaningful to them and mindful of the new direction of curricular change. Li and Rao (2005) report that prior to the reforms, China had adopted a subject-centred curriculum based on a Soviet model. Since the 1980s, an integrated curriculum had been promoted, based on ideas about early learning that were unfamiliar to early childhood teachers in China. In an attempt to provide guidance that would bridge the gap between the progressive theories of the integrated curriculum and the realities of teachers' everyday experiences in ECEC settings, the Ministry of Education of the People's Republic of China (PRC) (2001) published *Trial Guidance on Kindergarten Education*. The guidance (*You'eryuan Jiaoyu Zhidao Gangyao*) includes the aims of education in relation to society, stating that children will learn how to:

- actively and confidently participate in activities
- be willing to communicate with, help, co-operate, share with and be sympathetic to other people
- understand and follow basic rules of social behaviour in everyday life
- strive to accomplish tasks on their own, be able to overcome challenges and take on responsibilities
- love their parents, the elderly, teachers and friends as well as collective living, their home town and the state.

These aims reveal elements of both traditional Chinese culture (greatly influenced by Confucian principles) as well as 'Marxist-Leninist Mao Zedong Thought'. The difficulty for Chinese teachers is to marry these ideals with imported theories and approaches to early childhood education. Further, adult–child ratios of possibly 35 children or more to one teacher (Zhu and Wang, 2005) presents huge challenges to changing practice. The pressures on early childhood education teachers come not just from changing logistical issues and approaches to early learning, but also from shifting social and economic expectations in China. China's children are seen in relation to their potential contributions in the country's modernization drive, the need for a well-educated workforce of the future (Ministry of Education of the PRC, 1995: Article 5) and the hopes of parents for their children's (mostly 'only' children) success in an increasingly competitive education system (Ebbeck and Wei, 1996; Powell, 2002).

Finally, curriculum guidance has been shaped by China's research and development activities. Systematic explorations of other countries' models and approaches to ECEC, analysed and modified to suit Chinese culture, have been transformed into early childhood policies and guidance. Developing the accessibility of early childhood education for all children will be a challenge that, if overcome, is expected to benefit children today and the state tomorrow.

Learning from other countries 2: early childhood education and care in New Zealand

Policy is both text and action, words and deeds; it is what is enacted as well as what is intended. Policies are always incomplete insofar as they relate to or map on to the 'wild profusion' of local practice. (Ball, 1994: 10)

Both practitioners and educationalists often cast around, worldwide, seeking affirmation of their practice, inspiration for new practices, innovations or simply connections to research from 'elsewhere'. New Zealand has come to the attention of many because of the combined strength and flexibility of the early years curriculum policy and the inspirational metaphor of interwoven principles and aims in *Te Whariki* (Ministry of Education, 1996). From a distance it appears that in New Zealand there are other forces driving the care and education of young children than an academically driven policy discourse, and that these are inclusive and holistic.

As New Zealand is a relatively young country it is possible to track back the quite recent influences on its systems for educating and caring for young children. For example, the emphasis on the health and well-being of both children and their mothers is evident in May's extract from the 1947 Bailey Report (May, 2002: 5), with its suggestion of a middle-class Victorian England and in which pre-school was said to provide:

- companionship for children
- stimulating play environments
- parent education
- transition to school
- health supervision
- relief for mothers from the emotional strain of full-time parenting
- time for mothers for shopping and appointments
- support for mothers to have more children.

Although the first policies for early childhood education in New Zealand were designed to combat disadvantage, it was soon apparent that early childhood education services would benefit all children, their families and communities.

Play and companionship were given emphasis in that government review 60 years ago in New Zealand, similarly support for mothers was prominent in policy, and this history of ECEC has formed the bedrock upon which later policies have been built.

Further, there is evidence of the government's wide consultation – with the indigenous population, with parents generally and with 'the sector', a term which suggests an apparently homogenous group. Indeed, in the introduction to *Te Whariki*, the early childhood curriculum in New Zealand, it is claimed that the policy had been born 'in response to initiatives from the early childhood sector' (Ministry of Education, 1996: 7) and that somewhat disparate groups had contributed through curriculum development, research, 'shared knowledge and agreed understandings' to such a common curriculum. This kind of inclusive consultation represents a core constituent of *Te Whariki*, which is that, beyond the initial interwoven principles and aims, there is opportunity for difference and diversity in the patterns that may emerge and that this is dependent on community and culture. Hence the idea that the 'woven mat' exists for all to stand on, ensuring opportunities for full participation.

While many countries continue to agonize about disadvantage and social inequity, in New Zealand there appears to have been a strong political will to address this through their early childhood policies. Both the geography of the country and the history of the restoration of the rights of the Maori population have influenced the New Zealand government's emphasis on participation and inclusion in education from birth. The 'principles' of *Te Whariki* (holistic development, empowerment, family and community and relationships) and the 'strands' or aims (well-being, belonging, contribution, communication and exploration) closely reflect their stated intention to embrace the needs of individual children, their families and communities. Bronfenbrenner's (1979) model of Russian nested dolls is reproduced in *Te Whariki* to represent the significance of the environment and community in which children live, grow and learn.

Te Whariki is only one strand of the 10-Year Strategic Plan for Early Childhood Education in New Zealand (Ministry of Education, 2002). This plan promised to address the social, educational and economic health of the nation with a vision focusing on participation, relationships and quality. The plan seeks to acknowledge diversity in provision, within and across cultures, ensure regulation of services and increase requirements for training and qualifications. However, unlike more familiar policy here in England, the New Zealand plan claims that central government can fund, regulate, inform and support, and use a mixture of all approaches. Significantly, to overcome the tension between quality and costing implications, it states that 'The Government will fund services so that increased teacher quality does not come at the cost of decreased participation' (Ministry of Education, 2002). As in other countries however, suggestion of regulation brings with it concerns of centralized control, particularly in New Zealand where many settings in rural or geographically distant areas are unused to such regulative attention.

The other key issue that New Zealand faces, with its claims to a bicultural education system, is that of participation rates among Maori and Pacific Island children and families. Combined with this is increased migration from Asia, Africa and Europe, putting additional strain on a system built upon and celebrating relationships with parents, families and communities (May, 2002). However, if *Te Whariki*'s aim to permit 'local weaving' is successful and the curriculum can be 'locally responsive and achievements can be locally legitimated' (Cowie and Carr, 2004: 7), the needs of diverse community groups, as well as diverse national groups, should be met. Aims such as the provision of 'sociable, loving and physically responsive adults who can tune into an infant's needs' (Ministry of Education, 1996: 22) suggest that this is a universal curriculum that could serve the interests of children from any culture or country.

One of the central claims of both *Te Whariki* and the New Zealand 10-Year Strategic Plan for Early Childhood is that they are research and sector informed. *Te Whariki* has been frequently defined as a socioculturally informed curriculum (Anning et al., 2008; Cowie and Carr, 2004; May, 2002; Rogoff 1990; Wenger 1998; Wertsch 1991). May claims that in New Zealand a strong political statement about children was being made in 1996 when *Te Whariki* was introduced, in relation to 'their uniqueness, ethnicity and rights in New Zealand society ... a curriculum space where language and cultures could be in the foreground and not an add-on' (May, 2002: 12). Equally, a strong research statement was being made in relation to the difference between traditional early childhood interests in developmental approaches and ideas about children learning in communities of practice and in the company of informed professionals, thus requiring new strands of professional knowledge, understanding, and skills.

If, as Bennett (2008) argues, no single country has the entire story in relation to provision and practice, it may also be the case that no single country has the entire story in relation to the research paradigm informing and underpinning practice. While the unique nature of the political will New Zealand demonstrates concerning quality in ECEC and the apparent unity in sharing common aims, the research discourse currently dominating New Zealand research, policy and practice may need to be reappraised in order to also ensure participation at this level. Most important, however, is the will of the New Zealand government to 'demonstrate the kind of political courage that gives real substance to political rhetoric of putting children first' (May, 2002: 14).

So what can we learn about ECEC from other countries?

The questions raised by these two examples hopefully cause reflection on provision in one's own country. Like reflections in curved funfair mirrors, ECEC provision for babies and young children in other countries may highlight features we see as key, as well as those that are hidden. Additionally, international research sometimes causes the global early childhood community to reach similar conclusions.

For example, the issue of fixed ideas about child development and implications for practice is challenged by research arguing that contexts (extra-child influences) need to be taken into account because development is contingent (Morss, 1990). This then links to the education and training of early childhood professionals, which is crucial if children are to experience the kind of sensitive and relevant curriculum that is implied in describing the *Te Whariki* as a curriculum that can 'serve the interests of children from any country or culture' – a curriculum not based on subject knowledge and particular skills, but on rich, complex experiential processes involving the co-construction of social reality with people they love, who love them. As Soler and Miller (2007: 66) point out, the *Te Whariki* 'provides the main values, orientations and goals ... but does not define how these goals should be achieved'. The central issue seems to be to establish curricular aims and principles based on agreed values, rather than specific content which may not equip children for futures we cannot envisage.

Both our examples question the role of research. In China, explorations of ideas and practices from abroad have resulted in the dissemination of theories that have originated in other cultural contexts where childhood and 'teacherhood' (the evolving roles and identities as teacher) have different meanings and purposes from those traditionally recognized, causing challenges for practitioners. As in many other countries, research in New Zealand could be more participatory (David et al., 2003; Goouch, 2008; Powell and Goouch, 2005).

A further development would be greater interaction among practitioners, as well as researchers, across national boundaries. There is clear evidence that policy-makers share ideas – for example, at the same time as *Birth to Three Matters* (DfES, 2003) was being developed in England, Portugal had initiated similar work and Germany recently published its own guidelines. Maybe England owes its Ten Year Strategic Plan to New Zealand or Australia. In England one does not have to venture too far to be able to explore differences in developments – Wales, Scotland, Northern Ireland and the Republic of Ireland (see Clark and Waller, 2007) offer opportunities to consider the questions posed earlier in the chapter and generally do not involve complexities related to terminology and differences in meaning, which can be lost in translation.

A 'world picture' would benefit from information from more countries, particularly those in the Majority World. As Bar-On (2004: 82) points out in discussing provision in Africa, focusing on Botswana, 'where parents want to preserve their culture, Western notions of "good" and "bad" childrearing practices cannot be uncritically accepted and should be juxtaposed with local notions on the subject and local realities'. He also argues that organized ECEC in sub-Saharan Africa is expected to expand substantially in the next few years with help from the World Bank.

It is to be hoped that such plans are unaffected by the 2008 crisis in the world economy. Worldwide, 75,000,000 primary school age children are not in education and one-third who do attend are believed to enter school having suffered brain damage due to malnutrition during their early years (Shepherd, 2008).

In the previous edition of this book the 'world picture' chapter ended with a quote from Keating[5] and Mustard (1993) indicating that those societies which practise capitalism in a less selfish, broader social context have a much better record concerning individual and societal health and well-being. Similarly, arguing for integrated education and care, Gammage (2006: 242–3) points out 'good early childhood experience *can be seen* as a social "glue" in a well-functioning democracy … appropriately embedded in the community, it seems to help create a better social atmosphere and greater community security' (our italics).

Points for discussion

- Why might a country lack ECEC provision for children aged between birth and 3? Why might you advocate the development of such provision?

- In what ways do ECEC professionals have a responsibility to the world and how does this link with work with young children?

- How can we learn from each other, across nations and cultures, without simply transplanting models?

Further reading

Bar-On, A. (2004) 'Early childhood care and education in Africa: the case of Botswana', *Journal of Early Childhood Research,* 2(1): 67–84. One of the few but hopefully growing body of available articles in western/northern academic journals about early childhood in the majority world.

Bennett, J. (2003) 'The persistent division between care and education', *Journal of Early Childhood Research*, 1(1): 21–48. An excellent critique based on involvement in the 20-country OECD study and earlier experience working with UNESCO.

Morss, J. (1990) *The Biologising of Childhood.* Hove. Lawrence Erlbaum. This is an exciting and challenging book about child development, sadly out of print but available on inter-library loan.

Organization for Economic Cooperation and Development (OECD) (2006) *Starting Strong II.* Paris: OECD. The international study of 20 countries' provision for young children.

Rosenthal, M. (2003) 'Quality in early childhood education and care', *European Early Childhood Research Journal*, 11(2): 101–16. This article provides a thoughtful approach to understanding why young children are treated differently in different societies.

Notes

1   The school entry age in China is 6, but in some areas children do not start school until 7 years of age and may be enrolled in pre-primary classes in their sixth year.
2   It is unclear whether this refers to *tuo'ersuo* or to ECEC and care providers more broadly.
3   *Beijing Shifan Daxue* – a Chinese 'normal' university traditionally offers teacher education and training.
4   Bredekamp, S. (ed.) (1987) *Developmentally Appropriate Practice in Early Childhood Programs Serving Children from Birth through Eight*. Washington, DC: National Association for the Education of Young Children.
5   Keating took the role of Thinker in Residence with the South Australian Government between 2006 and 2007. He clearly raised awareness of ECEC in Australia, where new developments are ensuing.

References

Anning, A., Cullen, J. and Fleer, M. (eds) (2008) *Early Childhood Education: Society and Culture*. 2nd edn. London: Sage.

Ball, S.J. (1994) *Education Reform: A Critical and Post-Structural Approach*. Buckingham: Open University Press.

Bar-On, A. (2004) 'Early childhood care and education in Africa: the case of Botswana', *Journal of Early Childhood Research*, 2(1): 67–84.

Bennett, J. (2003) 'The persistent division between care and education', *Journal of Early Childhood Research*, 1(1): 21–48.

Bennett, J. (2008) 'Public policy and early childhood systems in Europe', keynote Address, 18th EECERA Annual Conference, Stavanger, Norway.

Bronfenbrenner, U. (1979) *The Ecology of Human Development*. Cambridge, MA: Harvard University Press.

China News (2006) 'Two thirds of chinese families can't afford kindergartens', 28 December. www.china.org.cn

China Today (2001) 'Chinese families spend heavily on children's education', 23 November. www.china.org.cn

Clark, M. and Waller, T. (eds) (2007) *Early Childhood Education and Care: Policy and Practice*. London: Sage.

Corter, C., Janmohammed, Z., Zhang, J. and Bertrand, J. (2006) *Selected Issues Concerning Early Childhood Care and Education in China*. UNESCO. http://unesdoc.unesco.org/images/0014/001492/149200e.pdf

Cowie, B. and Carr, M. (2004) 'The consequences of socio-cultural assessment', in A. Anning, J. Cullen and M. Fleer (eds), *Early Childhood Education, Society and Culture*. London: Sage.

David, T. (2006) 'The world picture', in G. Pugh and B. Duffy (eds), *Contemporary Issues in the Early Years*. London: Sage.

David, T., Goouch, K., Powell, S. and Abbott, L. (2003) *Birth to Three Matters: A Review of the Literature*. Research Report 444. London: DfES.

Department for Education and Skills (DfES) (2003) *Birth to Three Matters*. Nottingham: DfES.

Ebbeck, M. and Wei, Z.G. (1996) 'The importance of pre-school education in the People's Republic of China', *International Journal of Early Years Education*, 4(1): 27–34.

Gammage, P. (2006) 'Early childhood education and care', *Early Years,* 26(3): 235–48.

Goouch, K. (2008) 'Narratives of experience in the lives of teachers of young children'. Unpublished PhD thesis, University of Kent, Canterbury.

Keating, D.P. and Mustard, F.J. (1993) 'Social economic factors and human development', in D. Ross (ed.), *Family Security in Insecure Times.* Ottawa: National Forum on Family Security.

Kilburn, M.R. and Datar, A. (2002) 'The availability of child care centers in China and its impact on child care and maternal work decisions', *Labor and Population Program Working Paper Series 02-12.* www.rand.org/labor/DRU/DRU2924.pdf

Li, H. and Rao, N. (2005) 'Curricular and instructional influences on early literacy attainment: evidence from Beijing, Hong Kong and Singapore', *International Journal of Early Years Education,* 13(3): 235–53.

Liu, Y., Pan, Y.J. and Sun, H.F. (2005) 'Comparative research on young children's perceptions of play' – an approach to observing the effects of kindergarten educational reform', *International Journal of Early Years Education,* 13(2): 101–12.

May, H. (2002) 'Early childhood care and education in Aotearoa – New Zealand: an overview of history, policy and curriculum', *McGill Journal of Education,* 37(1): 19–36.

Ministry of Education (1996) *Te Whariki He Whaariki Matauranga: Early Childhood Curriculum.* Wellington: Learning Media.

Ministry of Education (2002) *Pathways to the Future: Nga Huarahi Aratiki. A 10-Year Strategic Plan for Early Childhood Education.* Wellington: Learning Media.

Ministry of Education of the People's Republic of China (PRC) (1995) *Education Law of the People's Republic of China.* WWW.MOE.EDU.CN/ENGLISH/LAWS_E.HTM

Ministry of Education of the People's Republic of China (PRC) (2001) *Trial Guidance on Kindergarten Education.* (In Chinese.) Beijing: Ministry of Education.

Morss, J. (1990) *The Biologising of Childhood.* Hove: Lawrence Erlbaum.

National Education Commission of the People's Republic of China (PRC) (1989) *Regulations on Kindergarten Education Practice.* (In Chinese.) Beijing: National Education Commission.

Neuman, M. (2005) 'Governance of early childhood education and care', *Early Years,* 25(2): 129–42.

Organization for Economic Cooperation and Development (OECD) (2001) *Starting Strong.* Paris: OECD.

Organization for Economic Cooperation and Development (OECD) (2006) *Starting Strong II.* Paris: OECD.

Powell, S. (2002) 'Constructions of Early Childhood in China', Unpublished PhD thesis. University of Kent, Canterbury.

Powell, S. and Goouch, K. (2005) 'Reflections on a project exploring young children's views of play', paper presented at the Warwick International Conference, University of Warwick, March.

Renmin Ribao (2007) 'Preschool education largely ignored in China', 7 November, *China News Service.* www.china.org.cn

Rogoff, B. (1990) *Apprenticeship in Thinking.* Oxford: Oxford University Press.

Rosenthal, M. (2003) 'Quality in early childhood education and care', *European Early Childhood Research Journal,* 11(2): 101–16.

Shanghai Evening Post (2006) 'Dispute over kindergarten tuition fee', 21 November. www.china.org.cn

Shepherd, J. (2008) 'It's young lives that count, not numbers', *Guardian,* 24 September.

Soler, J. and Miller, L. (2007) 'The struggle for early childhood curricula', *International Journal of Early Years Education,* 11(1): 57–67.

United Nations Educational, Scientific and Cultural Organization (UNESCO) (2008) *UIS Statistics in Brief. Education in China*. UNESCO Institute for Statistics. http://stats.uis.unesco.org/unesco/TableViewer/document.aspx?ReportId=121&IF_Language=eng&BR_Country=1560

Wang, H.M. (2003) 'Report on the early childhood education development situation', (In Chinese.) *Journal of Early Education*, 5: 2–5.

Wenger, E. (1998) *Communities of Practice*. Cambridge: Cambridge University Press.

Werstch, J.V. (1991) *Voices of the Mind*. Cambridge, MA: Harvard University Press.

Xinhua News Agency (2008) 'China legislature member proposes free nursery school for one year', *Chinaview* 31 August. http://news.xinhua.com/english/2008-08/31content_9744371

Zhao, L. and Hu, X. (2008) 'The development of early childhood education in rural areas in China', *Early Years*, 28(2): 197–210.

Zhu, J.X. (2002) 'Early childhood care and education in P.R. China', paper presented at 2002 KEDI-UNESCO Bangkok Joint Seminar and Study Tour on Early Childhood Care and Education, Seoul, Korea. www.zhujx.com/show.php/232/2

Zhu, J.X. and Jie, Z. (2008) 'Contemporary trends and developments in early childhood education in China', *Early Years,* 28(2): 173–82.

Zhu, J.X. and Wang, X.C. (2005) 'Contemporary early childhood education and research in China', in B. Spodek and O.N. Saracho (eds), *International Perspectives on Research in Early Childhood*. Charlotte, NC: Information Age Publishing. pp. 55–78.

CHAPTER 4

QUALITY IN EARLY CHILDHOOD EDUCATION: EVIDENCE FOR LONG-TERM EFFECTS

Kathy Sylva and Fiona Roberts

Chapter Contents

- What is quality?
- The Effective Pre-school and Primary Education 3–11 project
- Measuring quality through a classroom observation rating scale
- Key findings at age 11 – do the effects last?
- The impact of the EPPE 3–11 project on policy and practice

What is 'quality'?

There are many ways to describe quality in early childhood education. One way is for stakeholders to reflect on their own experiences to try to arrive at a set of 'quality practices' they think will benefit children. Another way is to ask experts such as inspectors or advisers what they judge, as professionals, to be the kind of environments or practices that are of high or low quality (often using formal written criteria). This method is closely related to national standards, that is, the expert might be judging how well an individual setting meets written standards. A third way is to use an observational rating scale containing criteria that research has shown to be important for children's development. The ECERS-R (Harms et al., 1998) is the most well-known and is usually administered by independent trained researchers skilled in scoring reliably with one another. One further way to identify quality is in terms of children's developmental outcomes; settings are thought to be high in quality if children can be shown to thrive in them. This last approach to quality is a *post hoc* one; a judgement is made about a setting after studying the outcomes of its children. In this chapter, the outcomes approach of assessing settings is referred to as an 'effectiveness' judgement rather than a 'quality' one. We distinguish between effectiveness and quality because a setting may promote strong developmental progress in a domain of development, for example language and literacy, but we would not call it a high-quality setting if the staff used aversive control to achieve such outcomes. Such a hypothetical 'high punishment' setting might be 'effective' in one sense but we would not call it high in 'quality'.

The four ways to identify quality outlined above – stakeholder views, expert judgement, systematic classroom observations and child outcomes – are all valid, but they rest on different standards of evidence.

A supporting view considered here is that of Munton et al. (1995), who identified two basic dimensions that can be taken into account when describing the quality of early childhood settings: structure and process. The structure includes the more easily measurable features such as facilities (for example, physical environment and furnishings) and human resources (for example, the child–adult ratio and staff qualifications). Process refers to the education and care children experience every day (for example, adult–child interactions and appropriate timetables). Munton also referred to the outcomes, or the longer-term consequences of the education and care, as relevant to quality but not synonymous with it.

The structural and process descriptions of quality are often highly correlated: good things tend to go together. The US large-scale study of childcare (NICHD, 1999) reported that early childhood settings rated as safer, cleaner and with better adult–child ratios (better structure) tended to have more sensitive caregivers who provided a more cognitively stimulating experience (better classroom processes).

Lilian Katz (1993) has written in a different way about the quality of early education. She argues that quality can be seen from a 'top-down' perspective, as viewed by visitors or observers, a 'bottom-up' perspective, as experienced by the children themselves, an 'outside-in' perspective, as seen by parents, and an 'inside' perspective, as considered by the staff. Katz's categories overlap with those outlined above but focus not on the characteristics of quality but on the perspective from which a setting or programme is viewed. Differing perspectives may lead to differences in the relative importance of various criteria.

This chapter will first describe observation instruments used to measure aspects of structure and process quality and then go on to examine the effects of this quality on children's later development. Most of the chapter will focus on a large longitudinal study investigating the effectiveness of early childhood education, the Effective Pre-school and Primary Education (EPPE) project

(Sylva et al., 2004; 2008). Findings from the EPPE 3–11 study highlight the factors associated with high quality and give a guide to the kind of practices that lead to good developmental progress for children across a range of cognitive, social-behavioural and dispositional outcomes. This chapter will also discuss how findings from the EPPE study have influenced national policy on early childhood, especially policy related to quality of provision.

The Effective Pre-school and Primary Education (EPPE 3–11) project

The Effective Pre-school and Primary Education project is a major European longitudinal study which investigated the effect of pre-school education and care on children's development. Co-leaders of the project are Kathy Sylva (University of Oxford), Edward Melhuish (Birkbeck College, London), Pam Sammons (University of Nottingham), Iram Siraj-Blatchford and Brenda Taggart (both at the Institute of Education, University of London). These researchers have followed children's development since 1997 (for an introductory paper see Sylva et al., 1999; for the most recent findings see Sylva et al., 2008). EPPE is an 'educational effectiveness' study of a national sample of randomly selected children aged 3–11 years old throughout England. The EPPE 3–11 team collected a wide range of information on 2,800 children who were recruited at age 3+ and studied longitudinally until the end of Key Stage 2. Data were collected on children's developmental profiles (between the age of 3 and 11 years), background characteristics related to their parents, the child's home learning environment, and the pre-school settings children attended. A sample of 300+ 'home' children, who had no or minimal pre-school experience, were also recruited to the study for comparison with the pre-school group.

Settings (141) were drawn from a range of providers that included local authority day nurseries, centres integrating care with education, playgroups, private day nurseries, nursery schools and nursery classes. All the early childhood settings in the EPPE 3–11 study were observed and rated according to two quality 'profiles' (to be described below). To establish the effects of quality in each pre-school setting on children's outcomes, the developmental progress each child made between entry to pre-school and entry to school was measured. In addition, account was taken of children's background factors such as family socio-economic status (SES), mother's education and the ways that parents stimulate their children's learning at home. After controlling for baseline and background factors, the 'value added' to children's development by the quality of the setting they attended could be calculated. Although children's development has been assessed at 5, 6, 7, 10 and 11 years, this chapter focuses only on age 11.

A similar longitudinal study conducted in the US by the NICHD (1998) also aimed to investigate links between childcare experiences and children's developmental outcomes. In-depth study of childcare predictors showed that childcare *quality* was a consistent predictor of child functioning after taking account of the social and family background. EPPE 3–11 also found that the quality of each individual pre-school influenced children's developmental progress across the pre-school period (Sylva et al., 2008) and this finding will be addressed in more detail in the sections that follow.

Measuring quality through a classroom observation rating scale

In the EPPE 3–11 project, the quality of early childhood settings was measured using two internationally recognized observation instruments. The first measure was the Early Childhood Environment Rating Scale – Revised (ECERS-R; Harms et al., 1998). This is a 'global' measure of quality, incorporating both process and structural aspects of quality while focusing equally on 'care' and 'education'. The second measure used was the Early Childhood Environment Rating Scale – Extension (ECERS-E; Sylva et al., 2003, revised 2006), which is concerned with pre-school curriculum and aims to measure 'educational' quality related to children's learning.

The ECERS-R

The Early Childhood Environment Rating Scale – Revised (ECERS-R) is a measure of quality that has been developed in the USA and is used widely in research and professional development. It was devised by early years practitioners and researchers to create a numerical profile for rating the 'quality' of a setting across a broad set of seven sub-scales, each dedicated to a different aspect of practice. This measure describes the characteristics of the *physical* environment but, as important, it also rates the quality of the *social* and *pedagogical* environment which children experience. The ECERS-R has 43 items divided into seven sub-scales: space and furnishing, personal care routines, language and reasoning, activities, social interactions, organization and routines, adults working together. Each item is rated on a seven-point scale (1 = inadequate, 3 = minimal/adequate, 5 = good, 7 = excellent). The ECERS-R has been widely used in research assessing the quality of early childhood settings, and has been shown to have good psychometric properties and good predictive validity in being significantly related to children's developmental outcomes (for example, Burchinal et al., 2002; De Kruif et al., 2000; Gilliam, 2000; Jaeger and Funk, 2001; Peisner-Feinberg and Burchinal, 1997; Phillips et al., 1987).

The word 'environment' in the ECERS-R is taken in its broadest sense to include the quality of social interactions, strategies to promote all round learning, and relationships between children as well as between adults and children. The emphasis in the instrument is very much on a balanced and 'whole child' programme. For example, the organization and routine sub-scale has an item called 'schedule' which gives high quality ratings to a balance between adult-initiated and child-initiated activities. To score a 5 the centre must have 'a balance between structure and flexibility' but a score of 7 requires 'variations to be made in the schedule to meet individual needs, for example a child working intensively on a project should be allowed to continue past the scheduled time'.

The importance in the ECERS-R of high-quality interaction is illustrated by the many observational indicators which give high scores to the way staff engage with children, even when that is not the explicit focus of a particular item. For example, in 'supervision of gross motor activities', a score of 7 requires that 'staff help children develop positive social interactions (e.g., help children to take turns on popular equipment; provide equipment that encourages cooperation such as a two-person rocking boat, walkie-talkie communication devices)'. The 'interaction' sub-scale places importance on the development of respect among the children, and on supervision and discipline which is 'negotiated' rather than 'imposed'. Throughout many of the items there are criteria for scoring that take into account the role of the staff. For example, in 'using language to develop reasoning skills' (in the language and reasoning subscale) a score of 5 requires that 'staff talk about logical relationships while children play with materials that stimulate reasoning' while for a 7, staff must 'encourage children to reason throughout the day, using actual events and experiences as a basis for concept development'. So, despite its title of 'Environment Rating Scale' the ECERS-R describes the social processes of the educational and care environment even more than the physical space and materials on offer.

The ECERS-E

In the EPPE 3–11 research, the ECERS-R rating scale was supplemented by a new scale, the Early Childhood Environment Rating Scale – Extension (ECERS-E; Sylva et al., 2003, revised 2006). This new, supplementary scale was designed because the ECERS-R was thought to be insufficiently detailed in its assessment of curricular provision for literacy, numeracy and science. These are important curricular areas for children's intellectual and linguistic progress in the run-up to school. The ECERS-E was developed to extend the ECERS-R, especially in 'emergent' literacy, numeracy and science; these are now reflected in three of the four subscales. The fourth sub-scale, diversity, assesses the extent to which the curriculum is tailored to children of different genders, cultures/ethnicity and ability levels. Some sample items from the ECERS-E appear as an appendix to this chapter.

The four sub-scales of the ECERS-E (literacy, mathematics, science/environment, diversity) are based on the *Curriculum Guidance for the Foundation Stage* (DfEE/QCA, 2000), and are compatible with the national 'learning goals' (statutory curriculum objectives) and some 'stepping stones' (developmental steps children take before reaching each statutory goal) in the Early Years Foundation Stage (EYFS; DCSF, 2008). Thus, the ECERS-E is specifically designed to tap the dimensions of quality which should support the children in achieving many of the learning goals in the published guidance. For example, consider the ECERS-E literacy sub-scale item 'sounds in words'. In it, high scores are obtained by settings where members of staff explicitly highlight rhyme, alliteration and syllabification in everyday activities such as nursery rhymes and clapping games. This relates closely to the early learning goals (in the EYFS curriculum) related to children's 'linking sounds and letters'. Other examples include the ECERS-E mathematics sub-scale item 'shape and space' which assesses the capacity of the setting to nurture children's development in the area of 'shape, space and measures' which are part of the statutory learning goals. Finally, the diversity item 'multicultural education' in the ECERS-E is closely linked to the early learning goals specified under 'confidence and self-esteem' in the EYFS document.

Key findings at age 11 – do the effects last?

The researchers rated all 141 settings that the EPPE children attended. Child assessments were made over time so that children's developmental progress could be measured and investigated in light of the quality of their pre-school settings. When the children were about to leave their primary schools, the researchers collected scores from the National Assessment Tests in English and mathematics at age 11. These were administered in the same week according to standardized instructions and marked on a government marking scheme. Classroom teachers also completed a social/behavioural rating scale (adapted from Goodman, 1997) for each child from which four factors were derived using confirmatory factor analysis: self-regulation, pro-social behaviour, hyperactivity and anti-social behaviour. The specific items associated with each of the four social/behavioural factors are shown in Table 4.1.

Measurement of the cognitive and social behavioural progress of children in the EPPE sample until the age of 11 has allowed the authors to investigate the long-term effects on children's development of their experiences at pre-school age (Sylva et al., 2008). In terms of cognitive gains, pre-school attendance (compared to none) had an effect on English and mathematics attainment at Key Stage 2 (Year 6, age 11). Furthermore, all children who attended pre-school had an advantage for 'pro-social' behaviour in Year 6 compared with children who did not attend pre-school ('home' children). For other social/behavioural outcomes at the end of Year 6, there are no longer statistically significant effects of simply attending pre-school. Thus, just attending *any* pre-school showed modest effects at age 11. However, the *quality* of the pre-school attended was found to have a more powerful and significant effect on children's development.

Turning to quality, in Figure 4.1 we can clearly see the impact of the quality of pre-school (measured by the ECERS-E) on children's academic outcomes in English and mathematics. Each bar shows the numerical effect on English (or mathematics) of low/medium/high quality compared to remaining at home. The only statistically significant difference here, however, is between the children who attended medium- and high-quality pre-schools, and the children who did not attend pre-school at all, which suggests that low-quality pre-school has little effect on children's academic gains; in fact, its effect may be similar to staying at home.

Table 4.1   Items associated with each social/behavioural dimension in Year 6 (age 11)

'Self-regulation' $(\alpha = 0.87)$

1. Likes to work things out for self; seeks help rarely
2. Does not need much help with tasks
3. Chooses activities on their own
4. Persists in the face of difficult tasks
5. Can move on to a new activity after finishing a task
6. Open and direct about what she/he wants
7. Confident with others
8. Shows leadership in group work
9. Can take responsibility for a task

'Pro-social' behaviour $(\alpha = 0.87)$

1. Considerate of other people's feelings
2. Shares readily with other children (treats, toys, etc.)
3. Helpful if someone is hurt, upset or feeling ill
4. Kind to younger children
5. Often volunteers to help others (teachers, other children)
6. Offers to help others having difficulties with a task
7. Sympathetic to others if they are upset
8. Apologises spontaneously

'Hyperactivity' $(\alpha = 0.87)$

1. Restless, overactive, cannot stay still for long
2. Constantly fidgeting or squirming
3. Easily distracted, concentration wanders
4. Thinks things out before acting
5. Sees tasks through to the end, good attention span
6. Quickly loses interest in what she/he is doing
7. Gets over excited
8. Easily frustrated
9. Impulsive, acts without thinking
10. Can behave appropriately during less structured sessions
11. Fails to pay attention
12. Makes careless mistakes

'Anti-social' behaviour $(\alpha = 0.75)$

1. Often fights with other children or bullies
2. Often lies or cheats
3. Steals from home, school or elsewhere
4. Vandalizes property or destroys things
5. Shows inappropriate sexual behaviour toward others
6. Has been in trouble with the law

Results showed that the two measures of pre-school quality (ECERS-R, Harms et al., 1998; and ECERS-E, Sylva et al., 2003, revised 2006) had a statistically significant impact on positive social/behavioural outcomes at age 11. Children who had attended medium- and high-quality pre-schools showed higher levels of 'self-regulation' in Year 6 than others. Further, children who attended low-, medium- or high-quality pre-school were rated by teachers as displaying more 'pro-social' behaviour compared with children who had stayed at home. Note that the difference is most marked for those who attended high-quality settings (see Figure 4.2).

In terms of negative social/behavioural outcomes, pre-school quality also had an impact on 'anti-social' behaviour, and results indicated that children who attended high-quality pre-schools had lower 'anti-social' behaviour in Year 6 than 'home' children (see Figure 4.3). Finally, the 'home' group and the high-quality pre-school

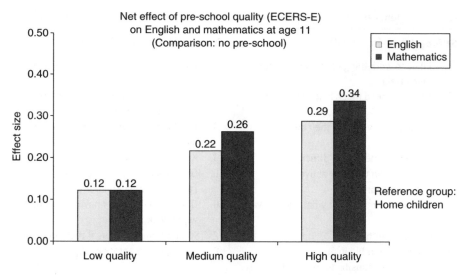

Figure 4.1   The impact of pre-school quality (ECERS-E) on English and mathematics in Year 6

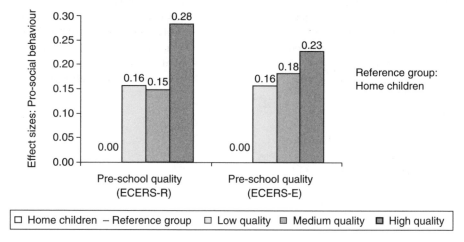

Figure 4.2   The impact of pre-school quality (ECERS-R and ECERS-E) on 'pro-social' behaviour in Year 6

group were rated by teachers as displaying significantly less 'hyperactivity' in Year 6 than children who had attended low-quality and medium-quality pre-school.

Overall these findings suggest that attending a high- or medium-quality pre-school has a lasting effect in promoting or sustaining better social/behavioural outcomes leading to increased 'self-regulation', higher 'pro-social' behaviour and lower 'anti-social' and 'hyperactive' behaviour levels at age 11.

EPPE 3–11 not only investigated the effects of varying types of pre-school experience on all children, but also examined in detail the ways in which early childhood experience affected different groups of children: according to

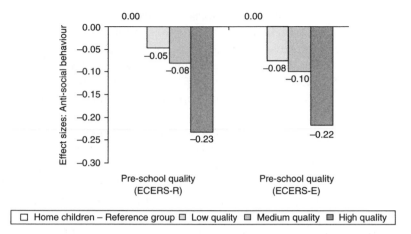

Figure 4.3   The impact of pre-school quality (ECERS-R and ECERS-E) on 'Anti-social' behaviour in Year 6

gender, eligibility for free school meals (FSM), low versus high levels of mother's qualifications, low versus high levels of multiple disadvantage, and whether or not a child had been identified as having a special educational need (SEN). The findings are interesting because, although high-quality benefits *all* children, its benefits are stronger for some groups rather than others.

The EPPE analyses indicate that boys benefit more than girls from attending a high-quality pre-school in terms of increased levels of 'self-regulation' and 'pro-social' behaviour, and lower levels of 'hyperactivity' and 'anti-social' behaviour in Year 6. Overall, girls have much better scores on all four social/behavioural outcomes than boys. However, boys are more sensitive to quality and so gain greater benefit from it. Although high quality is beneficial for both boys and girls, it may be more important for boys since they gain significantly more from it.

Children identified as having a special educational need (SEN) during primary school gained more from attending a higher quality pre-school setting in terms of increased 'self-regulation' and 'pro-social' behaviour, and lower 'hyperactivity' and 'anti-social' behaviour in Year 6. Overall, children who were never identified as having a SEN have better scores on all four social/behavioural outcomes than children with SEN. However, the effect of quality was stronger for children identified as having a SEN. This finding is important for children with elsewere SEN: medium- and especially high-quality pre-school can serve as a protective factor and benefit their all-round social/behavioural development.

Children from all SES groups benefit from higher-quality provision, indicating that quality is vital in all SES groups; it is not something that only benefits the poor. However, the EPPE 3–11 findings suggest that children who come from a high multiple disadvantage background benefit more from attending a high-quality pre-school (versus none, low or medium quality) than children of low multiple disadvantage. ('Multiple disadvantage' is measured using the Multiple Disadvantage Index, a summary measure based on various child and family predictors, such as low birth weight or living in a family with low socio-economic status, which are associated with an increased risk of lower attainment and poor social/behavioural outcomes). Children with high multiple disadvantage are more sensitive to the quality of their pre-school compared to children with low disadvantage. These findings are consistent with other recent studies in the USA, which suggest that children who come from a high family risk level benefit more from pre-school than children coming from a low family risk level (Niles et al., 2008).

To summarize, pre-school quality is important in shaping both academic and social/behavioural outcomes at age 11. Taken together, the two observational measures (ECERS-R and ECERS-E) demonstrate that quality of pre-school attended is positively related to children's developmental outcomes, and its continuing effect seems to be of greater impact than type (for example, a playgroup or a private day nursery) and the length of a child's attendance. Quality seems to be of even greater importance for particular groups within the EPPE 3–11 sample, with boys, children with multiple disadvantage and children with SEN gaining more from high-quality pre-school education in comparison to others in the study. The EPPE 3–11 study suggests that raising the quality of pre-school provision may help promote boys' attainment levels and possibly reduce the gender gap. It will also help children with SEN and those of high multiple disadvantage.

A final note on the two different quality measures: the more 'educational' aspects of quality measured by the ECERS-E predict academic attainment whereas the more 'care' oriented aspects of quality measured by the ECERS-R predict social-behavioural development.

The impact of EPPE 3–11 on policy and practice

EPPE 3–11 has been influential in shaping government policy (see Sylva and Pugh, 2005, for details). The findings demonstrate the importance of pre-school, and especially the importance of enhancing its quality. The impact of EPPE 3–11 has been seen at three levels.

First, it can be seen in national policy through evidence at Parliamentary Select Committees, ministerial briefings, contributions to the Treasury Spending Reviews and evidence to teams preparing government reports and policy documents. For example, the *ten-year strategy for childcare* (HM Treasury, 2004) quoted EPPE evidence in its rationale for increasing spending on early education and care, while the *Policy Review of Children and Young People* (HM Treasury, 2007) cites the EPPE as the basis for many government services for children. Furthermore, the 2005 Childcare Bill (House of Commons, 2005) used EPPE evidence to show how the new policies outlined in the Bill would benefit families and children. EPPE evidence was also used in the formation of the Early Years Foundation Stage (EYFS; DCSF, 2008), which was established under the Childcare Act 2006 (UK Parliament, 2006) and became law for early years settings in September 2008. Finally, EPPE is quoted in various government publications on quality (for example, The National Strategies Early Years handbooks on improving quality; The National Strategies, 2008a; 2008b).

Secondly, EPPE can be seen to influence local authority policy. The EPPE findings have been disseminated to local officers and elected members of local authorities seeking to reconfigure their early years services. EPPE also has an influence locally through workshops and training organized by local authority Early Years Development and Care Partnerships. EPPE 3–11 has been reported widely in practitioner publications, for example *Nursery World* and *Primary Practice*. One of the unanticipated impacts of EPPE 3–11 has been the way it has raised awareness of rigorous methods in carrying out 'policy-sensitive research'. There is anecdotal evidence showing that people at every level of expertise are now asking 'Where is your evidence?'.

Finally, EPPE has influenced the research community by publishing technical papers, explicitly showing the workings out of the analyses and descriptions of the research instruments. EPPE 3–11 has contributed to the debate about methods for establishing the effects of education, especially the 'mixed method', combining quantitative and qualitative approaches (Siraj-Blatchford et al., 2006).

The research is now extended in a continuation study: Effective Pre-school, Primary and Secondary Education 3–14 (EPPSE 3–14), also funded by the DCSF, to discover if the effects of early education and its quality that were evident at age 11 continue through to secondary school.

The chapter began with various views on quality, and then continued by showing how the EPPE 3–11 research used an 'educational effectiveness' research design to demonstrate how the quality of pre-school affects children's later academic and social/behavioural development. Quality was measured through the observational rating scales ECERS-R and ECERS-E. One of EPPE's most striking findings is that the quality of the individual settings attended by children still has a measurable impact on their developmental progress up to age 11. High quality benefits all children but its effects are stronger for boys, children with multiple disadvantage and children with SEN. Thus quality has an important role to play in supporting the development of vulnerable children.

Summary of the effects of pre-school at age 11

- *Impact of attending pre-school*

  - Pre-school attendance, compared to none, had significant benefit for English and mathematics attainment at Key Stage 2
  - Attending any pre-school versus none was also related to higher scores on 'pro-social' behaviour but not on other social-behavioural outcomes

- *Effects of quality*

  - *Academic gains:*

    - Attending a medium-or high-quality pre-school leads to higher scores in English and mathematics
    - Children who attend a low-quality pre-school had comparable scores to those who stay at home.

(Continued)

(Continued)

– *Social/behavioural outcomes:*

- A medium-to high-quality rating on the ECERS-R had a strong impact on 'pro-social' and 'anti-social' behaviour.
- Children who attended high-quality pre-school had lower levels of 'hyper-acitivity' than children who attended low- or medium-quality pre-school.

- **Differential effects of quality**

  – *Boys:*

  - Boys are more 'sensitive' to the effects of quality of pre-school than girls are.
  - Quality effects are stronger for boys on:

    o 'Self-regulation'
    o 'Pro-social' behaviour
    o 'Hyperactivity'
    o 'Anti-social' behaviour

  – *Special educational needs (SEN):*

  - The effects of quality of childcare for children with SEN are greater than such effects for children without SEN
  - The differential effects of quality on children with SEN were in these areas:

    o Higher levels of 'self-regulation' and 'pro-social' behaviour, and
    o Lower levels of 'hyperactivity' and 'anti-social' behaviour

  – *Multiply disadvantaged children*

  - Children with backgrounds of high multiple disadvantage benefit more from high-quality pre-school than do children from low levels of multiple disadvantage.

 Points for discussion

1. The two ECERS instruments provide a view of quality as seen from the 'outside' (see Katz, 1993). How do the scales achieve objectivity in their assessments?

2. How would you go about discovering the 'insiders' view of quality? What if people disagreed with one another?

3. What are the implications for policymakers of the EPPE findings on the lasting effects of quality?

 **Further reading**

Harms, T., Clifford, M. and Cryer, D. (1998) *Early Childhood Environment Rating Scale – Revised Edition (ECERS-R)*. New York: Teachers College Press. The reference for the ECERS-R, one of the rating scales discussed in the chapter:

Siraj-Blatchford, I. (2007) 'Creativity, communication and collaboration: the identification of pedagogic progression in sustained shared thinking', *Asia-Pacific Journal of Research in Early Childhood Education*, 1: 3–24. This paper considers the contribution of 'sustained shared thinking' to pedagogical practice:

Sylva, K., Melhuish, E., Sammons, P., Siraj-Blatchford, I. and Taggart, B. (2008) *Effective Pre-school and Primary Education 3–11 Project (EPPE 3–11) Final Report from the Primary Phase: Pre-school, School and Family Influences on Children's Development during Key Stage 2 (age 7–11)*. Research Report DCSF-RR061. Nottingham: DCSF Publications. The final report of the primary school phase of the EPPE project, showing the contribution of pre-school quality to children's outcomes at age 11.

Sylva, K., Siraj-Blatchford, I. and Taggart, B. (2003, revised 2006) *Assessing Quality in the Early Years: Early Childhood Environment Rating Scale – Extension (ECERS-E): Four Curricular Subscales*. Stoke-on-Trent: Trentham Books. The reference for the ECERS-E, the other rating scale discussed in the chapter:

Sylva, K., Siraj-Blatchford, I., Taggart, B., Sammons, P., Melhuish, E., Elliot, K. and Totsika, V. (2006) 'Capturing quality in early childhood through environmental rating scales', *Early Childhood Research Quarterly*, 21: 76–92. An article describing how rating scales attempt to 'capture' the essence of quality through identifying the behaviours of children and staff in pre-school settings that are of high or low quality.

References

Burchinal, M., Howes, C. and Kontos, S. (2002) 'Structural predictors of child care quality in child care homes', *Early Childhood Research Quarterly*, 17: 87–105.

De Kruif, R., McWilliam, R., Ridley, S. and Wakely, M. (2000) 'Classification of teachers' interaction behaviours in early childhood classrooms', *Early Childhood Research Quarterly*, 15: 247–68.

Department for Children, Schools and Families (DCSF) (2008) *Early Years Foundation Stage*. Nottingham: DCSF Publications.

Department for Education and Employment/Qualifications and Curriculum Authority (DfEE/QCA) (2000) *Curriculum Guidance for the Foundation Stage*. London: DfEE/QCA.

Gilliam, W. (2000) *The School Readiness Initiative in South-Central Connecticut: Classroom Quality, Teacher Training, and Service Provision. Final Report of Findings for Fiscal Year 1999*. Retrieved 2 December 2002 from http://nieer.org/resources/research/C3RI1999.pdf

Goodman, R. (1997) 'The strengths and difficulties questionnaire: a research note', *Journal of Child Psychology and Psychiatry*, 38(5): 581–6.

Harms, T., Clifford, M. and Cryer, D. (1998) *Early Childhood Environment Rating Scale, Revised Edition (ECERS-R)*. Vermont: Teachers College Press.

Her Majesty's (HM) Treasury (2004) *Choice for Parents, the Best Start for Children: A Ten Year Strategy for Childcare*. London: The Stationery Office.

Her Majesty's (HM) Treasury (2007) *Policy Review of Children and Young People: A Discussion Paper*. London. Her Majesty's Stationary Office.

House of Commons (2005) *Childcare Bill*. London: The Stationery Office.

Jaeger, E. and Funk, S. (2001) 'The Philadelphia Child Care Quality Study: an examination of quality in selected early education and care settings. A technical report submitted to the Improving School Readiness project of the united way of South-Eastern PA'. Retrieved 2 December 2002 from http://psych.sju.edu/faculty/Jaeger/JaegerFunk2001.pdf

Katz, L. (1993) 'Multiple perspectives on the quality of early childhood programmes', *European Early Childhood Education Research Journal*, 1(2): 5–9.

Munton, A., Mooney, A. and Rowland, L. (1995) 'Deconstructing quality: a conceptual framework for the new paradigm in day care provision for the under eights', *Early Child Development and Care*, 144: 11–23.

NICHD Early Child Care Research Network (1998) 'Early child care and self-control, compliance and problem behavior at twenty-four and thirty-six months', *Child Development*, 69: 1145–70.

NICHD Early Child Care Research Network (1999) 'Child outcomes when child care center classes meet recommended standards for quality', *American Journal of Public Health*, 89: 1072–7.

Niles, M.D., Reynolds, A.J. and Roe-Sepowitz, D. (2008) 'Early childhood intervention and early adolescent social and emotional competence: second-generation evaluation evidence from the Chicago Longitudinal Study', *Educational Research*, 50(1): 55–73.

Peisner-Feinberg, E. and Burchinal, M. (1997) 'Relations between pre-school children's child care experiences and concurrent development: the Cost, Quality and Outcomes study', *Merrill–Palmer Quarterly*, 43: 451–77.

Phillips, D., McCartney, K. and Scarr, S. (1987) 'Child care quality and children's social development', *Journal of Applied Developmental Psychology*, 23: 537–43.

Sammons, P., Sylva, K., Melhuish, E., Siraj-Blatchford, I., Taggart, B., Elliot, K. and Marsh, A. (2004) *The Continuing Effects of Pre-school Education at Age 7 Years. Technical Paper 11*. London: DfES/London Institute of Education.

Siraj-Blatchford, I., Sammons, P., Sylva, K., Melhuish, E. and Taggart, B. (2006) 'Educational research and evidence based policy: the mixed method approach of the EPPE project', *Evaluation and Research in Education*, 19(2): 63–82.

Siraj-Blatchford, I., Sylva, K., Muttock, S., Gilden, R. and Bell, D. (2002) *Researching Effective Pedagogy in the Early Years*. London: DfES.

Sylva, K. and Pugh, G. (2005) 'Transforming the early years in England', *Oxford Review of Education*, 31: 11–27.

Sylva, K., Melhuish, E.C., Sammons, P., Siraj-Blatchford, I. and Taggart, B. (2004) *The Effective Provision of Pre-School Education (EPPE) Project: Technical Paper 12 – The Final Report: Effective Pre-School Education*. London: DfES/Institute of Education, University of London.

Sylva, K., Melhuish, E., Sammons, P., Siraj-Blatchford, I. and Taggart, B. (2008) *Effective Pre-school and Primary Education 3–11 Project (EPPE 3–11) Final Report from the Primary Phase: Pre-school, School and Family Influences on Children's Development during Key Stage 2 (Age 7–11)*. Research Report No. DCSF-XXXX. Nottingham: DCSF Publications.

Sylva, K., Sammons, P., Melhuish, E.C., Siraj-Blatchford, I., and Taggart, B. (1999) *The Effective Provision of Pre-School Education (EPPE) Project: Technical Paper 1 – An Introduction of EPPE*. London: DfEE/Institute of Education, University of London.

Sylva, K., Siraj-Blatchford, I. and Taggart, B. (2003, revised 2006) *Assessing Quality in the Early Years: Early Childhood Environment Rating Scale – Extension (ECERS-E): Four Curricular Subscales*. Stoke-on Trent: Trentham Books.

The National Strategies (2008a) *Early Years Quality Improvement Support Programme (EYQISP)*. Department for Children, Schools and Families: Nottingham.

The National Strategies (2008b) *Early Years Consultant's Handbook*. Nottingham: Department for Children, Schools and Families.

UK Parliament (2006) *The Childcare Act*. London: The Stationery Office.

Appendix

Example ECERS-E item "Adult reading with the children", taken from the *literacy* subscale

Item	Inadequate 1	2	Minimal 3	4	Good 5	6	Excellent 7
Item 3. Adult reading with the children							
	1.1 Adults rarely read to the children. *		3.1 An adult reads with the children most days. **		5.1 Children take an active role in group reading during which the words and/or story are usually discussed.		7.1 There is discussion about print and letters as well as content.
			3.2 Children are encouraged to join in with repetitive words and phrases in the text (where appropriate).		5.2 Children are encouraged to conjecture about and comment on the text.		7.2 There is support material for the children to engage with stories by themselves e.g. tapes, flannel board, displays etc.
							7.3 There is evidence of one to one reading with some children.

Notes for clarification

* Score yes if no reading with the children is seen during the observation (formal or informal, include reading with small groups or individuals).

** Score yes if you observe an adult reading with groups or individual children during the observation.

Source: Sylva et al. (2003)

Example ECERS-E item "Food preparation" taken from the *science/environment* subscale

Item	Inadequate		Minimal		Good		Excellent	
	1	2	3	4	5	6	7	

Item 5. Science Activities: Science processes: Food preparation

Note + In order to assess this you must have observed staff interacting with children. For higher levels, look for evidence for engagement with children in scientific processes i.e. close observation, raising questions/making guesses (hypothesising), experimenting (see what happens) and communicating and interpreting results (why has this happened).

Inadequate (1)	Minimal (3)	Good (5)	Excellent (7)
1.1 No preparation of food or drink is undertaken in front of the children.	3.1 Food preparation is undertaken by adults in front of the children.	5.1 Food preparation/ cooking activities are provided regularly.	7.1 A variety of cooking activities in which all children may take part are provided regularly.
	3.2 Some children can choose to participate in food preparation. But this is random, not planned in advance.	5.2 Most of the children have the opportunity to participate in food preparation.	7.2 The ingredients are attractive and the end result is edible and appreciated, e.g. eaten by children, or taken home.
	3.3 Staff discuss with the children food that has been prepared by adults, where appropriate, e.g. burnt toast or new biscuits or food brought in by children.	5.3 The staff lead discussion about the food involved and use appropriate terminology, e.g. melt, dissolve.	7.3 The staff lead and encourage discussion on the process of food preparation, such as what needs to be done to cause ingredients to set or melt.
		5.4 Children are encouraged to use more than one sense (feel, smell, taste) to explore raw ingredients.	7.4 Staff draw attention to changes in food and question children about it, e.g. what did it look like before, what does it look like now, what has happened to it?

Source: Sylva et al. (2003)

CHAPTER 5

INSPECTING AND EVALUATING THE QUALITY AND STANDARDS OF EARLY YEARS AND CHILDCARE PROVISION

Caroline Jones

Chapter Contents

- The impact of policy on accountability
- Early years and childcare provision
- Reversing the trend: from quality to compliance
- Inspecting EYFS: towards coherence
- Leading to excellence
- Leadership, self-evaluation and improvement
- Joint Area Reviews of children's services

The theme of 'quality' is a crucial aspiration of policy development for early childhood. Effective regulation and inspection are seen as a vital aspect in ensuring that providers meet acceptable standards in the delivery of services for children and their families. A vision for the care and education of children was expressed in the Green Paper, *Every Child Matters* (ECM) (DfES, 2003), which led to the 2004 Children Act. The radical restructuring of early years provision and the continued investment and expansion, which has evolved in response to the Every

Child Matters agenda, has resulted in changes to the ways in which early years and childcare providers are registered, regulated and inspected. The Childcare Act 2006, a pioneering piece of legislation, heralds further attempts to bring cohesion to the quality assurance and inspection of early years provision under the long term umbrella philosophy of *Every Child Matters.*

This chapter examines the changing context, nature and purposes of inspection and evaluation of early years and childcare provision. It begins with a brief overview of the recent political backdrop to regulation and inspection. It moves on to comment on new registration and inspection arrangements under the Childcare Act 2006, the first ever concerned exclusively with childcare and early childhood services. We then review the extent to which the introduction of the Early Years Foundation Stage (EYFS) and associated common inspection schedules provide an opportunity for the long-awaited 'level playing field' across the maintained and non-maintained sectors, asking whether it is possible for one size to fit all in the context of diverse patterns of provision. Tensions are highlighted between inspections based on compliance to new minimum General Childcare Register (GCR) Requirements, and those based on the EYFS for the purpose of evaluating quality underpinned by effective leadership, self-evaluation and improvement. Measures in the 2006 Act formalized the strategic role of local authorities (LAs) through a set of new duties, requiring them to undertake work in ensuring children have the best start in life by working with partners, reducing inequalities and improving outcomes. With local authorities retaining responsibility for information, advice and training and support for early years practitioners in a multi-agency context, we provide a brief overview of how LAs themselves are inspected for the quality of their services for children and young people.

The impact of policy on accountability

Evaluation serves a variety of purposes and is inherently linked to the wider policy context. Those involved in delivering early years services are generally accountable to the funding body or the public purse. Hence evaluation can be used as evidence of accountability and value for money. Evaluation can also contribute to the formation and interpretation of government policy vision (Jones and Leverett, 2008). The Green Paper *Every Child Matters* (DfES, 2003) continually emphasized the importance of early years services as essential for working parents. Children's day care has become a particularly significant element in government economic policies designed to reduce social exclusion and the number of children living in poverty. The government's pledge for greater provision for the early years was consolidated through the 10-year national strategy for childcare, *Choice for Parents, the Best Start for Children: A Ten Year Strategy for Childcare* (HMT, 2004). The focus was on moving children out of poverty via the workforce participation of their parents. The strategy involved not only expansion of places but also called for a simplified and independent registration and inspection framework, to be provided by Ofsted. This was based on the premise that the inspection process prompts regular self-evaluation and offers service providers an independent assessment of their strengths and weaknesses, so they can target their improvement efforts. It also allows parents to make informed choices encouraging the market to deliver high quality (DfES/DWP, 2006)

The Childcare Act 2006 was a significant milestone in changing the way provision was registered, delivered and inspected and took forward fundamental commitments from the Childcare Strategy. Part 1 set out new duties of local authorities in England in relation to well-being and specific duties in relation to early childhood services. Local authorities were charged with securing sufficient childcare for working parents and providing information, advice and assistance to parents and providing training and advice to childcare providers. Evaluation and inspection, however, remained at arm's length from local authorities with Ofsted, a non-ministerial independent government department, renamed in April 2007, the Office for Standards in Education, Children's Services and Skills but still known as Ofsted. The *Framework for the Regulation of Daycare and Childminding* (Ofsted, 2006: Annex D) sets out a number of clear principles which apply to all inspection activities carried out by, or on behalf of Ofsted. These are intended to make sure that the findings of the inspection contribute to improvement and that the process of inspection promotes inclusion. This ensures that the inspection is carried out openly with those being inspected and the findings of the inspection are valid, reliable and consistent. The principles include:

- Inspection acts in the interests of children, young people and adult learners and, where relevant, their parents, to encourage high-quality provision that meets diverse needs and promotes equality.
- Inspection is evaluative and diagnostic, assessing quality and compliance and providing a clear basis for improvement.
- Inspection invites and takes account of any self-evaluation by those inspected. Inspection is carried out by those who have sufficient and relevant professional expertise and training.
- Judgements are based on systematic evaluation requirements and criteria, are reached corporately where more than one inspector is involved, and reflect a common understanding in Ofsted about quality.

The Early Years Foundation Stage (DfES, 2007), introduced the first common quality framework for early years provision regardless of age group or sector. This provided an opportunity to develop these principles and bring greater consistency to the inspection across all early years providers. It necessitated, from 1 September 2008, a revised registration and inspection framework for children in early years provision, which also impacted on registration for older children.

Early years and childcare provision

Arrangements under the Children Act 1989 were replaced from 1 September 2008, with new registers under the Childcare Act 2006. The type of inspection carried out now depends on the type of registration, which in turn is determined by the child's age and type of setting attended. In spite of intentions to simplify arrangements, the registration system has become arguably more complex. The Childcare Act 2006 introduced two new childcare registers, one for 'early years' and one for 'later years' provision.

The Early Years (EY) Register is compulsory for:

- maintained schools or independent schools directly responsible for children under 3
- childcarers, such as childminders, day nurseries, pre-schools and private nursery schools providing for children from birth to the 31 August following their fifth birthday (Ofsted, 2008a).

There is ostensibly more cohesion in that schools are, for the first time, required to register where they are directly responsible for under threes. Yet there are still anomalies between the schools and the private, voluntary and independent (PVI) sector, for example, in schools, children who are 3 in the term in which they start to attend or 'rising 3s' can be treated as 3-year-olds. Settings registered on the EY register will be known as 'early years providers'.

The 2006 Act removed the traditional distinction between 'education' and 'care' as far as early years registration and inspections were concerned, replacing them with the umbrella term 'early years provision', part of a broader spectrum of early years services. The EYFS also maintains a distinction between 'welfare' and 'learning and development', in effect retaining the distinction between the two dimensions of childcare provision. To add to the complexity, childcarers on the EY register who provide for children over 5, or 'later years' provision, may also need to register on the second register, the 'general childcare register' (Childcare Act 2006: 16). Even more confusing for providers, the first part (Part A), of this childcare register (CR) is compulsory and the second part (Part B), is voluntary, for those not required to be registered on the compulsory or EY register, for example those caring for children over 8 but under 18. A lone childminder caring for a baby, a 5-year-old and a 9-year-old after school, could be on all three registers and inspected against all three sets of requirements Accountability and raising standards is a priority but one that needs to be supported by equitable levels of funding, training and advice. There is a danger that some non-maintained early years settings, already under financial pressure due to the graduate leadership initiative and the wider economy, will close due to the pressure and cost of adapting to an unwieldy external 'context neutral' inspection and quality framework. Interestingly, schools providing 'later years' provision do not have to register on the childcare register but should have regard to its requirements.

Reversing the trend: from quality to compliance

The general childcare register (GCR) bears over 40 separate requirements, based on the statutory Childcare (Inspections) Regulations (2008) some of which are applicable to both parts, others to Part A and others to Part B only. Attempts at simplification have resulted in childcare standards overall being much less comprehensive in content and guidance than the previous National Standards, with inspection criteria matched to five types of childcare provision – full day care, sessional day care, crèches, out-of-school care and childminders (DfES, 2001). The EYFS welfare requirements, applicable solely to under 5s, have absorbed and replaced the *National Standards for Under Eights Daycare and Childminding* (DfES, 2001). The regulation and inspection of childcare for children over 5 has been reduced to random inspections or inspections following a complaint, and related to compliance rather than quality. As Ofsted suggests, 'The purpose of the inspection is to check that you are continuing to meet the requirements of your registration and any conditions we may have imposed on it' (Ofsted, 2008a: 6).

The 2006 Act places a duty on local authorities to ensure sufficient childcare places for working parents, encouraging ever-increasing numbers of school age children into childcare. At the same time these changes to inspection of childcare represent a retrograde step, particularly for children over compulsory school age. In attempting to develop a 'one size fits all', the different criteria, formerly tailored to respond to the diverse needs of day care and childminding have been lost. For providers on both registers, there are also some minor inconsistencies between the EYFS welfare requirements (WRs) and the CR requirements. In relation to complaints, for example, the EYFS statutory welfare requirements state that providers should respond within 28 days (DfES, 2007: 23) whereas the CR requirements cite 20 days (CR 7.4).

By contrast to later years inspections the purpose of early years inspections is to 'evaluate the quality and standards' of early years provision 'in line with the principles, and general and specific requirements of the EYFS' (Ofsted, 2008a). This suggests an emphasis on quality as well as an element of compliance.

Inspecting Early Years Foundation Stage: towards coherence

The Children Act 1989 inspections of childminding and day-care provision for children under 8 were traditionally undertaken by local authorities. It took the establishment of Ofsted through the 1992 Act to cause all maintained schools, including nursery schools, to be inspected on a regular cycle, which began in September 1994. In 2001, Ofsted became responsible not only for inspection but also registration, investigation and enforcement in relation to childminders and day-care providers. Ofsted's priority was to review an approach to inspection that was initially concerned with compliance rather than quality and establish a national, coherent regulatory system across the range of early years providers. By April 2003, Ofsted had revised its Children Act inspection framework to identify providers that not only met the national standards but provided good quality care. This work paved the way for the development of a combined framework for judging both care and education, and reporting the findings in a single report.

Changing and diverse patterns of educational provision brought a blurring of the boundaries resulting in renewed demands for integrated approaches to quality assurance through inspection and self-evaluation. The Childcare Act 2006 formalized further reforms to the early years inspection and evaluation. In addition the gap between 'care' and 'education' providers was narrowed as, for the first time, maintained provision was subject to meeting welfare requirements, as well as promoting learning and development. Conversely, the EYFS brought new territory for childcare providers, including those caring for children under 3 who are required to be accountable for externally imposed 'educational' programmes via the learning and development requirements for every child under 5, whether or not they provide government-funded places. While this brings coherence, it also raises an issue of whether it is possible or practicable or even desirable to create a system of inspection and evaluation where one size fits all.

Leading to excellence

An Ofsted report based on inspections of 19,000 non-maintained funded nursery education providers concluded that 'over half the childcare provision is good; the overwhelming majority of the remainder is at least satisfactory; and a third of nursery education provision is of high quality with children making very good progress towards the early learning goals' (Ofsted, 2005: 3). A more recent report on childcare and early education, *Leading to Excellence* (Ofsted, 2008b), based on evidence from a variety of sources, including inspections of 84,000 settings between April 2005 and March 2008, states that almost all (97 per cent) settings provided at least satisfactory childcare. The proportion of day-care providers inspected with good or outstanding childcare has risen in 2007–08, These statistics beg the question as to whether the recent overhaul of inspection and evaluation was really necessary.

From September 2008 a common early years evaluation schedule has been included in all inspection frameworks. Although EYFS provision in schools (run by governing bodies) will be inspected as part of their school inspections, the early years part will use the same schedule. The intention is to ensure that early years provision in schools and in early years registered settings is evaluated in the same way. In all sectors the report will include key judgements accompanied by an evaluation of the effectiveness of early years provision. Inspections, with little or no notice, will be shorter and sharper. The five outcomes for children set out in *Every Child Matters* have provided the theme that reconciles the different inspection frameworks. Although a common framework has not been developed, common judgements (see Table 5.1) are now applied to all settings delivering EYFS, with a separate section in school reports, a new report format and a more extensive self-evaluation in the non-maintained sector. From September 2008 early years provision not based on school sites will be subject to a 'stand alone' inspection, enabling shorter, but comparable reports which

Table 5.1   The six judgements evaluated on a four-point judgement scale

How effective is the provision in meeting the needs of children in the Early Years Foundation Stage?*
How well do children in the EYFS achieve?
How good are the overall personal development and well-being of the children in the EYFS?
How effectively are children in the Early Years Foundation Stage helped to learn and develop?*
How effectively is the welfare of the children in the Early Years Foundation Stage promoted?*
How effectively is provision in the Early Years Foundation Stage led and managed?*

Source: Ofsted, 2008c: 7

give an overview of outcomes for children to be generated across all registered early years provision. Provision on school sites will be inspected either with a single or parallel inspection.

All provision on a school site that is *managed by the governing body* will be inspected in a 'single inspection' under the existing section 5 framework from the 2005 Education Act. Childcare for older pupils, not part of the EYFS, will also be inspected proportionately as part of section 5 inspections. Registered childcare provision on a school site that is *not managed by the governing body* will be inspected under section 42 of the Childcare Act 2006 using the Early Years Evaluation Schedule (Ofsted, 2008c), at the same time as the school where practically possible as a 'parallel inspection event'. However, the inspections and reports will remain separate.

The four asterisked judgements in Table 5.1 are common to all providers within the EYFS whether in early years' settings or in schools. The other two judgements (non-asterisked) are outcome judgements which are made in maintained schools under the common inspection framework. These two judgements will also be made in independent schools. They will not be applied to the private and voluntary sector.

Inspection methodology remains the same. Inspectors will consider a range of evidence obtained mainly from first-hand observation of children and how adults interact with them; discussions with managers and staff members; discussions with parents; talking with children and considering documents, including planning and assessment records. Inspection will also focus on how providers meet the needs of the children by reporting on any groups which are disadvantaged by race, gender or ability. Working in partnership is also a key theme of the EYFS and of inspection. This includes working with parents, local authorities, early years professionals and other settings that work with a provider to give children full EYFS provision. There will be a greater expectation that all providers, not just those delivering the free entitlement, will plan for and assess children's progress.

The four-point judgement scale remains the same as in the previous framework, with updated descriptors to reflect the ECM outcomes and EYFS (Table 5.2).

The inspection framework follows its predecessors into the trap of being too comprehensive. It is rendered somewhat inelegant by the complexity of its many inspection criteria, judgements and sub-judgements, and this can distract from rigorous evaluation. How can Ofsted ensure that sound decisions are

Table 5.2 Evaluating overall effectiveness: the four point judgement scale descriptors

Outstanding (1)	Exemplary: the setting is highly effective at making sure children's progress across the five ECM outcomes is consistently good and is exemplary in significant elements. All major aspects of the provision are at least good, and exemplary in most respects. Children's learning and development are impressive in relation to their starting points and capabilities. Provision for their physical and emotional well-being is excellent. Exemplary partnerships between providers, parents and other agencies ensure children's needs are met and their protection is assured. Highly effective systems lead to improvement. All other judgements are at least good and some are outstanding. The overarching requirements of the EYFS are met.
Good (2)	Children make good progress in their learning. They enjoy their time in school. Learning opportunities help to meet all children's needs well and keep them actively engaged. Good arrangements exist to ensure their safety and health and encourage their involvement in their community. Effective links with parents/carers help to involve them in their children's care and education, and they are kept very well informed of their progress. Those in charge work in partnership with other agencies and providers to ensure that children's learning and welfare needs are met. They have an accurate understanding of the strengths and weaknesses of the provision and take effective steps to improve it. There are no breaches of specific requirements that have a significant impact on the children or on the extent to which the overarching requirements are met.
Satisfactory (3)	The EYFS is satisfactory in all key judgements, and may be good in some respects. There are no breaches of specific requirements that have a significant impact on the children or on the extent to which the overarching requirements are met
Inadequate (4)	Overall effectiveness is likely to be judged inadequate if any of the key judgements are inadequate. Learning opportunities have significant weaknesses that restrict the progress and personal development of children. Children are not cared for adequately so their safety and/or health are at risk. Those in charge do not give other staff an adequate sense of direction. Those in charge disregard or are unaware of weaknesses and show insufficient capacity to make improvements. Communication with parents and carers is not focused on children's learning and development. There are breaches of the overarching requirements that have a significant impact on the children.

Source: Ofsted, 2008c: 8–9

made concerning the EYFS in schools when inspectors may only have a few hours for this aspect of the school's work? How can the same judgements be applied to every setting regardless of individual differences in funding, building, size, numbers of children and levels of training?

Inspectors (and providers) will need be thoroughly conversant with the detailed inspection framework and guidance, the EYFS learning and development requirements, principles, themes and commitments as well as the welfare requirements and in some cases the CR requirements. Inspection reports produced under sections 49 and 50 of the Childcare Act 2006, contain a description of the setting, list of what the setting needs to do to improve and evaluate quality under three headings:

1   Overall effectiveness of the early years provision – a general statement summarizing overall effectiveness.
2   Leadership and management – commenting on systems for self evaluation and continuous improvement, partnership with parents, safeguarding children from harm or neglect, including recruitment procedures.
3   Quality and standards – covering the EYFS welfare and learning and development requirements and the five ECM outcomes.

Although parents are more likely to choose a setting based on reputation and location than on the Ofsted report, this record provides a clear basis of comparison between provision. However, as the majority will be 'good' it will be the presence of the other judgements which distinguish one report from another, as well as the content of the report itself. The limit to only four points in a scale makes it hard to differentiate, for example, between a 'good' in the sense of almost outstanding and 'good' in the sense of just better than satisfactory. A scale with more points, and clear specific criteria linked to each point, would give settings guidance as to what needs to be done to move to the next level of overall effectiveness. The phrase 'significant impact' is relative as perceptions of what constitutes significant and what is less than significant may differ between individual inspectors depending on their own varying background, qualifications and experiences.

The crucial inspection judgement on the quality of leadership and management appears to underpin the inspection outcome. Jones and Pound (2008) describe leadership and management as a problem-solving, culturally influenced process of reflection and concerted efforts by individual practitioners working together with others to improve outcomes for children. This is reflected during inspections by the inclusion of a sub-judgement on capacity to improve as well as the effectiveness of self-evaluation which goes wider than progress with actions or recommendations set at the most recent inspection.

Leadership, self-evaluation and improvement

Inspection frameworks have been very influential in promoting self-evaluation (Matthews and Sammons, 2004) with a completed self-evaluation form (SEF) forming part of the inspection process in both the maintained and non-maintained sectors. As the inspection process has become increasingly transparent, there has been a growing tendency for schools and other providers to ask the same questions of themselves as inspectors ask. Their perceived success in doing this has resulted in the school inspection system adapting so as to use the outcomes of self-evaluation to shape the inspection agenda. In the maintained sector the SEF itself has traditionally been more detailed than in non-maintained settings, where it only elicited basic operational information. The revised framework introduced a more extensive SEF, based on the EYFS and ECM outcomes, to be completed at various (non-specified) intervals between inspections and submitted online. The latest version is to be used by inspectors as a starting point for all early years inspections. It will form the basis of a number of inspection hypotheses that they will test out during the inspection.

This assumes that all early years providers not only have the information and communications technology (ICT) and written communication skills to submit an online form, but that they will have or need to develop the complex knowledge, skills and ability to reflect upon and evaluate their practice and identify what needs to be done in order to improve. Some early years providers already demonstrate excellent practice in this art. Others will need extensive training and support. Initially, at least, there may be a tendency for the 'registered person' or manager of the setting to complete the SEF. It will be interesting to see how many settings grade themselves as inadequate! Inspectors will be faced with the additional challenge of how to comment on the quality of self-evaluation, which, in spite of comprehensive guidance, will vary in style, length and content. In some cases the SEF may not even be completed as it is not mandatory.

The concept of self-improvement through reflection and self-evaluation has potential, but care must be taken not to narrowly interpret self-evaluation as a tool for ensuring practitioners merely 'deliver' and 'comply' with the EYFS. There is a danger that the SEF becomes a limited assessment of conformity to externally imposed frameworks in a technical sense or a purely mechanical procedure rather than a tool for stepping back in order to reflect, analyse and improve. The outcome of self-evaluation should be a revised and better informed improvement plan, regardless of the timing of inspection. The SEF may endorse competent settings and in the long term, help instil an ethos of self-improvement but will it help improve those that are barely satisfactory or even inadequate? With the demise of the annual inspection and the removal of local authority involvement it seems unrealistic to expect inspection to be both formative and summative. An alternative would be to establish regional inspectorates or quality assurance procedures which can feed into the local authority advice, support and training teams. If settings were visited annually for interim monitoring and local inspectors were able to build a rapport with those in charge of settings then improvement is more likely to be sustained. A different inspector, with no knowledge of the setting or context, arriving unannounced every three years, may not prove to be the most effective evaluation process. As local authorities are charged with promoting the well-being of all children and young people in the area, they could and perhaps should be trusted to monitor as well as support the quality of services in the area. Their inspections of early years provision could then form part of the assessment of local authorities.

Joint Area Reviews of children's services

Under the Children Act 2004, inspectorates started working together for the first time to inspect and report on the quality of services for children within a local authority. This involved two complementary processes: Annual Performance Assessments (APAs) and Joint Area Reviews (JARs). The APAs form an integral element of the improvement cycle, acting as a risk assessment for the JAR. The JARs, including fieldwork, reported on the well-being of *all children and young people* in a local area following up any area of weakness identified in the APA. The three-year reviews covered universal, preventive and targeted services incorporating education, health and social services. Particular attention is given to joint action by local services on behalf of those groups of children and young people who are vulnerable to poor outcomes. They described the outcomes achieved by children and young people growing up in the area, and evaluated the way local services, taken collectively, contribute to their well-being. Specific judgements, on the same four-point scale shown above, were made about the quality, management and leadership of the council's children's services. Hudson (2005) identified three 'inspecting principles' within the process of inspection in local authorities:

1 The co-ordinating principle – the APA bringing together procedures carried out by Ofsted and the Commission for Social Care Inspection (CSCI).
2 The proportionate inspecting principle – inspection in proportion to identi-fied strengths and weaknesses.
3 Engagement and involvement principle – including gathering evidence from parents, children, front line workers and senior officers.

These should be retained in the proposals, under consultation, for new Comprehensive Area Assessments (CAAs) (Ofsted, 2008d). This new performance framework for local public services began on 1 April 2009. It replaces the cur-rent Comprehensive Performance Assessment of councils (CPA) led by the Audit Commission and Ofsted's APAs and JARs. The proposals are being tested in national trials in 10 areas.

Conclusions

The usefulness of external inspections has been hotly debated, particularly in schools. Improvements have been made but there are still issues to be addressed. More research is needed into the potential negative as well as positive effects of 'arm's length' inspection. Although there is greater integration the legacy of the two separate inspection frameworks remains intact. School inspections are still carried out under section 5 of the Education Act 2005 with the non-maintained sector coming under sections 49 and 50 of the Childcare Act 2006. There is no longer a separate inspection judgement for 'care' and 'education' but a single visit inspecting the overall effectiveness of the early years provision as a whole. Early years inspections now provide increased emphasis on leadership, reflection, self-evaluation and ongoing improvement. The EYFS demands highly trained inspectors with recent and relevant experience and extensive in-depth knowledge of child development and early learning. The proposed move by Ofsted to privatize early years inspections may compromise the quality and consistency of inspections. As there is usually only one inspector, consistency between inspectors and inspections needs to be monitored between settings and sectors.

Bringing together the evaluation of early years services in a single quality framework to encompass all types of childcare from birth to 5 may have unwittingly damaged the ability of individual providers to respond to their own unique communities and contexts of childcare and education. It could be argued that a 'one size fits all approach' undermines the idea of quality in diversity and does not take account of different philosophies, traditions and priorities, qualifications and training experiences. Diverse patterns of provision may demand more diverse patterns of inspection. A formative approach to evaluation that encourages dialogue and improvement to policy and practice does not sit comfortably with the separation of the local authority duty to provide information, advice and training from the responsibility for monitoring quality. It remains to be seen if the proposed CAAs will have an impact on local early years services. Finally, the continued focus on leadership and management needs to be matched with help and support for all those in leadership roles. This would enable all providers to implement ongoing rigorous self-evaluation and improvement systems, to the point where inspections are simply endorsing everyday high-quality practice, taking place regardless of whether or not 'an inspector calls'.

 Points for discussion

- Do the outcomes for children provide a sufficiently comprehensive basis for assessing care and education provision and safeguarding their well-being, needs and interests?

- What are the implications of reliance on more extensive self-evaluation and less on direct inspection?

- Is it reasonable to have a compliance model of inspection of 'later years childcare?

- Is it practicable, possible or desirable to achieve common inspection and evaluation systems across complex and diverse patterns of provision?

- What are the implication of a single quality framework for leadership and management ?

Further reading

Jones, C. and Pound, L. (2008) *Leadership and Management in the Early Years: From Principles to Practice*. Maidenhead: Open University Press/McGraw Hill. Leadership and management underpins inspection judgements, so this is an invaluable book for those interested in accountability in early years provision.

Matthews, P. and Sammons, P. (2004) *Improvement Through Inspection*. London: Ofsted and the Institute of Education, University of London. An in-depth look at inspection and evaluation principles, processes and practices.

Office for Standards in Education, Children's Services and Skills (2008) *Early Years: Leading to Excellence*. Ref 080044. London: Ofsted. A clear overview of the Ofsted perspective on quality with some interesting data relating to inspection judgements.

Office for Standards in Education, Children's Services and Skills (2008) *Are You Ready for Your Inspection? A Guide to Inspections of Provision on Ofsted's Childcare and Early Years Registers*. Ref. 080023. London: Ofsted. An up-to-date overview of precisely which documents providers needs ready for their inspection, and the purpose and nature of inspections.

Office for Standards in Education, Children's Services and Skills (2008) *Inspecting the Early Years Foundation Stage: Guidance for Inspectors, September 2008*. ofsted.gov. uk/content/download/6796/70134/file/ (accessed 21 November 2008). Useful to see the insformation given to inspectors to help them to make decisions on judging quality. Interesting perspectives on how to reach the various judgements and work towards consistency.

References

Department for Education and Skills (DfES) (2001) *National Standards for Under Eights Daycare and Childminding: Full Day Care*. Nottingham: DfES.

Department for Education and Skills (DfES) (2003) *Every Child Matters*. Green Paper. London: The Stationery Office.

Department for Education and Skills (DfES) (2007) *The Early Years Foundation Stage: Setting the Standards for Children's Learning, Development and Care for Children from Birth to Five*. Nottingham: DfES.

Department for Education and Skills/Department for Work and Pensions (DfES/DWP) (2006) *Choice for Parents, the Best Start for Children: Making it Happen*. London: DfES/DWP.

Her Majesty's Treasury (HMT) (2004) *Choice for Parents, the Best Start for Children: A Ten Year Strategy for Childcare*. London: The Stationery Office.

Hudson, B. (2005) '"Not a cigarette paper between us": integrated inspection of children's services in England', *Social Policy and Administration*, 39(5): 513–27.

Jones, C. and Leverett, S. (2008) 'Policy into practice: assessment, evaluation and multi-agency working with children', in P. Foley and A. Rixon (eds), *Changing Children's Services: Working and Learning Together*. Bristol: Policy Press in association with The Open University.

Jones, C. and Pound, L. (2008) *Leadership and Management in the Early Years: From Principles to Practice*. Maidenhead: Open University Press/McGraw-Hill Education.

Matthews, P. and Sammons, P. (2004) *Improvement Through Inspection*. London: Ofsted and the Institute of Education, University of London.

Office for Standards in Education (Ofsted) (2005) *Early Years: Firm Foundations*. London: Ofsted.

Office for Standard in Education (Ofsted) (2006) *Framework for the Regulation of Daycare and Childminding.* www.ofsted.gov.uk/publications/2601 (accessed 13 May 2007).

Office for Standards in Education, Children's Services and Skills (Ofsted) (2008a) *Are You Ready for Your Inspection? A Guide to Inspections of Provision on Ofsted's Childcare and Early Years Registers*. Ref. 080023. London: Ofsted.

Office for Standards in Education, Children's Services and Skills (Ofsted) (2008b) *Early Years: Leading to Excellence.* Ref. 080044. London: Ofsted. www.ofsted.gov.uk/Ofsted-home/Leading-to-excellence (accessed 21 November 2008).

Office for Standards in Education, Children's Services and Skills (Ofsted) (2008c) *Inspecting the Early Years Foundation Stage: Guidance for Inspectors September 2008*. ofsted.gov.uk/content/download/6796/70134/file/ (21 November 2008).

Office for Standards in Education, Children's Services and Skills (Ofsted) (2008d) *Comprehensive Area Assessment: Proposals for Assessing Local Authority Services for Children and Young People*. Ref. 080187. London: Ofsted. www.ofsted.gov.uk (accessed 21 November 2008).

PART 2

PRACTICE

CHAPTER 6

LISTENING TO YOUNG CHILDREN: ENABLING CHILDREN TO BE SEEN AND HEARD

Y. Penny Lancaster

Chapter Contents

- Defining listening to young children within the context of the UNCRC and *Every Child Matters*
- Our view of childhood: a tapestry of assumptions
- Exploring the strands of a 'seen and heard' view of childhood
- Imagined boundaries

The past eight years have been an exciting era in which the emphasis on listening to young children's views in matters that affect them has wrought a dramatic shift in thinking and practice within early years. The assumptions, values and beliefs that underpin the United Nations Convention on the Rights of the Child (UNCRC) and *Every Child Matters* (ECM) have played a central role in constructing this emphasis. They have signposted young children's entitlement to expressing their perspectives of their experiences, facilitated an increased understanding of what it means to work with children respectfully and have countered the stance that children are passive recipients in their daily lives. They have largely quashed the adage that children should be seen and not heard and have brought an end to the practice of 'paying lip service' to children's perspectives. As a result, children are increasingly being recognized as active participants in their daily lives, whose perspectives of service provision are valuable within the planning and delivery of children services. The themes and principles that are embedded in the Early Years Foundation Stage (EYFS) endorse children's status as stakeholders of early years settings and the importance for practitioners to embark on effective practice that is respectful of children's views as well as their well-being. The EYFS guidance acknowledges that effective practice involves:

- understanding that children have an entitlement to be listened to and have their views valued
- practitioners respecting what children express, whether they are communicating what they have to say visually or verbally
- encouraging children to plan the layout of their environments
- involving children in decision-making, including their own learning journey.

In this chapter, within the context of the UNCRC and *Every Child Matters*, I will explore the assumptions and values that underpin the practice of listening to young children within early years contexts. I will also consider how current thinking about the notions of 'being' and 'becoming' has implications for listening to young children. Throughout this chapter, I will also include examples of how practitioners are already listening to young children.[1] First, however it is important to explain what we mean by listening to young children.

Defining listening to young children

Listening to young children, which is interchangeable with young children's participation, is defined here as opportunities in which children are participating in decision-making about matters that affect them in their daily lives (Lancaster, 2003). Time, space and choice are key features of these opportunities; time for children to formulate their views, spaces in which children feel comfortable to express their perspectives in ways that they prefer, and genuine choice to participate or not (see Lancaster, 2006a; 2006b). Listening to young children offers children opportunities to participate in decision-making while at the same time learning a range of decision-making skills. They are not only expressing their perspectives of their experiences, but also learning how to listen respectfully to the views of others and to negotiate a way forward with those who hold competing or alternative views. Within these opportunities adults are taking seriously children's perspectives, whether these are articulated through visual representations, body language or talk, and are ensuring that children receive feedback as to how their perspectives have influenced, or not, outcomes.[2] The responsibility for any outcomes, however rests with the adult, who is accountable for decisions ultimately made. The following example illustrates listening to young children and ensuring adults are making the ultimate decision.

Young children involved in complaints and compliments procedures

What was the activity?

The children were given images of happy faces and sad faces and asked to distinguish what feelings the faces expressed. We explained to the children that the faces would be kept in the entrance area and when the children arrived, they could choose if they wanted, to put a happy or sad face in a photograph wallet along with their name card. Later in the day the children would have the opportunity to discuss their face choice with either their key person or in circle time or if it was a complaint with management.

Who was involved?

Children, staff, and management in a nursery.

What opportunities do children have to express their perspectives?

Children were encouraged to discuss how they are feeling, what makes them happy about nursery and anything that they dislike.

What next?

The management committee will need to act upon any complaints made by the children. This could involve buying new resources, getting rid of inappropriate resources, dealing with conflict, staff supervision, sharing information with the policy group, discussion with the parents group or adding to the development plan. Staff could work closely with children to carry out any changes and it would be good practice to ensure these issues were written up or incorporated into the development plan.

Source: Kirklees Early Years Service, 2008

... within the context of the UNCRC

Article 12 of the UNCRC provides all children with a legal entitlement to express their perspective on matters that concern them. However, this is not an unqualified right. This entitlement includes the condition that adults will give 'due weight' to children's views. Adults are obligated to consider seriously children's perspectives in light of their age and maturity. There is an expectation that the role adults play in assessing children's understanding of the issues at hand will forge a protective shield around outcomes affecting children. Article 12 is only partially emancipatory. Children's entitlement to have a say in matters that affect them is in effect a space with boundaries. How adults understand the 'due weight' they should afford children's contributions determines the extent to which children's perspectives influence decision-making. Children have an entitlement to participate in decision-making, but it is adults who decide the extent of children's understanding and therefore are by implication ultimately responsible for any decisions made.

Article 5 of the UNCRC also obligates the significant adults in children's lives to take into account the evolving nature of children's cognitive, physical, social, emotional and moral development within decision-making. This is not a passive obligation or a one-off commitment, but rather an active and recurrent responsibility to ensure that the direction and guidance given to children within decision-making is continually adjusted to match children's evolving yet varying social, emotional, cognitive and moral capacities. Article 5 provides children with two significant entitlements: to have increasing autonomy in decision-making according to their evolving capacities *and* to be protected from being responsible for outcomes because of their unevolved capacities (Lansdown, 2005). This, again, is an article which balances children's entitlement to participate in matters that affect them and protecting them from the responsibility of decisions that are ultimately made. Children are entitled to being encouraged to increasingly participate in decision-making, but within an adult-led supportive framework that protects them from being exposed prematurely to responsibilities beyond their capacities. The boundaries that determine children's participation are not fixed. The boundaries are expected to move, to progressively broaden, so that children gain increasing autonomy in matters that concern them.

How adults are making sense of their obligation to judge the extent to which children are understanding their experiences is, however, likely to be underpinned with their particular belief system. The particular values and assumptions that they hold about what children understand socially, cognitively and emotionally within childhood will mediate what they ultimately understand to be the appropriate 'due weight' they need to place on children's perspectives.

Together Article 12 and Article 5 provide all children with a legal entitlement to engage in decision-making, within a space that ebbs and flows according to their understanding of the particular issue at hand – even babies, as the following example illustrates.

Planning in response to babies' learning experiences

What was the activity?

A young baby was given a treasure basket with various resources in it to explore and handle. Staff observed the baby at play and monitored which resources he enjoyed and disliked.

Who was involved?

Child and key person in a nursery.

What opportunities do children have to express their perspectives?

As the activity was with a young baby, it was important to recognize the different ways of communication other than verbal

- facial expressions
- body language
- noises
- time spent with items.

What next?

A key person could use the information about likes and dislikes to produce a specific treasure basket for that child containing all the items that they like. This could be used to comfort them when they are upset.

Source: Kirklees Early Years Service, 2008

... within the context of *Every Child Matters*

Every Child Matters is in many ways a unique policy initiative. Never before has an inquiry about one child wrought such radical service reform across social, health and educational services for children. Lord Laming's recommendations, that became the foundation for ECM, emphasized the need for practitioners to see children as their primary clients, as the primary stakeholders of early years services. Since its arrival on the social policy scene in 2003 as a Green Paper, it has become a much broader conduit of social and educational initiatives that are concerned with improving outcomes for socially and educationally disadvantaged children. Underpinning all these is an explicit assumption that *children and young people learn and thrive when they are healthy, safeguarded from harm, and engaged* (DfES, 2004). The five interdependent outcome indicators,[3] of the ECM Outcomes Framework provide a clear set of indicators that map out how this can be achieved and are together steering an emphasis towards understanding effective service provision as one, which reflects the needs and interests of children. While each of these outcome indicators are amenable to taking into account the direct views of children and their families (Lancaster, 2006a), it is the outcome of 'making a positive contribution' that explicitly provides a set of progressive aims and objectives that aspire to encourage children engage in decision-making. Underpinning ECM is an aspiration that children are involved in the designing and planning of service provision such as the following example.

Young children planning learning experiences

What was the activity?

Creating a 'What shall we do today?' book by photographing equipment to support children choose equipment to play with.

Who was involved?

Childminder, childminder assistant and children.

What opportunities do children have to express their perspectives?

- Selecting what they would like to do.
- Being involved in setting up activities.
- Planning together with the adult.

What next?

We will continue to photograph new resources and add them to the wallet and use these as part of our planning system. I plan to start taking the children to the toy library so we can create photo cards of these resources but make them different to our photo cards so the children can distinguish which toys we have borrowed.

Source: Kirklees Early Years Service, 2008

Despite this, the notion of children 'making a positive contribution' is problematic. The values and assumptions embedded in the particular aims and objectives of this indicator have given rise to a set of mixed messages and as a result is defining 'making a positive contribution' as children:

- engaging in decision-making and supporting the community and environment
- engaging in law-abiding and positive behaviour in and out of school
- developing positive relationships and choosing not to bully and discriminate
- developing self-confidence and successfully dealing with significant life changes and challenges
- developing enterprising behaviour.

On the one hand, the emphasis on children engaging in decision-making implies that children's perspectives of service delivery are integral to developing effective service provision. This raises children's status. It ascribes children as stakeholders, as people who are not passive recipients of service provision, but rather consumers of services whose views are valid and legitimate within decision-making about service planning and delivery. Recent reports on the ECM website have acknowledged that while the process of children engaging in decision-making may not always be a straightforward process, it needs to be pursued because children's perspectives are integral to ensuring effective service provision.

On the other hand, the rest of their aims and objectives of 'making a positive contribution' emphasize that if children's contributions to their communities are to be positive, they need support. They need direction on how to develop particular personal and social skills that promote their well-being, to be involved in good works, and reduce the behaviour that puts them at risk. While all this is well intended and in children's best interests, 'making a positive contribution' in this sense is about normalizing children's behaviour according to predetermined indicators because they are not yet the appropriate social beings they need to be (Prout, 2005). These objectives focus on shaping children towards becoming an appropriate member of society.

The images of children that are embedded in the aims and objectives of 'making a positive contribution' are problematic. The image that children's views are integral to informing effective children's services is in conflict with the image that children need to be socialized to contribute to society appropriately. This raises all kinds of questions. How are practitioners making sense of what 'making a positive contribution' means? What are children's experiences of engaging in decision-making within a framework that is also committed to socializing children to make an appropriate contribution to society?

Our view of childhood: a tapestry of assumptions

Both the UNCRC and ECM are potential mechanisms for listening to young children in matters that affect them. They both provide a platform from which children's status as active participants of their communities can be realized. However, as Prout (2001) has argued, the starting point for listening to young children is not the policy initiative, or intention to involve children in decision-making, but rather the belief system that individual practitioners bring to their practice. The set of assumptions that we hold about children and childhood shapes children's experiences of decision-making. Children's experiences of early years provision is determined by how practitioners are making sense of the policies they are encouraged to implement (Borko, 2004). Subsequently 'making a positive contribution' has the potential to be understood as nothing more than an exercise in learning what is already determined as 'appropriate' decision-making behaviour and skills rather than supporting children to increasingly participate in decision-making that genuinely includes their perspectives of what it means to deliver effective early years provision.

Each one of us has in our possession a unique social and cultural lens through which we attempt to make sense of the world and our experiences. This lens is made up of a particular set of assumptions, values and beliefs that we have acquired from our families, social networks, our experiences of education and the workplace, and from our faith community. The particular set that we develop over time helps us to make sense of our experiences and the experiences of others (Borko, 2004; Prout, 2001; Rogoff, 1990; Vygotsky, 1962). These different strands of assumptions and values weave together, so to speak, a tapestry that ultimately informs our practice. They determine the expectations we have of children. For instance, do we have an expectation of children participating in the recruitment of staff, as in the following example, and if so how?

Young children involved in recruitment

What was the activity?

The children devised questions to ask short-listed applicants for the post of centre manager. The children worked with their key worker to think about:

- what a manager does
- the questions they would like to ask
- the kind of person they would like.

The interview process involved applicants spending time with children in the 3–5's room. During this time, the children were encouraged to ask the questions that they had already discussed and talk to the manager about the post. Staff also asked some of the questions that the children had thought of and recorded the applicants' responses.

Who was involved?

Children, staff, applicants, interview panel in a nursery.

What opportunities do children have to express their perspectives?

The children had the opportunity to express what they thought was important for a manager to do and what they understood the role of a manager should be. The questions they thought of allowed them to be involved in the process and to respond to the answers that were given by the applicants.

What next?

After observing applicants with the children, feedback would be shared with the interview panel regarding how the applicants communicated with the children and responded to the questions. The children could also be asked which applicant they like the most v. When the manager is appointed they could ensure that the children's requests/questions are a priority in order to build up a relationship with the children and show that their contributions are valued and important.

Source: Kirklees Early Years Service, 2008

Our values and assumptions help us think about what children should and should not do and say in different sociocultural contexts and at different stages within their journey through childhood to adulthood. They also inform the role we believe we should play in children's development; the responsibilities we should shoulder in supporting children to reach their potential, cognitively, socially, emotionally and socially, and the particular relationship we should build with children to achieve this.

We are aware of some of the assumptions and values that are informing our practice. However, we also have a set of implicit assumptions. These tend to be deeply entrenched in 'taken for granted' and 'common-sense' language that others may be aware of, but we ourselves are not (Fairclough, 1989; Foucault, 1984; Prout, 2001; Rogoff, 1990; Vygotsky, 1962). Subsequently we may not, at any point in time, ever understand fully the diverse set of assumptions that informs our practice, but what we do have is the option to be committed to pursue awareness and understanding. This involves subscribing to a reflective practice (Lancaster, 2003; 2006b) which involves continually examining our view of childhood and our preferred way of working with children. It is a reflective and dialogical space in which to think and discuss critically our view of childhood; to what extent we understand children as socially active participants whose perspectives of their experiences are integral in developing effective service provision. It likewise enables us to raise our awareness and understanding the role our talk plays, including our body language, in enabling or hindering children's experiences of decision-making.

Exploring the strands of a 'seen and heard' view of childhood

Listening to young children is underpinned by the standpoint that children from birth are people in their own right and as such should be recognized as socially active participants of their families, communities, and societies. This assumption fits with the emerging sociology of childhood in which children are ascribed the status of social actors (James and Prout 1997). Children are active in the construction and determination of their own social lives and the lives of those around them. This locates children as active participants in their lives rather than passive recipients, who have an inherent desire and competency to actively engage with other human beings from birth. Childhood in this view is understood as a social construction and as such makes a distinction between biological and social maturity. Empirical evidence from educationalists, psychologists, anthropologists and sociologists is demonstrating how different children are already accomplishing in a range of childhood contexts (see, for instance, Alderson, 2000; Brooker, 2002; Christensen, 2004; Christensen and James, 2000; Clark and Moss, 2001; Corsaro, 2005; David, 1986; Dunn, 1988; Ennew, 1994; James, 2007; James and Prout, 1997; Jenks, 2005; Malaguzzi, 1993; Mayall, 1996; Prout, 2001; Woodhead, 1997). This understanding has led to a vanguard of advocacy to move beyond understanding children as people who are simply learning and practising for the future. Understanding children as incomplete and in need of childhood to prepare for membership of society, as social 'becomings', is recognized as no longer reflecting children's childhoods.

Recent work on brain maturation (see, for instance, Shonkoff and Phillips, 2000; Woodhead, 2005) has shown that children's cognitive, emotional and social development is inextricably linked to the physical and social context in which children are living. This has implications for how we view children's development. Children raised in environments that stimulate their capacities are developing enhanced cognitive, emotional and social skills, and moral capabilities. Children are not acquiring competencies merely as a consequence of age, but rather through experiences, the culture they are a member of and the levels of adult support and expectation that are proffered (Lansdown, 2005). This has given rise to reconceptualizing children's development as a combination of social and cultural practices and processes of maturation (Woodhead, 2005), which ultimately leads to children developing their capacities in diverse ways. This nature and nurture framework understands that the various encounters children experience in different sociocultural contexts in combination with their individual brain maturation will give rise to differing capacities evolving. This view of children's development challenges the idea that children's maturation traverses a linear trajectory that is comprised of fixed age-related maturation indicators. As Woodhead (2005) and others (see James and Prout, 1997; Prout, 2005; Qvortrup, 1997) argue the nature and nurture framework assumes that children's participation in decision-making will facilitate the development of their social, cognitive, and emotional capacities, as the following example of children involved in decision-making illustrates.

Young children influencing the general outdoor environment

What was the activity?

To develop the outdoor play area in full consultation with both children and parents. As part of this consultation process, the children visited a local garden area to understand the task, and form an opinion of what they liked/disliked. The children were then given a plan of the current outdoor area so they could draw what they hoped to see.

Who was involved?

Children, parents, staff, landscape gardeners and advisory teacher in a nursery.

What opportunities do children have to express their perspectives?

Children talked about what they would like to have and then drew and painted plans to show what they hoped to see within the garden areas. They took photos of the things that they particularly liked or disliked. They were involved in purchasing resources, for example, seeds, equipment and collaborated with adults in improving, planning and designing the physical spaces.

What next?

This work was incorporated into the development plan. Children reviewed the garden once completed to discuss what may need to be changed. They will be involved in the ongoing upkeep of the garden areas given that they had designed them and now have ownership of them.

Source: Kirklees Early Years Service, 2008

A 'seen and heard' view of childhood draws on the understanding that children are socially active participants, who are already contributing to their daily lives, yet who are dependent upon adults to provide stimulating environments that continually facilitate their participation in decision-making, consistent with their evolving understanding, interests and preferred ways of communicating (Lansdown, 2005; Woodhead, 2005).

Imagined boundaries

The empirical evidence of children that has gathered illustrating children as social actors has helped to shift thinking about how we understand children and childhood. Children are now being understood as socially prepared, adequate and capable of actively contributing to their social lives and environment, just like adults. This has led to a call to move away from the thinking that children are social becomings and instead acknowledge children as social beings. Subsequently, the binary of 'adults are social beings and children are social becomings' is now for the most part discarded as no longer relevant. But is the notion of 'social becomings' obsolete? Recent thinking about how we understand evolving capacities within adulthood has implications for rethinking the notions of social beings and social becomings.

Lee (2001) claims that adulthood can no longer be understood as a state of completeness and competency. The recent emphasis, for instance, on lifelong learning, with its opportunities to re-skill so as to make employment changes during the life course, has given rise to an understanding that adulthood is a site in which adults are continually evolving their capacities. This is ascribing adulthood as a period within the life course which is not complete; it has an evolving and by implication an unfinished nature. Jenks (2005) suggests that since the process of individuals evolving their capacities is contingent on the presence and communication of 'others' (see Rogoff, 1990; Vygotsky, 1962; 1978) this gives rise to a state of 'becoming'. Recent empirical evidence is illustrating that not only is adults' development contingent on 'others' being an adult, but children are found to be supporting their parents develop all kinds of technological competencies, for example, with DVD recorders and the computer. The 'other' in this process can therefore be a child (Lee, 2001; Uprichard, 2008). How are we making sense of this interdependence? And if adulthood is a state of 'becoming' how are we reconciling this with the recently discarded notion of children as 'becomings'. What implications does this have on how we understand the notion of social beings?

Lee (2001) contends that we need to reconceptualize children and adults as both 'social beings *and* social becomings'. We need to understand that adults and children alike are active social beings who are competently contributing to their daily lives and environments. Likewise we need to understand that children and adults are both in the process of evolving their capacities. This dual conceptualization is not a step towards restoring the former imagined binary of 'social becomings or social beings'. Rather it is a call to reinstate the notion of children as 'social becomings' without compromising their status as 'social beings' and within an account of childhood and adulthood that is interdependent in nature (Prout, 2005). The thinking that understands children as both 'social beings *and* social becomings' provides a more inclusive and more comprehensive description of their daily lives. It helps us to see children in processes of evolving their capacities while they are likewise competently contributing to their daily lives, as the following example illustrates.

Young children planning healthy snacks

What was the activity?

To consult the children aged birth to 5 on their preferences for the food available for snacks. To feed back the gathered information to the centre cook to ensure children's preferences are considered when planning for healthy snacks.

Who was involved?

Children and adults in a nursery.

What opportunities do children have to express their perspectives?

The children were given a fruit basket containing a selection of fruits and were given the opportunity to use their five senses to explore and self-select the contents at their own pace and preference. A pictorial tally chart of the fruits sampled was included as an additional visual opportunity for the children and adults to collect the data. Adults and peers gave verbal descriptions and language around preferences and differences of food, building vocabulary and classification. The key questions put to the children included:

- Which fruit/vegetable would you like to try?
- What is it called?

- Which is your favourite fruit/vegetable?
- Which shall we ask Mandy (the cook) to give us for snack?

For the youngest children the key person placed the basket on the floor so the contents could be easily accessed and the children could self-select. Adults observed and took photos to indicate the preferences of those children with developing vocabulary. For the older children the fruit was placed on the snack table and they were provided with equipment to peel/cut up the fruit as they explored, and a key person supported the children with indicating whether or not they liked the varied fruits.

What next?

When this activity is revisited, it would be useful for the key person to record what the children said/did in their individual learning journeys. This activity can be extended to include a shopping trip for the children to select and purchase the fruit. The nursery cook was given the results and has included the children's preferences into the menus. This activity will be repeated within the next six months and extended to include vegetables.

Source: Kirklees Early Years Service, 2008

Conclusion

The UNCRC and ECM provide a context in which children's status as active participants of their communities can be realized. However, practices ultimately rely on the assumptions, beliefs and values that we bring to the workplace. Understanding which assumptions and values are mediating our practice requires a commitment to an ongoing reflexivity. Being self-critical of how we understand children and childhood will help us to understand how we are making sense of children engaging in decision-making; of informing and shaping the services we provide.

However, this is not a static process. The listening to young children journey is continually facing challenging nudges, step changes and shifts of thinking. The thinking that is leading to the call to reinstate understanding children as 'social becomings', without the loss of status of being understood as active 'social beings' is one of these nudges. This dual-natured reconceptualization takes into account the reality that both adults and children are in processes of evolving their capacities while they are competently contributing to their daily lives. This helps to make visible the learning that occurs between adults and children without the 'other' being understood as not yet grown up, or incomplete or incompetent. Understanding the life course as 'social beings and social becomings' helps us to see that opportunities for listening to young children, in which their views are being sought to ensure effective services, is an inclusive and stimulating space in which children and adults are learning from one another, but where adults are retaining ultimate responsibility for outcomes.

Points for discussion

- How are you making sense of listening to young children?
- What values and assumptions are mediating your practice of listening to young children?
- What role does your talk and body language play when children are engaging in decision-making?
- How are children making sense of the opportunities you are offering them to inform and shape the services you provide?

 Further reading

Dahlberg, G., Moss, P. and Pence, A. (1999) *Beyond Quality in Early Childhood Education and Care*. Abingdon: RoutledgeFalmer. Focuses on the role values and perspectives play in how we understand quality.

Lancaster, Y.P. (2006) *RAMPS: A Framework for Listening to Young Children*. London: Daycare Trust. Explores a set of principles with examples from which to guide the development of a listening culture within early years settings.

Lansdown, G. (2005) 'The evolving capacities of the child', *Innocenti Insight*. Florence: UNICEF Innocenti Research Centre. A readable piece of advocacy in which we are challenged to evolve our practice strategies so that they match children's evolving abilities.

Woodhead, M. (2005) 'Early childhood development: a question of rights', *International Journal of Early Childhood*, 37(3): 79–98. Makes the case for children's development to be understood as a rights-based and sociocultural practice.

Woodhead, M. and Brooker, L. (2008) 'A sense of belonging', *Early Childhood Matters*, 111: 36. Explores the concept of belonging as an important aspect of supporting children be active contributors in their communities.

Notes

1 My thanks to Gillian Butterfield from Kirklees Early Years Service (KEYS) for kindly giving permission for these examples to be used in this chapter. They are part of the *Listening Book* that documents their journey of listening to young children.
2 Underpinning all this is a set of ethical principles, which likewise help to understand the nature of young children's participation. There is no scope to discuss these principles here but see for instance Lancaster (2006b), Alderson and Morrow (2004), Farrell (2005), Lancaster (2003).
3 • Staying safe: protected from harm and neglect and to grow up to look after themselves.
  • Being Healthy: enjoying good physical and mental health and living a healthy lifestyle.

- Enjoying and achieving: getting the most out of life and develop broad skills for adulthood.
- Achieving Economic well-being: overcoming socio-economic disadvantage to achieve their full potential.
- Making a Positive contribution: to the community and society.

References

Alderson, P. (2000) 'Citizenship theory and practice: being or becoming citizens with rights', in D. Lawton, J. Cairns and R. Garner (eds), *Education for Citizenship*. London: Continuum.

Alderson, P. and Morrow, V. (2004) *Ethics, Social Research and Consulting with Children and Young People*. Borkingside: Barnardo's.

Borko, H. (2004) 'Professional development and teacher learning: mapping the terrain', *Educational Researcher*, 33(8): 3–15.

Brooker, L. (2002) *Starting School: Young Children Learning Cultures*. London: Open University Press.

Christensen, P.H. (2004) 'Children's participation in ethnographic research: issues of power and representation', *Children & Society*, 18(2): 165–76.

Christensen, P.H. and James, A. (2000) *Research with Children*. London: Falmer Press.

Clark, A. and Moss, P. (2001) *Listening to Young Children: The Mosaic Approach*. London: National Children's Bureau.

Corsaro, W.A. (2005) *The Sociology of Childhood*. Thousand Oaks, CA: Pine Forge Press.

David, T. (1986) 'One picture is worth a thousand words', *Education 3–13*, 14(2): 23–7.

Department for Education and Skills (DfES) (2004) *Every Child Matters: Change for Children*. Nottingham: DfES.

Dunn, J. (1988) *The Beginning of Social Understanding*. Oxford: Blackwell.

Ennew, J. (1994) 'Time for children or time for adults?', in J. Qvortrup, M. Brady, G. Sgritta and H. Wintersberger (eds), *Childhood Matters: Social Theory, Practice and Politics*. Aldershot: Avebury.

Fairclough, N. (1989) *Language and Power*. Harlow: Longman.

Farrell, A. (ed.) (2005) *Ethical Research with Children*. Maidenhead: Open University Press.

Foucault, M. (1984) 'Space, knowledge and power', in P. Rabinow (ed.), *The Foucault Reader*. London: Penguin. pp. 239–56.

James, A. (2007) 'Ethnography in the study of children and childhood', in P. Atkinson, C. Amanda, S. Delamont, J. Lofland and L. Lofland (eds), *Handbook of Ethnography*. London: Sage Publications .

James, A. and Prout, A. (eds) (1997) *Constructing and Reconstructing Childhood: Contemporary Issues in the Sociological Study of Childhood*. London: RoutledgeFalmer.

Jenks, C. (2005) *Childhood*. London: Routledge.

Kirklees Early Years Service (2008) *The Listening Book*. Kirklees: Kirklees Council.

Lancaster, Y.P. (2003) 'Promoting listening to young children: the reader', in Y.P. Lancaster and V. Broadbent (eds), *Listening to Young Children*. Maidenhead: Open University Press.

Lancaster, Y.P. (2006a) 'Listening to young children: respecting the voice of the child', in G. Pugh and B. Duffy (eds), *Contemporary Issues in the Early Years*. London: Paul Chapman/Sage.

Lancaster, Y.P. (2006b) *RAMPS: A Framework for Listening to Young Children*. London: Daycare Trust.

Lansdown, G. (2005) 'The evolving capacities of the child', *Innocenti Insight*. Florence: UNICEF Innocenti Research Centre.

Lee, N. (2001) *Childhood and Society: Growing up in an Age of Uncertainty*. Buckingham: Open University Press.

Malaguzzi, L. (1993) 'History, ideas and basic philosophy', in C. Edwards, L. Gandini and G. Forman (eds), *The Hundred Languages of Children*. Norwood, NJ: Ablex.

Mayall, B. (1996) *Children, Health and the Social Order*. Buckingham: Open University Press.

Prout, A. (2001) 'Representing children: reflections on the Children 5–16 programme', *Children & Society*, 15(3): 193–201.

Prout, A. (2005) *The Future of Childhood: Towards the Interdisciplinary Study of Children*. London: RoutledgeFalmer.

Qvortrup, J. (1997) 'A voice for children in statistical and social accounting: a plea for children's right to be heard', in A. James and A. Prout (eds), *Constructing and Reconstructing Childhood: Contemporary Issues in the Sociological Study of Childhood*. London: RoutledgeFalmer.

Rogoff, B. (1990) *Apprenticeship in Thinking: Cognitive Development in Social Context*. New York: Oxford University Press.

Shonkoff, J.P. and Phillips, D.A. (eds) (2000) *From Neurons to Neighbourhoods: The Science of Early Childhood Development*. Washington, DC: National Academy Press.

Uprichard, E. (2008) 'Children as "beings and becomings": children, childhood and temporality', *Children & Society*, 22(4): 303–13.

Vygotsky, L.S. (1962) *Thought and Language*. Cambridge: MIT Press and Wiley.

Vygotsky, L.S. (1978) *Mind in Society*. Cambridge, MA: Harvard University Press.

Woodhead, M. (1997) 'Psychology and cultural construction of children's needs', in A. James and A. Prout (eds), *Constructing and Reconstructing Childhood: Contemporary Issues in the Sociological Study of Childhood*. London: RoutledgeFalmer.

Woodhead, M. (2005) 'Early childhood development: a question of rights', *International Journal of Early Childhood*, 37(3): 79–98.

CHAPTER 7

THE EARLY YEARS CURRICULUM

Bernadette Duffy

Chapter Contents

- Do we need a curriculum for the youngest children?
- What is the curriculum?
- Why was the *Early Years Foundation Stage* (EYFS) introduced?
- What is the EYFS?
- What has been the response to EYFS?
- What are the challenges in implementing the EYFS?
- How does EYFS link with Key Stage 1?
- Where does the early year's curriculum need to go next?

Many years ago when I complained to a civil servant that government did not recognize the importance of early education, he replied that they were starting to but one day I might look back nostalgically to the days when they did not and early years practitioners were left to their own devices. I understand what he meant. The early years curriculum is now something every one has a view on. For the Department for Children, Schools and Families the learning and development opportunities offered in the early years are a vital element in addressing a key objectives of closing the gap between children who are doing well and those are disadvantaged (DCSF, 2007; DfES, 2007). In local authorities the outcomes duty within the 2006 Childcare Act (HMG, 2006) has lead to greater scrutiny of the Early Years Foundation Stage Profile results and increased focus on the experiences being offered in their early years settings. For some, early years provision should be about ensuring that childhood is protected from negative influences from the wider world and the pressures of schoolification (Open Eye, 2007; 2008) and the curriculum offered should reflect this; while for others it is about providing children with a head start to schooling in a competitive world. It is perhaps not surprising that some practitioners look back with longing to the days when planning was a simple spider web diagram on one side of A4! Reconciling these differing views on what the curriculum in the early years should be and do is no easy task.

Do we need a curriculum for the youngest children?

Increasingly, children are experiencing provision outside the home at a younger age. Most 3- and 4-year-olds now attend early years settings and an increasing number of children under 3 attend some form of provision, and this is likely to continue (HMT, 2004). Children are born with the desire to learn and make sense of the world around them. Fortunately, adults are usually keen to help them to do this (Gopnik et al., 2001). At home, parents are supporting babies and young children they know extremely well and are in tune with. However, adults outside the home may not share this level of understanding; indeed they are unlikely to when we consider the diverse backgrounds that children entering our provision come from. These adults need guidance to help them fulfil their role, to understand what is important for children at different ages and how best to support children from a range of backgrounds. As more schools and early years settings offer longer hours, it is becoming increasingly important to think carefully about what children are experiencing during these times and to ensure that the provision offered is what they actually need.

While most people would agree that practitioners need guidance, for many the use of the term 'curriculum' with reference to the age range from birth to 5, and especially birth to 3, raises particular questions. Practitioners and the wider public have been concerned that the use of the term will lead to formalized learning and introduce pressure for children to conform too early to targets for their development (Abbott and Langston, 2005). To avoid this the terms 'education' and 'curriculum' are rarely used in the *Early Years Foundation Stage* framework (DfES, 2007). However this has not stopped it being labelled as the 'nappy curriculum' (Paton, 2008). The term 'curriculum' will be used to describe any framework to support young children's learning so we need to make the term our own and ensure that it is defined in ways that stress responsiveness to the particular needs of children in the early years. I would also argue that using the term 'curriculum' for this age group is about giving the youngest children the same status as older children. It is showing that the learning and development of a 1-year-old is as important as, if not more important, than that of a 15-year-old.

What is the curriculum?

There has always been much debate about how the curriculum should be defined (Kelly, 2004). Does it include the 'hidden curriculum', that is, the things children learn through the way in which the setting or school is planned and organized and the materials that are provided, for example, such things as identity? Does it include the 'planned' and 'received' curriculum, that is, the experiences the practitioner intends to offer and what the child actually understands and learns? Does it include the 'formal' and 'informal', that is, the elements that are seen as part of the 'school' day and those that are seen as extra-curricular? Does it only include 'school'-aged children and those in receipt of public funding, or does it also include the youngest children, the babies and young children up to 3 who are increasingly part of early years settings?

Recent definitions of the term show that the curriculum is much more than a body of knowledge to be transmitted, subjects to be delivered, formal learning contexts or schooling. The *National Curriculum Handbook for Primary Teachers in England* (QCA, 1999: 2) defines the curriculum as 'all the learning and other experiences that each school offers'. The *Curriculum Guidance for the Foundation Stage* states 'The term curriculum is used to describe everything children do, see, hear or feel in their setting, both planned and unplanned' (QCA, 2000: 2). According to Kelly the curriculum is 'the totality of the experiences the pupil has as a result of the provision made' (2004: 8).

The early years curriculum needs to include all the learning that goes on, whether explicitly planned and intended or that which happens as a by-product of our planning and practice. In the early years the curriculum describes all the experiences the child has in their setting.

Wood and Attfield point out that 'all curriculum models reflect a set of beliefs and values about what is considered to be educationally and developmentally worthwhile in terms of children's immediate needs, their future needs and the wider society' (Wood and Attfield, 2005: 138). As a society we need to agree what is important for children based on evidence from research and experience, and make sure that children get what they need to promote their well-being, learning and development. Education is not just about what goes on in the school or setting, it is about the child as part of community and society, and provision should reflect the child's culture.

This requires a curriculum framework to support practitioners and answer the questions:

- What do we believe is important for the youngest children and why do we believe this? These are the values, aims and principles that our curriculum is based on.
- When do we think it is best to focus on particular learning experiences and how should we do this? This includes our understanding of children's likely patterns of development and our understanding of the processes involved in learning and teaching, sometimes referred to as pedagogy.

We need a curriculum that can grow and evolve. The curriculum must be able to develop in response to changes in society and our understanding about how children learn – neither stand still and nor should the curriculum.

The introduction of the *Early Years Foundation Stage*

In recent years all four countries of the United Kingdom have reviewed their curriculum frameworks for the youngest children. In England this has resulted in the *Early Years Foundation Stage* (DfES, 2007). This brings together the *Curriculum Guidance for the Foundation Stage* (*CGFS*) and *Birth to Three Matters* (*BTTM*) (DfES, 2002). The *CGFS* was introduced in 2000. In 2002 the Foundation Stage was made a statutory part of the National Curriculum to ensure that it had the same status as the curriculum for older children. The guidance was warmly welcomed by most practitioners (QCA, 2004) and the Foundation Stage as a distinct phase in education was seen as a success (HMT, 2004). *Birth to Three Matters* signalled an acceptance that practitioners needed guidance for their work with the very youngest children. Happily the introduction and reception of *BTTM* showed that practitioners welcomed guidance (Abbott and Langston, 2005). Although the framework did not use the term 'curriculum', it did reflect the definition of curriculum used in this chapter. Both documents helped to show that working with the youngest children requires knowledge, skills, insights and commitment and that those who work with this age group are to be valued.

While each document was well received by practitioners it was clear from the start that there was a lack of continuity between their status, principles, aims, pedagogy and content . While the *CGFS* was statutory curriculum guidance for the age range from the term after a child's third birthday to the end of the academic year in which they became 5, *BTTM* was guidance. *Birth to Three Matters* focused on what we want the child to be and the experiences that will promote this, while the *CGFS* focused on what we want children to achieve. 'This guidance is intended to help practitioners to plan to meet the diverse needs of all children so that most will achieve and some, where appropriate, will go beyond the early learning goal by the end of the foundation stage' (QCA, 2000: 5). The principles for *BTTM* stressed the importance of relationships, while in comparison the Foundation Stage principles focused on what practitioners should do in order to work effectively – there were a lot more 'shoulds, 'musts' and 'requires'! *Birth to Three Matters* used a format and language which was more accessible to the multi-agency teams who are increasingly working in early years setting and a more flexible approach to promoting learning and development which worked well in integrated settings. The tone in the two documents was not the same and showed the different periods in which they were written. Though there is only two years between them, *BTTM* reflects a move to person-focused approaches that are more in tune with the *Every Child Matters* (HMT, 2003) agenda.

This lack of continuity between *BTTM* and the *CGFS* and the increasing recognition of the importance of high-quality early education lead to the decision to create a single framework as part of the 10-year childcare strategy, *Choice for Parents, the Best Start for Children* (HMT, 2004).

The 10-year childcare strategy builds on *Every Child Matters*. Its ambition is to ensure that every child gets the best start in life and to give parents more choice about how to balance work and family life. The strategy's rationale is underpinned by evidence from research such as Effective Provision of Pre-School Education (Sylva et al., 2004, and see Chapter 4). There is a recognition that the quality of provision can vary, which undermines parents' confidence, and at its worst has a harmful impact on children's development. The strategy's view is that good quality early education experiences can transform children's lives. *The Children's Plan: Building Brighter Futures* has continued the emphasis on the importance of the early years: 'High quality early years education ensures that children are ready to succeed at school and is particularly beneficial to those from disadvantaged backgrounds' (DCSF, 2007: 8).

The single quality framework for services from birth to 5 announced in the 10-year strategy has developed into the EYFS. Proposals were brought forward in 2006 and, following wide consultation with practitioners, the final version was published in 2007 and became statutory in September 2008.

The framework brings together *BTTM* and the *CGFS*, and incorporates the national standards for day care and childminding. The aim is to build a coherent and flexible approach to care and learning. The framework seeks to encourage an integrated approach to care and education and a play-based approach to promoting children's development and learning. All providers are required to use the EYFS to ensure that whatever setting parents choose, they can be confident that their child will receive a quality experience that supports their development and learning (DfES, 2007).

What is the *Early Years Foundation Stage*?

The EYFS is a statutory framework. It sets out the legal requirements relating to learning and development (the early learning goals; the educational programmes and the assessment arrangements) and the requirements relating to welfare (safeguarding and promoting children's welfare; suitable people; suitable premises, environment and equipment; organization; and documentation).

At the heart of the EYFS are four principles that must underpin practitioners' work with young children whichever setting they attend:

- A *Unique Child* recognizes that every child is a competent learner from birth who can be resilient, capable, confident and self-assured.
- *Positive Relationships* describes how children learn to be strong and independent from a base of loving and secure relationships with parents and/or a key person.
- *Enabling Environments* explains that the environment plays a key role in supporting and extending children's development and learning.
- *Learning and Development* recognizes that children develop and learn in different ways and at different rates, and that all areas of learning and development are equally important and interconnected.

The principles are each broken down into four commitments describing what practitioners need to know and do to put them into practice and ensure that the EYFS meets the overarching aim of improving outcomes for children.

Alongside the statutory framework is additional guidance to help practitioners implement the framework. This includes the booklet, *Practice Guidance for the Early Years Foundation Stage,* with learning and development grids from birth to 5 years, a CD-ROM, poster and Principles into Practice cards.

Responses to *Early Years Foundation Stage*

There is much to recommend in the new framework, and the response from many practitioners has been positive. Following the launch, the British Association for Early Childhood Education welcomed the introduction of the EYFS, especially the principles and commitments, and stated that their members would find much that they recognized and valued in the new framework (British Association for Early Childhood Education, 2007). In March 2008 *Nursery World* magazine reported support for EYFS from nursery managers (Vevers, 2008) and a survey for the *Times Educational Supplement* in August found that nine out of 10 teachers supported the introduction of the EYFS (Ward, 2008).

However, the EYFS has not met with universal approval. There are those who think it goes too far and is too prescriptive (Open Eye, 2007; 2008) and those who think it does not go far enough and should insist on higher requirements on issues such as adult:child ratios, qualifications and outside play (*Nursery World,* 2008). Many are concerned that EYFS contains early learning goals for literacy which are inappropriate and these concerns have led to the DCSF initiating a review of these goals.

Implementing the early years curriculum

The EYFS is being implemented at a time when other aspects of early years provision are changing in response to the Childcare Act 2006 (HMG, 2006). These changes are influencing how practitioners are putting EYFS into practice and present a number of challenges.

Outcomes duty

The Childcare Act 2006 places an outcomes duty on local authorities. From April 2008, local authorities have a duty to reduce inequalities and improve outcomes of all the young children in their area through the planning and provision of early childhood services, including the free entitlement. National and local statutory targets were set by April 2008 based on Early Years Foundation Stage Profile results. The aim of this duty is to be applauded – namely, to improve outcomes for all children, especially the most disadvantaged, and to close the gap in attainment between different groups of children. However, there are concerns that the unintended impact of the duty may be a narrowing of the curriculum and a focus on the goals at the end of EYFS rather than what is best for children at an earlier stage of development.

Flexible offer

As outlined in the 10-year childcare strategy, from 2010 the government has committed to extending the free entitlement of nursery education hours, accessible from the term following a child's third birthday, from 12.5 to 15 hours a week for 38 weeks a year. Parents who wish to will be able to take up the free entitlement more flexibly across a minimum of three days. They can also use their entitlement at more than one provider. These changes will have an impact on the way in which the curriculum is organized and offered.

Traditionally the early years curriculum has been linked to a pattern of two and half hours per day, five days per week attendance often with one provider. In the future, children's attendance patterns could be much more varied. For example, a child could attend Monday to Wednesday five hours per day or 10 hours on Monday, four on Tuesday afternoon and one hour on Friday. If parents opt to use more than one provider there will be additional challenges in co-ordinating children's experiences. Increased flexibility does not necessarily result in quality. Careful attention will need to be given to ensuring that provision is sufficiently flexible to meet the needs of local parents while still maintaining the quality and consistency of experience we know is vital for young children. For our youngest children this consistency is about being with the same small group of adults and children in a familiar setting. It is about a routine that flows with the child, offering an appropriate balance between stimulation and rest, child- and adult-initiated activity.

Linking with Key Stage 1 (KS1)

The EYFS ends at the end of the academic year in which children become 5, and KS1 of the National Curriculum starts in the autumn of the year in which they become 6. The Office for Standards in Education (Ofsted) has found a lack of continuity between the curriculum and assessment frameworks for the Foundation Stage and KS1 which impacts on learning and teaching (Ofsted, 2004). This is partly due to the transition between the early years curriculum organized around six areas of learning, and the 10-subject national curriculum for KS1 (NFER, 2005). It is also due to some Year 1 teachers not making sufficient use of the information that is provided by reception teachers, in particular the Early Years Foundation Stage Profile. There have been calls to move the EYFS into year one of KS1, or even year two as has been done in Wales (QCA, 2004). Sir Jim Rose has been asked to undertake an independent review of the primary curriculum (DCSF, 2008) including the transition from EYFS to KS1. To improve continuity the interim report recommends six areas of learning that will dovetail with the EYFS framework and ease transition. The six areas of learning are:

- Understanding English, communication and languages
- Mathematical understanding
- Scientific and technological understanding
- Human, social and environmental understanding
- Understanding physical health and well-being
- Understanding the arts and design.

The interim report hopes that this approach will give more flexibility for young children to consolidate their learning from the EYFS and ensure that learning through play continues to be stressed into KS1. It will be interesting to see how the recommendations are received and, if adopted, how much they impact on practice.

Where next?

In the early years we have moved from a situation of no guidance to a plethora of guidance. The EYFS is a lengthy framework and includes 69 early learning goals with related developmental matters. As well as the EYFS framework the National Strategies have produced a range of guidance materials aimed at early years practitioners. Many practitioners focused on the *CGFS* stepping stones and there is a concern that they will now concentrate on the goals and a rigid use of the developmental matters rather than the principles, commitments and guidance on teaching and learning. A focus on predetermined goals can lead practitioners to miss the learning that is actually occurring and underestimate the children's knowledge and understanding.

The EYFS will be reviewed in 2010 and this will be an opportunity to think again. It may be time to review the guidance we are providing for practitioners to help them focus on what is most important for children, indeed there may well be a strong argument for doing less but doing it better

Moving away from a subject-based curriculum

Certain subjects have been part of the curriculum since the eighteenth century and came from the desire to understand the nature of God by dividing knowledge into discrete units or subjects. These are now so familiar and well established that often they are not questioned. But knowledge is changing fast and we cannot hope to give children all the knowledge they need to know for their future lives. Instead we need to help them to develop supple and nimble minds to cope with real life in a complex world (Claxton, 2005). A continued focus on knowledge is likely to fail the children and us.

In October 2005 the QCA published the 'Futures' paper (QCA, 2005) which recognized that we are living in a rapidly changing world. We need people who can be more enterprising, adaptable and flexible, and the curriculum needs to change to ensure that this happens. 'Education only flourishes if it successfully adapts to the demands and needs of the time' (QCA, 2005: 1).

At the same time as the EYFS has been introduced the primary curriculum has been under review (DCSF, 2008) and the interim report is recommending a framework which moves away from 10 subjects to six areas of learning. Dividing the curriculum into discrete subject chunks is not making sense and there is a need to reintegrate the curriculum.

Using the term 'areas of learning' will not necessarily mean that practitioners understand that children's learning is interconnected and that the different areas overlap and interrelate. While 'area of learning' rather than 'subject' is used in the EYFS it is clear in the introduction to each section that most areas of learning draw on subject knowledge. For example, knowledge and understanding of the world is described as the foundation for later work in science, design and technology, history, geography and information and communication technology, and the aspects are clearly laid out to reflect this. This can influence how practitioners offer the curriculum. Subjects do have a role to play in the curriculum. The EPPE study (Sylva et al., 2004) found that practitioners' subject knowledge was a key element in outcomes for children. The subjects provide the 'stuff', the content to explore. But they should not be centre stage, they are there to promote what we believe is important for children. We need to move away from the six areas of learning as the focus and, building on the positive response to the EYFS principles and commitments, ensure that we are all clear about the elements that should be at the heart of the early years curriculum.

Messages from research

The *Researching Effective Pedagogy in the Early Years* (REPEY) project (2002) found 'that for most practitioners the declared priorities in the early years were the development of positive dispositions to learning, safety, confidence and independence' (Siraj-Blatchford, et al., 2002: 10). This view is reflected in research. In recent years we have learned more and more about what works for children. Gopnik et al. (2001) show how brain research has revolutionized our ideas about childhood, the human mind and the brain. Babies' brains are designed to enable them to make sense of the world around them. Babies and young children think, draw conclusions, make predictions, experiment and look for explanations. The reason they can do so much so early is because they have the help of the people who care for them (Gopnik et al., 2001). Gerhardt (2004) points out that love is essential to brain development in the early years of life as baby's earliest relationships shape their developing nervous systems. We need to use this information to ensure that all children, but especially the youngest, experience warm loving relationships that nurture them in our settings.

For the brain to develop effectively it is important that babies and young children have a secure and steady source of positive emotion, a nutritious diet and stimulation of the senses (though not all at the same time!) in an atmosphere free from stress but with a degree of pleasurable intensity. There needs to be a series of novel challenges that are neither too hard nor too easy, social interaction and active participation rather than a passive observation (Diamund and Hopson, 1998).

The EPPE project (Sylva et al., 2004, and see Chapter 4) identified the importance of a form of interaction between children and adults they call 'sustained shared thinking' in promoting children's learning and development and this is now part of EYFS. Sustained shared thinking is when practitioners and children work together in an intellectual way to solve a problem, clarify a concept, evaluate an activity or extend a narrative.

Blakemore (2001) in his paper 'Early learning and the brain' argues that we have much to learn from cognitive psychologists about the kinds of things that appear to emerge at particular stages of development and how we can act on this knowledge in our work with children. Our sense of being an individual emerges between 6 to 8 months and 2 years, and between 1 and 4 years we are developing a sense of ourselves and our beliefs in relation to others. For Blakemore these are the things that our brains are set up to develop in the early years – learning about ourselves, others, co-operation and collaboration – all the things society needs and which, if we combine them with creativity, enable us to respond to the challenges we face as individuals and as a society (Duffy, 2006).

The importance of practitioners

The curriculum is only as good as the people who offer it to the children. Practitioners are a key element in the curriculum and the experience of the child will depend on them. It is not possible to 'practitioner proof' the curriculum; it is impossible to provide schemes of work or support materials that practitioners will use the way the planner intended (Kelly, 2004).

Each child and setting is unique, and the curriculum offered needs to reflect this. This requires every practitioner to be reflective, to be able to use underpinning theory, research and evidence from practice to develop the curriculum that works best for the children in the setting they are in. This is a highly skilled role. It requires the practitioner to differentiate, to understand each child as an individual and personalize the curriculum content to match their needs and interests.

What do we need from the curriculum?

What we need from the curriculum today depends on who we think children are, what we believe they need now, how we think they develop and learn, and what we want for children in the future. I would argue that, while there are many things that children can be doing in the early years, we need to focus our curriculum on what is most important for them, the things they need to be doing at this particular stage of their development. It seems to me that looking at research and practice the most important things are:

- *Being social* – making attachments; being with others and sharing experiences; being flexible and independent; showing care for one's self, others and living things; understanding that people have different needs, views, cultures and beliefs that need to be treated with respect.
- *Being positive* – developing positive dispositions and attitudes; a willingness to try new things; showing confidence and enjoyment; displaying high levels of involvement and persisting for extended periods; having a sense of pride in own achievements.
- *Being a communicator* – enjoying using words/gestures to communicate; developing a wide vocabulary; speaking to others about wants and interests; interacting with others; listening and taking account of what others say; using talk to resolve disagreements, negotiating and taking turns; listening with enjoyment and responding to stories, rhymes etc; exploring sounds and letters; finding out about books and writing; using ICT.

- *Being creative* – being curious, investigating, exploring and experimenting; questioning; noting similarities and difference; seeing patterns; pretending and imagining, constructing, combining ideas and materials, making connections, representing, responding to comments and questions.
- *Being healthy and safe* – developing an understanding of healthy practices with regard to eating, sleeping dressing/undressing and personal hygiene; handling tools, objects, construction and malleable materials safely with increasing control; moving with control and co-ordination; feeling safe and secure, demonstrating a sense of trust and belonging, having a positive self-image and being comfortable with themselves, standing up for own rights.

None of this is new – all these things are already in the current guidance and appear across the aspects and areas of learning. The only problem is that for many practitioners at the moment they are hidden by the words that surround them.

Conclusion

The curriculum needs to link theory with practice. It needs to develop from a theoretical underpinning which informs the practitioner's work and helps them to grow the curriculum with the child to reflect children's changing interests and developing abilities (Goldschmeid and Jackson, 2004). By focusing our attention on what is most important for children at this stage of their lives we can make the most difference for them. We do not have to do everything in the early years, after all there are 11 more years of statutory schooling to follow! But we must do what we do to the best of our ability to ensure that we promote each child's learning, development and well-being.

 Points for discussion

- What do you consider to be the values which should underpin the curriculum in the early years?
- Where do they come from?
- Why do you hold these values?

 Further reading

Blakemore, C. (2001) 'Early learning and the brain', Royal Society of Arts lecture, 4 February. This paper looks at brain research and its implications for educators.

Department for Children, Schools and Families (2008) *The Independent Review of the Primary Curriculum: Interim Report*. Norwich: HMSO. This report, also known as the 'Rose Review', puts forward recommendations for the development of the primary curriculum.

Department for Education and Skills (2007) *Early Years Foundation Stage*. Norwich: HMSO. This pack contains the statutory framework for providers in England and additional guidance on implementing the framework.

Duffy. B. (2006) *Supporting Creativity and Imagination in the Early Years*. Maidenhead and New York: Open University Press. This book expands on a number of the themes addressed in this chapter, in particular the importance of creativity in the early years curriculum.

Gopnik, A., Metfzoff, A. and Kuhl, P. (2001) *How Babies Think*. London, Phoenix. This book provides a synthesis of research in philosophy, psychology, computing and neuroscience on babies and what they know.

References

Abbott, L. and Langston, A. (2005) *Birth to Three Matters – Supporting the Framework of Effective Practice*. Maidenhead: Open University Press.

Blakemore, C. (2001) 'Early learning and the brain', Royal Society of Arts lecture, 4 February.

British Association for Early Childhood Education (2007) Press release, 13 March.

Claxton, G. (2005) 'Learning to learn: a key goal in the 21st century curriculum', in *Futures; Meeting the Challenge – a Curriculum for the Future*. London: QCA.

Department for Children, Schools and Families (DCSF) (2007) *The Children's Plan: Building Brighter Futures*. Norwich: TSO.

Department for Children, Schools and Families (DCSF) (2008) *The Independent Review of the Primary Curriculum: Interim Report*. Norwich: TSO.

Department for Education and Skills (DfES) (2002) *Birth to Three Matters – a Framework to Support Children in their Earliest Years*. London: DfES.

Department for Education and Skills (DfES) (2007) *Early Years Foundation Stage*. Nottingham: DfES.

Diamund, M. and Hopson, I. (1998) *Magic Trees of the Mind*. New York: Dutton.

Duffy, B. (2006) *Supporting Creativity and Imagination in the Early Years*. Maidenhead: Open University Press.

Gerhardt, S. (2004) *Why Love Matters*. Hove: Brunner–Routledge.

Goldschmeid, E. and Jackson, S. (2004) *People under Three; Young Children in Day Care*. London: Routledge

Gopnik, A., Metfzoff, A. and Kuhl, P. (2001) *How Babies Think*. London: Phoenix.

Her Majesty's Government (HMG) (2006) *Childcare Act 2006*. Norwich: HMSO.

Her Majesty's Treasury (HMT) (2003) *Every Child Matters*. London: The Stationery Office.

Her Majesty's Treasury (HMT) (2004) *Choice for Parents, the Best Start for Children: A Ten Year Strategy for Child Care*. London: The Stationery Office.

Kelly, A.V. (2004) *The Curriculum: Theory and Practice*. London: Sage Publications.

National Foundation for Educational Research (NFER) (2005) *A Study of the Transition from the Foundation Stage to Key Stage 1*. Slough: NFER.

Nursery World (2008) 'Controversies look set to make 2008 an interesting year – Opinion Column', 3 January.

Office for Standards in Education (Ofsted) (2004) *Transition from the Reception Year to Year 1: An Evaluation by Her Majesty's Inspectors*. London: HMSO.

Open Eye (2007) Open letter, *Timer Educational Supplement,* 30 November.

Open Eye (2008) Press release, 5 December.

Paton, G. (2008) 'Nappy curriculum a "threat to children", warn leading authors', *Daily Telegraph,* 24 July.

Qualifications and Curriculum Authority (QCA) (1999) *The National Curriculum Handbook for Primary Teachers in England.* London: QCA.

Qualifications and Curriculum Authority (QCA) (2000) *Curriculum Guidance for the Foundation Stage.* London: QCA.

Qualifications and Curriculum Authority (QCA) (2004) *Foundation Stage Monitering Report 2003/04.* London: QCA.

Qualifications and Curriculum Authority (QCA) (2005) *Futures; Meeting the Challenge – a Curriculum for the Future.* London: QCA.

Siraj-Blatchford, I., Sylva, K., Muttock, S., Gilden, R. and Bell, D. (2002) *Researching Effective Pedagogy in the Early Years (REPEY).* DfES Research Report 356. London: DfES/HMSO.

Sylva, K., Melhuish, E.C., Sammons, P., Siraj-Blatchford, I. and Taggart, B. (2004) *The Effective Provision of Pre-School Education (EPPE) Project: Technical Paper 12 – The Final Report: Effective Pre-School Education.* London: DfES/Institute of Education, University of London.

Vevers, S. (2008) 'Managers give EYFS qualified welcome', *Nursery World,* 26 March.

Ward, H. (2008) 'Teachers hail "nappy" plan', *Times Educational Supplement,* 1 August.

Wood, E. and Attfield, J. (2005) *Play, Learning and the Early Childhood Curriculum.* London: Paul Chapman Publishing.

CHAPTER 8

THE TOOLS OF ASSESSMENT: WATCHING AND LEARNING

Cathy Nutbrown and Caron Carter

Chapter Contents

- What is assessment?
- Why assess young children's learning and development?
- Values and vision underpinning assessment
- National policy on assessment of early learning
- Assessment for the purposes of teaching and learning

What is assessment?

The word 'assessment' is used in different contexts to mean different things. Nutbrown (2006) has suggested three different purposes for assessment, arguing that different tools are needed for different purposes. *Assessment for teaching and learning* involves identifying the details of children's knowledge, skills and understanding in order to build a detailed picture of their individual development and subsequent learning needs. *Assessment for management and accountability* prefers scores over narrative accounts of children's learning. Such assessments included the Baseline Assessment system which measured children's progress in predetermined objectives (SCAA, 1997) and allowed the 'value added' by the school to be calculated. *Assessment for research* includes (often numerical) assessments which are used specifically in research projects where quickly administered measures are needed and where uniformity of approach is necessary. Table 8.1 summarizes the characteristics of these three purposes of assessment.

Table 8.1   Some characteristics of the three purposes of assessment

Assessment for teaching and learning	Assessment for management and accountability	Assessment for research
Focus on individuals	Focus on age cohort	Focus on samples
Concerned with details about each individual learner	Concerned with a sample of group performance	Concerned with performance of the sample
Is ongoing	Occurs within specific time frame	Takes place at planned points in a study
'Takes as long as it takes'	Is briefly administered or completed from previous assessment for teaching	Can be brief, depends on assessment and ages
Needs no numerical outcome to be meaningful	Numerical outcome provides meaning	Numerical outcomes often essential
Is open-ended	Often consists of closed list of items	Often consists of closed items
Informs next teaching steps	Informs management strategy and policy	Informs research decisions, and findings – measures outcomes
Information relates primarily to individuals	Information relates primarily to classes, groups, settings or areas	Information relates to the sample, not to individuals or schools
Assessments required for each child	Some missing cases permissible	Some missing cases permissible
Main purpose is teaching	Main purpose is accountability	Purpose is to add to knowledge
Only useful if information is used to guide teaching	Only useful when compared with other outcomes (of other measures of cohorts)	Only useful as evidence of effectiveness of research study
Requires competence in insight into children's learning	Requires professional administration of the test	Requires competence in administration of the test
Depends on established relationship with individual children to be effective	Can draw on information derived through interaction with individual children, but not dependent on relationship	Often requires no previous relationship, but the ability to establish a rapport with the child at the time of the assessment
Requires on-going professional development and experience	Requires short training session/learning the test and practice	Requires short training session. Learning the test and practice.

Source: Nutbrown, 2006: 128

Assessment of young children, whatever the purpose, raises a number of concerns in relation to their well-being and self-esteem and how children come to see themselves as learners (Roberts, 1995).

Why assess young children's learning and development?

Children's learning is so complex, so rich, so fascinating, so varied, so surprising and so full of enthusiasm that to see it taking place every day, before one's very eyes, is one of the greatest privileges. Watching young children can open our eyes to their astonishing capacity to learn, and make us marvel at their powers to think, to do, to communicate and to create. As well as being in awe at young children's capacities, early childhood practitioners must understand, really understand, what they see when they observe.

Several pioneers (Froebel, Piaget, Vygotsky and Isaacs) and more recent researchers and commentators (Athey, 2006; Donaldson, 1983; Elfer et al., 2003; Nutbrown, 2006) have illuminated children's learning and development and provided practitioners with strategies for reflecting upon and interpreting their observations of children. This rich resource illuminates, the meanings of children's words, representations and actions. For example, those who work with babies and toddlers can draw on recent work to embellish their own understanding of the children (Abbott and Moylett, 1997; Elfer et al., 2003; Goldschmied and Jackson, 2004; Nutbrown and Page, 2008). When early childhood educators use the work of others as a mirror to their own, they can see the essentials of their own practice reflected more clearly and so better understand the learning and development of the children with whom they work.

The observations of Susan Isaacs can be useful to present-day educators as tools for reflection on children's processes of learning and as a means of moving from the specifics of personal experiences to general understandings about children's thinking. Isaacs' Malting House School, in Cambridge, was the setting (from 1924 to 1927) for her compelling accounts of the day-to-day doings of the children, which show clearly how children's intellectual development can result from reflecting on detailed anecdotal insights. Isaacs (1929) described the development of the basic concepts of biology (change, growth, life and death) illustrating the process with a rich body of observational evidence:

18th June 1925
The children let the rabbit out to run about the garden for the first time, to their great delight. They followed him about, stroked him and talked about his fur, his shape and his ways.

13th July 1925
Some of the children called out that the rabbit was dying. They found it in the summerhouse, hardly able to move. They were very sorry and talked much about it. They shut it up in the hutch and gave it warm milk.

14th July 1925
The rabbit had died in the night. Dan found it and said: 'It's dead – its tummy does not move up and down now'. Paul said, 'My daddy says that if we put it in water it will get alive again'. Mrs I said 'shall we do so and see?' They put it into a bath of water. Some of them said. 'It's alive, because it's moving.' This was a circular motion, due to the currents in the water. Mrs I therefore put [sic] a small stick which also moved round and round, and they agreed that the stick was not alive. They then suggested that they should bury the rabbit, and all helped to dig a hole and bury it.

15th July 1925
Frank and Duncan talked of digging the rabbit up – but Frank said, 'It's not there – it's gone up to the sky.' They began to dig, but tired of it and ran off to something else. Later they came back and dug again. Duncan, however, said, 'Don't bother – it's gone – it's up in the sky' and gave up digging. Mrs I therefore said, 'Shall we see if it's there?' and also dug. They found the rabbit, and were very interested to see it still there.

Isaacs's diary entries about the play and questioning of young children formed the basis of her analysis of children's scientific thinking and understanding and offer rich evidence of the development of children's theories about the world and what they find in it. Isaacs learned about children's learning through diligent and meticulous reflection on observations of their play. Practitioners need continued opportunity to practice their skills of observation as well as time to reflect with colleagues on those observations. Many researchers and practitioners have followed Isaacs's observational practices (Athey, 2006; Clark, 2001; Jenkinson, 2001; Nutbrown, 2006; Rinaldi, 1999). The pioneering practice of Reggio Emilia in northern Italy is developed largely through careful documentation which includes observations, notes, photographs and reflections upon the children's work as it unfolds in their learning communities (Abbott and Nutbrown, 2001; Filippini and Vecchi, 1996).

Goldschmied (1989) illustrates the importance of close observation of babies. Watching babies playing with the Treasure Basket can give the adult valuable insights into their learning and development. The following extract from an observation of Matthew shows the fine detail of this 9-month-old's persistent interests:

Kate places Matthew close enough for him to reach right into the basket. He immediately reaches in with his right hand and selects a long wooden handled spatula. 'oohh, ahh,' he says and looks directly at his mother. She smiles at him in approval. Still holding the spatula he proceeds to kneel up and lean across the basket in order to reach a long brown silk scarf. He pulls at the scarf and squeals in delight as he pulls the fabric through his fingers, 'oohh, ahh' he repeats. He lets go of the spatula and abandons the scarf to his side, his eyes rest on a large blue stone, he picks up the large stone with his right hand and turns it over on his lap using both hands. Still using both hands he picks the stone up and begins to bite it, making a noise as his teeth grind against the hard surface. He smiles; looking at his mother as he repeatedly bites the stone over and over again. He stops, holds the stone up to his face and looks at it intently then puts it to his mouth once more. He then picks up the wooden spatula again and whilst holding it firmly in one hand, he turns the contents of the basket over with his other hand, squealing loudly with delight as he discovers the matching long handled fork. Matthew looks at his mother and waves both items in the air smiling and rocking on his knees saying 'oohh, ahh'. He turns away from the basket and waves the long handled implements up and down in his hands, first one then the other then both together. (Nutbrown, 2005: 153)

Other reasons for observing and assessing young children centre around the adult's role as a provider of care and education. Young children's awesome capacity for learning imposes a potentially overwhelming responsibility on early years practitioners to support, enrich and extend that learning. When educators understand more about children's learning they must then assume an even greater obligation to take steps to foster and develop that learning further. The extent to which educators can create a high-quality learning environment of care and education is a measure of the extent to which they succeed in developing positive learning interactions between themselves and the children such that the children's learning is nurtured and developed.

'Quality' is often culturally defined and community-specific (Woodhead, 1996). But whatever their setting and wherever they are located, where educators watch children and use those observations to generate their own understandings of children's learning and their needs, they are contributing to the development of a quality environment in which those children might thrive. When educators observe young children they are working to provide high-quality learning experiences. The evaluative purpose of assessment is central for early childhood educators, for they cannot know if the environments they create and the support they provide for children are effective unless they watch and unless they learn from what they see. *Observation can provide starting points* for reviewing the effectiveness of provision and observational assessments of children's learning can be used daily to identify strengths, weaknesses, gaps, and inconsistencies in the curriculum provided for all children. *Assessment can be used to plan and review* the provision, adult involvement and teaching, as well as to identify those significant moments in each child's learning which educators can build upon to shape a curriculum that matches each child's pressing cognitive and affective concerns. *Observation and assessment can provide a basis for high-quality provision.* Curriculum, pedagogy, interactions and relationships can all be illuminated and their effectiveness reviewed through adults' close observation of children. Despite the introduction of the EYFS and the EYFS Profile, formal assessments continue to be used routinely to diagnose children's abilities and there is a danger that over-formalized assessment at the age of 4, can limit the opportunities which children are offered rather than opening up a broad canvas of opportunity for learning. It is important, however, to use the active process of assessment to identify for each child the next teaching steps, so that learning opportunities in the immediate future are well matched to the children to whom they are offered.

This focus on the next steps in teaching and learning takes us into the 'zone of proximal development' – a concept developed by Vygotsky (1978) who argued that assessment does not end with a description of a pupil's present state of knowing, but rather begins there. Vygotsky (1978: 85) wrote: 'I do not terminate my study at this point, but only begin it.' Effective assessment is dynamic, not static, and can be used by educators as a way of identifying what she or he might do next in order to support children's learning. Assessment reveals learning potential as well as learning achievements.

Watching and learning are the essential tools of assesment with which practitioners can both establish the progress that has already taken place and explore the future – the learning that is embryonic. The role of the adult in paying careful and informed attention to children's learning, and reflecting upon that learning, is crucial to the enhancement of children's future learning.

Values and vision

Against the backdrop, in England, of the EYFS Profile, and an emphasis on the acquisition of some identified elements of knowledge, skills and understanding, practitioners can assess children in ways which are appropriate to their age and learning stage. As devolution gathers pace around the UK, different policies are being developed to allow, to varying degrees, a freedom to practitioners to decide how and what to assess. Whatever the national policy, practitioners' bring to assessment, their personal and professional values and their beliefs about children. Whatever the framework for national assessment, wherever in the world that might be, how children are assessed depends upon adults' views on the nature of childhood, children's behaviour, children's feelings, and their personal approaches to living and learning. Whenever, wherever educators observe, assess and interpret young children's learning, they are influenced by personal beliefs and values.

Policy since the early 1990s shows a shift in the language about children and childhood and the purposes of early education and care which perhaps indicates a change in the dominant political view of childhood. The language in policy documents of the 1990s suggested that 'childhood' had been reconstructed for policy (or perhaps *through* policy) with very young children becoming 'pupils' and early 'experiences' designed to promote learning gave way to 'outcomes' (Nutbrown, 1998). In 2000, a more appropriate language re-emerged, with talk of 'foundations', 'play' and 'children'. However, target-driven assessment remained until 2002 when the Foundation Stage Profile heralded a more flexible approach to ongoing assessment of young children's learning and needs through observation. It is crucial that early childhood educators are supported in articulating their own personal vision of early experiences for children (how things might be), because such vision derives from the values they hold, and their own constructions of childhood. Practitioners must challenge the language of policy when it is at odds with a holistic and developmental view of children's early learning.

National policy on assessment of early learning

The *Early Years Foundation Stage* became statutory in September 2008. Education and care, brought together in a single framework, focus on the holistic development of each child (DfES, 2007a). *The Children's Plan* (DfES, 2007b: 60) states the vision for 'high quality play-based early learning that will allow children to reach their full potential'. At the heart of this philosophy is person-alized learning – with children's needs central and approaches to teaching and learning which allow them to develop at their own pace.

The Children's Plan (DfES, 2007b) viewed the *Early Years Foundation Stage* as a means to register children's development through early learning goals rather than a prescribed curriculum, but as the EYFS was introduced in all settings in September 2008 there remained doubt as to whether or not this was the case. The principle of development over curriculum seemed appropriate but, like any pol-icy document, the EYFS framework is subject to interpreted application in settings and so support for practitioners with little training and no or minimal qualifica-tions is essential to ensure that capabilities rather than deficits remain the focus.

Echoes of baseline assessment of the early 1990s rang in the ears of many who raised concerns about the new framework and its potential for misuse. The statu-tory framework for the Early Years Foundation Stage (DfES, 2007a) was paralleled by the Early Years Foundation Stage Profile – a summative assessment at the end of Foundation Stage 2 – just before children enter Key Stage 1. The intention was that evidence collected over two years was used to compile the profile, using observation, analysis and planning. The language used was formal and on a par with that used in Key Stage 1 and Key Stage 2 summative assessments. Additionally, there was an element of reporting and accountability not dissimilar to that of KS1 and KS2; local authorities are permitted access to the outcomes of the children's end of EYFS assessments which is across 13 scales. This means that the potential for 'league tables', 'value-added' judgements and versions of baseline assessment remains. Even with the EYFSP young children may, yet again, be invisible as individuals if settings, local authorities and government, resort to generalized statistics to demonstrate their overall success in 'raising standards'.

Despite changes in policy which emphasize observation and ongoing assess-ment of young children's learning and development, the tendency to use assessment for purposes of management and accountability remains. Though official league tables of performance for the youngest children no longer apply and despite the long-awaited abolition of SATS for pupils up to the age of 14, assessment is still used as a way of showing how well (or poorly) a setting has done. Assessment for management and accountability often involves numerical assessment of young children's progress and fear has been expressed that the EYFS Profile will result in 'checklist'-type assessments of babies, toddlers and young children which are given a percentage score. Settings and local authorities are often tempted to demonstrate their success in achievements by producing tables which list high-achieving institu-tions (and of course those who do not achieve high assessment scores are also identified). If such assessments are used it is important to remember that such assessments are not useful in teaching young children and, for that, different tools of observation and reflection are needed in order to identify next learning steps for each child. However, the underpinning philosophy of personalized learning in the EYFS will succeed if practitioners experience effective professional develop-ment, and receive appropriate support and leadership which accentuate *all* chil-dren's learning and lead to high-quality inclusive provision.

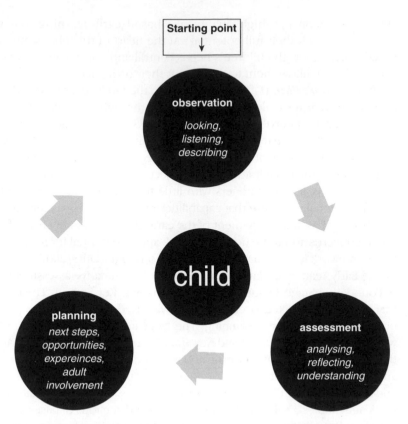

Figure 8.1   Using observation, assessment and planning to support children's individual learning

Personalized learning in the EYFS

The model of formative assessment advocated in the EYFS (DfES, 2007a) is similar to that in Figure 8.1. This OAP (observation, assessment, planning) model always begins with *observation,* which is then reflected upon in the *assessment* and then used for *planning* next steps which lead into the next OAP cycle.

The EYFS encourages 'snap shot' observations of children – both spontaneous and planned – to create individual portfolios, which document children's learning journeys. Table 8.2 summarizes four ways to document children's learning which can be used for formative and summative assessment.

Practitioners may need time to try different observation techniques for different purposes and to analyse or interpret observations and question how they inform practice or individualized children's learning. When it comes to learning it is not the case that 'one size fits all', and settings need to focus on individuals in order to remain distinctive in their ethos and pedagogy.

Elfer (2005) suggests that practitioners are better able to focus on the child if they observe *without* taking notes, spending 5–10 minutes watching a child

Table 8.2   Some types of observation and their main purposes

Observation	Purpose
Time sampling/target child	To capture detail relating to the behaviour and language of a child (Hobart and Frankel, 2004)
Learning stories	To look for behaviours that link in with the strands of the curriculum. Observation is woven into the curriculum with a focus upon strengthening learning dispositions (Clark, 2001; Palaiologou, 2008)
Snap shot	To record spontaneous or planned observations focusing on a short episode on any area of the curriculum
Observation without a notebook	A narrative observation that usually lasts about 10 minutes. The observer watches the child with no fixed agenda but a concern for overall holistic development. Significant events in the observation episode are recorded after the observer has stopped watching. Some things, such as the detail of dialogue could be lost but advocates of this approach say that essential details are remembered and recorded (Elfer, 2005).

then moving to a different space to write up their observation. The following is an example:

> Sophie has been in the setting for 30 minutes. She snuggles up on the lap of her key worker. She is sucking her thumb and strokes her face with her square of comfort blanket. They are sitting at a table with lego boards and bricks laid out ready for the children. Three other children are standing around the table. They have selected their boards and are busy building and chatting about their creations. Sophie is watching the lego building from the safety of her key worker's lap. She does not speak but her eyes watch the creation of the boy by her side. This continues for several minutes. Sophie's key worker then takes a board and starts to build. Sophie's attention is now diverted to her key worker. She watches for a couple of minutes and then she picks up a brick and offers it to her key worker. This is repeated several times until the design is complete and her key worker announces in a sing songy style 'Da-Dah!!' A smile forms from behind Sophie's thumb.

Elfer's point is that what has been learned remains in the mind of the observer with key events, information and emotions being written down later. Such observations can result in fewer words but a higher quality of observation and insight. Children's words and conversations are less likely to be recorded but, as part of a range of observational strategies the 'without a notebook' approach has an important place.

Using observations to inform planning

To achieve this aim of personalized learning, the EYFS advocates the use of PLOD planning (Possible Lines of Direction) (Whalley, 2007). This tool can be used to plan individual or small group learning across six areas of learning. All practitioners and parents can contribute suggestions to such planning tools. Figure 8.2 shows an example of a PLOD plan based on the interest and schemas of a small group of children. This form of personalized learning planning can be effective if based on observation, and practitioners should feel confident in experimenting with different planning formats and tools which are flexible and allow for spontaneous experiences to be developed (DfES, 2007b).

Observation is crucial to understanding and assessing young children's learning; effective and meaningful work with young children which supports their learning must be based on appropriate assessment strategies to identify their needs and capabilities. The fine mesh of learning requires detailed, ongoing and sensitive observations of children as they play. Importantly, aspects of respectful assessment can include the development of inclusive practices which seek to allow children to 'have their say' in the assessment of their own learning (Critchley, 2002).

Key aspects in assessing young children

If assessment is to work for children it is important to consider the following questions:

- *Clarity of purpose* – why are children being assessed?
- *Fitness for purpose* – is the assessment instrument or process appropriate?
- *Authenticity* – do the assessment tasks reflect processes of children's learning and their interests?
- *Informed practitioners* – are practitioners appropriately trained and supported?
- *Child involvement* – how can children be fittingly involved in assessment of their learning?
- *Respectful assessment* – are assessments fair and honest with appropriate concern for children's well-being and involvement, and do they inform planning of next learning steps?
- *Parental involvement* – do parents contribute to their child's assessment? (Adapted from Nutbrown, 2005: 14)

With due respect ...

This chapter has considered *why* early childhood educators should observe and assess young children in the context of assessment policy in England. Answers to remaining questions depend upon the principles on which early education and assessment are based. The principle of *respect* is crucial. Assessment must be carried out with proper respect for the children, their parents, carers and

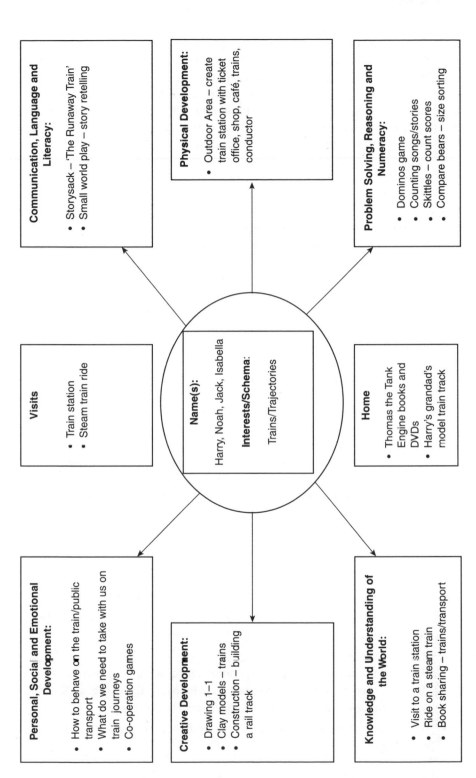

Figure 8.2   Flexible indididual and small group planning

their educators. Respectful assessment governs what is *done*, what is *said*, how *relationships* are conducted and the *attitudes* which practitioners bring to their work. Those who watch young children – really watch and listen and reflect on their learning – will know that time to watch and reflect is essential to really understanding what young children are doing. Observations which are not reflected upon are wasted effort. It is only when practitioners seek to understand the *meanings* behind what they have seen that the real worth of observational practices are realized.

Whatever the implications of the EYFS Profile in England, and policies and practices around the world, two things are essential: the involvement of parents and practitioners in generating respectful understandings of children's learning, and professional development for educators which is worthy of children's amazing capacity to learn. *Time* for teaching and assessment, *confidence* in educators' capabilities and *recognition* of the judgements practitioners make can create the important climate of *respectful early assessment*. The concept of *respect* can underpin and inform the way adults make judgements about young children's learning and how curriculum and assessment policies are developed and implemented: 'Respect is not about "being nice" – it is about being clear, honest, courteous, diligent and consistent' (Nutbrown, 1998: 14).

Teaching young children requires clarity, honesty, courtesy, diligence and consistency. It means identifying what children *can* do, what they *might* do and what their educators need to do next to support and challenge them in their learning. Despite repeated policy attempts to 'keep it simple', supporting young children as they learn can never be other than complex. Watching young children as they learn and understanding their learning moments is complex and difficult work, and places the highest of demands upon their educators. There are no short cuts, instead there are long, interesting and unique journeys.

 Points for discussion

- How do individual children and their needs underpin practice?

- Thinking about the EYFS/Children's Plan and personalized learning, what steps might be taken in your setting to further develop children's involvement in their assessment?

- Table 8.2 shows examples of observation types. Is there a place for each type of observation? Have you used any of these in your setting? Could you try and evaluate a method you have not used before?

- How can parents be involved in the assessment of their children's learning?

Further reading

Filippini, T. and Vecchi, V. (eds) (1996) *The Hundred Languages of Children: The Exhibit.* Reggio Emilia: Reggio Children. This 'catalogue' of the now internationally famous exhibition illustrates the importance of adults supporting children's learning over a sustained period of time, and of the place of careful close observation of and listening to children.

Isaacs, S. (1929) *The Nursery Years.* London: Routledge and Kegan Paul. A book filled with Susan Isaacs's observations of children at the Malting House School, which, though published in 1929, offers an unhindered example of why observation is essential to understanding young children's learning.

Nutbrown, C. and Page, J. (2008) *Working with Babies and Children: From Birth to Three.* London: Sage. This book includes numerous case studies and vignettes which highlight the importance of relationships to children's learning, development and well-being.

Vygotsky, L.S. (1978) *Mind in Society.* Cambridge, MA: Harvard University Press. A clear and unique exposition of the role of the adult in children's learning, providing an insight into the need for careful observation before intervention.

Drummond, M.J., Rouse, D. and Pugh, G. (eds) (1992) *Making Assessment Work.* London: NES Arnold/National Children's Bureau. Materials which provide a means for practitioners to examine their assessment practices in the context of their beliefs about children and the role of assessment. They are relevant, whatever the policy context in which practitioners work.

References

Abbott, L. and Moylett, H. (eds) (1997) *Working with the Under-Threes: Training and Professional Development.* Buckingham: Open University Press.

Abbott, L. and Nutbrown, C. (eds) (2001) *Experiencing Reggio Emilia: Implications for Preschool Provision.* Milton Keynes: Open University Press.

Athey, C. (2006) *Extending Thought in Young Children, a Parent–Teacher Partnership.* London: Paul Chapman Publishing.

Clark, M. (2001) *Assessment in Early Childhood Settings: Learning Stories.* London: Paul Chapman Publishing.

Critchley, D. (2002) 'Children's assessment of their own learning', in C. Nutbrown (ed.), *Research Studies in Early Childhood Education.* Stoke-on-Trent: Trentham.

Deparment of Education and Skills (DfES) (2007a) *The Early Years Foundation Stage: Setting the Standards for Learning, Development and Care for Children from Birth to Five.* Nottingham: DFES.

Deparment of Education and Skills (DfES) (2007b) *The Children's Plan: Building Brighter Futures.* Norwich: HMSO (TSO).

Donaldson, M. (1983) *Children's Minds.* London: HarperCollins.

Elfer, P. (2005) 'Observation matters', in L. Abbott and A. Langston (eds), *Birth to Three Matters: Supporting the Framework of Effective Practice.* Maidenhead: Open University Press.

Elfer, P., Goldschmied, E. and Selleck, D. (2003) *Key Persons in the Nursery: Building Relationships for Quality Provision.* London: David Fulton.

Filippini, T. and Vecchi, V. (eds) (1996) *The Hundred Languages of Children: The Exhibit.* Reggio Emilia: Reggio Children.

Goldschmied, E. (1989) *Infants at Work: The Treasure Basket Explained.* London: National Children's Bureau.

Goldschmied, E. and Jackson, S. (2004) *People Under Three: Young Children in Day Care.* London: Routledge.

Hobart, C. and Frankel, J. (2004) *A Practical Guide to Child Observation and Assessments.* 3rd edn. Cheltenham: Stanley Thornes.

Isaacs, S. (1929) *The Nursery Years.* London: Routledge and Kegan Paul.

Jenkinson, S. (2001) *The Genius of Play: Celebrating the Spirit of Childhood.* Stroud: Hawthorne Press.

Nutbrown, C. (1998) 'Early assessment – examining the baselines', *Early Years,* 19(1): 50–61.

Nutbrown, C. (2005) *Key Concepts in Early Childhood Education and Care.* London: Sage.

Nutbrown, C. (2006) *Threads of Thinking: Young Children Learning and the Role of Early Education.* London: Paul Chapman Publishing.

Nutbrown, C. and Page, J. (2008) *Working with Babies and Children: From Birth to Three.* London: Sage.

Palaiologou, I. (2008) *Childhood Observation.* Exeter: Learning Matters.

Rinaldi, C. (1999) 'The pedagogy of listening', paper given at the Reggio Emilia Conference, Reggio Emilia, Italy, 28 April.

Roberts, R. (1995) *Self-esteem and Successful Early Learning.* London: Hodder and Stoughton.

School Curriculum and Assessment Authority (SCAA) (1997) *National Framework for Baseline Assessment: Criteria and Procedures for the Accreditation of Baseline Assessment Schemes.* London: DfEE/SCAA.

Vygotsky, L.S. (1978) *Mind in Society.* Cambridge, MA: Harvard University Press.

Whalley, M. (2007) *Involving Parents in their Children's Learning.* 2nd edn. London: Paul Chapman Publishing.

Woodhead, M. (1996) *In Search of the Rainbow: Pathways to Quality in Large-Scale Programmes for Young Disadvantaged Children.* Early Childhood Development: Practice and Reflections Number 10. The Hague: Bernard van Leer Foundation.

CHAPTER 9

CHILDREN'S CENTRES

Caron Rudge

Chapter Contents

- The evolution of children's centres and government policy
- The aims of children's centres and the services offered
- The story of Fortune Park, now Golden Lane, children's centre.
- Challenges and issues facing children's centres.
- What makes a successful children's centre?

The evolution of children's centres and government policy

Children's centres are an exciting and promising initiative, offering a wide range of services encompassing health, education and social care. This chapter explores the concept and their development.

While integrated or combined centres have been with us since the 1970s they have developed most rapidly over the past decade. Their development has certainly proved challenging and the interpretation of an integrated centre that provides day care with education has been, until recently, translated into practice in a variety of ways.

The 'early excellence' programme (DfES, 1997) and Sure Start (DfES, 1999) are two key initiatives that have heavily influenced the development of children's centres. Early excellence centres (EECs) were created in 1997 as a means of disseminating models of effective integrated practice which incorporated a range of professionals and services often under one institution. The total number of EECs created by 2003 were 107. Early excellence centres were required to focus on the following core objectives:

- Provision of high-quality care and education over an extended day.
- Promoting and achieving parental involvement including developing parenting skills.
- Provision for support services for parents including: drop in services, counselling and family support.
- Provision and support to parents wishing to re-enter employment or access further adult education.
- Raising standards of integrated early years provision across all providers including childminders, voluntary and private providers.

In light of both the concept and workings of EECs it is clear to see how such an initiative contributed to not only the development of children's centres and extended schools, but also to many other aspects of the concept of children's services as set out in the Green Paper *Every Child Matters* (DfES, 2003).

The first Sure Start local programmes were set up in 1999 as the result of the 1998 Comprehensive Spending Review. They brought together early education, health and family support for the benefit of young children living in disadvantaged areas. Sure Start local programmes were an area-based initiative with the aim of improving the health and well-being of families and children from pre birth to 4, so that children were ready to flourish when they started their statutory education. Local programmes were concentrated in neighbourhoods where a high proportion of children were living in poverty.

Districts were selected to develop Sure Start local programmes according to the levels of deprivation within their areas, but decisions about catchment areas were decided locally. Catchment areas were identified as areas which had 20 per cent of the most deprived wards (as measured by the ODPM – Office of the Deputy Prime Minister – Index of Multiple Deprivation). Super Output Areas (SOAs) are now used to determine levels of deprivation. While services were designed to meet the needs of families within each catchment area and offered to those families first, many of the services developed were also available to those living outside the catchment area.

Building on the work of both the Sure Start local programmes and the early excellence programme, the government's 10-year strategy for childcare, *Choice for Parents, the Best Start for Children* (DfES, 2006) has crystallized what settings need to consider when addressing the needs of parents, particularly those who are either working or studying. The 10-year strategy (HMT, 2004) noted the importance of the following principles:

Choice and flexibility – parents to have greater choice about balancing work and family life.

Availability – for all families with children aged up to 14 who need it, an affordable, flexible, high-quality childcare place that meets their circumstances.

Quality – high-quality provision with a highly skilled childcare and early year's workforce, among the best in the world.

Affordability – families to be able to afford flexible, high-quality childcare that is appropriate for their needs.

The children's centre concept was initially promoted in the Interdepartmental Childcare Review report *Delivering for Children and Families* (DfES, 2002) and has been taken forward through the Green Paper *Every Child Matters*. It was enshrined in the Children Act 2004, supported further through the Childcare Act 2006 and is recognized within *The Children's Plan* (DCSF, 2007) as the key delivery mechanism for improving outcomes for children under 5 and their families.

Children's centres have been prioritized initially in areas which are defined as disadvantaged, perhaps due to economic conditions, or because of poor housing, or simply due to an inadequate provision of services. Local authorities have been given strategic responsibility for the delivery of children's centres. They are planning the location and development of centres to meet the needs of local communities, in consultation with parents, the private, voluntary and independent sectors, Primary Care Trusts, Jobcentre Plus and other key partners to deliver a range of services.

The government has contracted with a partnership of private-sector and public-sector organizations called Together for Children to provide delivery support on the ground for local authorities. By 2010 it is intended that there should be a children's centre in every community serving children and families from the antenatal period through to the end of the Early Years Foundation Stage. By the end of 2008 there were almost 3,000 children's centres, with the aim of there being 3,500 by 2010.

The aims of children's centres and the services offered

Children's centres provide an excellent opportunity to bring the elements of good practice together and extend the benefits of Sure Start to all children under 5 and their families in a local area. Day care, education, health and family support is integrated in order to meet the complex and changing needs of children and parents. The aim is to make a real difference to children's life opportunities by addressing health, social and educational inequalities and requiring professionals to work more closely together. Parents are at the heart of planning and delivery, so that services are more accessible – ideally in one place – and responsive to individual needs.

Table 9.1   Services provided in children's centres, as a percentage of all children's centres, 2007

Services for children	
Full day care for children under 5	77
Sessional day care for children under 5	73
Holiday provision	30
After school provision	25
Before school provision	23
Support for families	
Family support outreach and/or home visiting services	91
Employment advice links to Job Centre Plus	90
Literacy, language or numeracy programmes for parents/carers with basic skills needs	87
Support for parents with disabled children	87
Support for lone parents	86
Support for teenage parents	83
Support for families with drug or alcohol related problems	79
Support for people with mental health problems	76
Relationship support	76
Support for particular minority ethnic groups	75
Support for families of asylum seekers	68
Support for families with a parent in prison or involved in criminal activity	66
Any other services	66

Source: DCSF, 2008

Children's centres are service hubs where children under 5 years old and their families can receive integrated services and information. These services may vary according to each centre but Table 9.1 shows those that are most commonly available.

Children's centres are not about creating physical buildings, but building on the services that are already in place. In some areas, however, this may mean the need to set up entirely new facilities to enable services to come together.

Centres are open for 10 hours a day for 48 weeks a year and each serves a particular geographic area. Children from babies to 5 years old enjoy the benefits of good quality day care combined with education led by qualified early years teachers. Special needs are identified as early as possible so that the chances of addressing them are maximized and children can thrive both at home and when they get to school.

The development of children's centres is helping professionals to understand what services have to be provided to address the needs of parents, including families who are working or studying. The 10-year childcare strategy (DfES, 2006), the Laming report (DH/DfES/HO, 2003) and *Every Child Matters* (DfES, 2003) show that it is not merely about providing a service which provides flexible, high-quality care and education, but also one that has a woven structure of additional services including health, social care and employment advice which operates as one 'seamless provision'. Indeed the government's *Children's Plan* (DCSF, 2007) highlights the importance of partnership working, the role of parents/carers and high expectations.

Children's centres are multidisciplinary institutions that are influenced by the needs of the local community to ensure young children have the best possible opportunities for reaching their full potential. In the light of this and perhaps not surprisingly, children's centres are clearly based on the premise that providing high-quality integrated services (health, education, family support and childcare) leads to positive outcomes for children, families and their communities. They have evolved as a recognized model requiring high-quality provision within a multidisciplinary framework that is responsive to the needs of the local community in relation to the five *Every Child Matters* outcomes.

 ## Case study 9.1: developing a children's centre

I will now describe the development of Golden Lane Children's Centre which grew out of Fortune Park Centre. Fortune Park Early Years Centre was a purpose-built setting which was opened in 1995 to provide education with care for 85 children from 6 months to 5 years old. The centre was built with money from the London Borough of Islington, the Corporation of London, the City of Vienna (via money donated by way of an acknowledgement of damage to the City of London during the Second World War), the Cripplegate Foundation (a local independent charity that provides grants to organizations that work to improve the local area) and the Department for Education and Skills. The centre was located in the most southerly tip of Islington and bordered the City. It was a maintained local authority provision offering care with education for 48 weeks of the year from 8.00 a.m. to 6.00 p.m.

A third of the places were allocated to the centre from the Borough of Islington as 'children in need' (children deemed to be vulnerable but not necessarily having a child protection plan), 12 places were purchased by the City of London, six places were allocated to Islington's multi-agency panel for children with a range of complex special educational needs, and 12 places were marketed (place sold at a higher cost for people who worked or lived locally). The remaining places were for local Islington residents. The borough provided free half-day places for 3-year-olds and free core day places for 4-year-olds (a core day being from 9.30 a.m. to 3.30 p.m.). Access to provision outside the free offer was paid for by parents on a sliding scale according to income. The centre was one of 12 early years settings that were maintained by the local authority.

I was appointed Head of Centre in 1995 and felt very fortunate to be working in a borough that was already leading the way in developing integrated services and inclusive practice. In 1998 the centre was designated as an early excellence centre. I again felt very privileged to be working in a borough where I believe that any one of the maintained local authority settings could have been put forward for the rather onerous and yet honourable title of 'early excellence'. Two centres within Islington were designated – New River Green and Fortune Park – and the borough appointed an early excellence co-ordinator to support the dissemination of the good practice as effectively as possible.

As well as the pressures and excitement that came with this EEC title, it also brought with it an opportunity to empower staff, who realized that they had something of value in terms of sharing ideas relating to practice. Several practitioners rose to the challenge and began to deliver training locally, nationally and internationally.

At the same time as the development of early excellence centres, Sure Start local programmes were being opened in waves. Round 1 started in 1999 and round 6, the final wave, in 2003. Fortune Park Children's Centre benefited from being within round 6 and was able to learn a great deal from the earlier programmes. In autumn 2003 Fortune Park Early Excellence Centre and the local Sure Start programme became an early designated children's centre.

With early excellence funding we had appointed two family support workers to develop services within the local community and to encourage parents of young children to access these developing facilities. Social isolation had been identified as being a huge barrier to the developing community. The children's centre was a resource based within the local community and practitioners *would walk from setting to setting* in order to staff the various services that were being developed to meet the needs of the recently empowered community. Parents' voices were being heard through a parent forum, which met regularly on Saturday mornings, as well as through an advisory board that encompassed the Sure Start Local Programme management board and the management committee of the children's centre.

It was at this point that it became obvious that our wonderful purpose-built early years centre was no longer fit for purpose. Due to lack of space, we were already having to provide a 'stay and play' facility in another local primary school and had plans to place another within a local high-rise block of flats. The local childminders were using the centre on a day that the children were out of the building on educational outings, and offering courses to childcare and education practitioners or parent workshops was proving difficult to accommodate.

Coincidentally, our neighbouring primary school was also in a building that was no longer fit for purpose and therefore unable to fully develop as an extended school. Additionally, a local special school across the road was in a similar position, particularly in view of the borough's inclusion policy which stated 'a commitment to provide accommodation fit for the 21st century and to co-locate Islington's special schools onto mainstream school sites' and that 'old fashioned and unsuitable accommodation would be replaced by modern, custom-designed facilities. As this would provide … greater opportunities for students to benefit from high quality formal and informal education during and after school, at weekends and holidays, alongside their peers' (CEA, 2005). Consequently, the special school, too, would certainly require new accommodation to deliver on the borough's policy directive.

A proposal was put together, initially by the heads of the three settings, to develop a campus on one site. It was a proposal that became known locally as the 'dream'. The 'dream' was well received and was developed with enthusiastic governors and committed borough colleagues as a concept that has now come into being. The council, with its education partner CEA @ Islington, began the process of building new facilities to accommodate Fortune Park Children's Centre, the primary school and the primary department of the special school.

The primary school and the children's centre needed to be re-housed in order to build the new campus. The primary school moved onto the site of a former primary school, which underwent a rapid refurbishment (over a summer holiday) in order to accommodate the increased numbers of children, and operated here for three years and one term.

Fortune Park moved into another local primary school (one with a falling roll and, therefore, ample space), taking with it the nursery class of the closed school. The school had already accommodated our stay and play provision, so moving onto the site, temporarily but in our entirety, was not such an alien concept. The temporary move was actually a fortunate step for both settings as this primary school was also to develop a children's centre on site and therefore absorbed services already developed by Fortune Park. For Fortune Park it helped to support our developing relationships within our area and a rich partnership with our neighbouring children's centre.

In Islington children's centres have been planned to be located on, or very close to, primary school sites wherever possible, as well as to formulate integrated plans with schools to develop a range of 'extended school' services to transform their role in the community and offer a broader range of activities to pupils. The impact for children and families is potentially very significant, when considering the possibility of a truly 'joined up approach' to working with children from birth to 11 years of age. However, such ventures require a very clear and well thought out plan for implementation. It is my view that while the potential is vast, there is still a great need to explore the myriad of issues including governance, leadership models and pedagogy.

The two children's centres worked in partnership to deliver services across the south of Islington – known as the Finsbury area. This partnership has continued to date and certainly seems to make sense for the local community and for the developing Area Children's and Young Peoples Partnership.[1] The process of building the new campus was a long, exciting and demanding one that started with an architectural competition. This competition was won by Nicholas Hare architects (NHA) and so began a fruitful relationship with a project manager, building contractors, governors, staff and an interested group of parents. The architects worked closely with stakeholders to fulfil the 'dream'. This involved many late meetings and an amazing commitment from partners involved in the process but the resulting building has been well worth the effort even though we are just at the beginning of a journey for the building to realize its full potential.

The Golden Lane Campus opened the doors to children, families and the wider community in April 2008. It houses the primary school and children's centre and the primary department of the school for children with physical disabilities. The children's centre is one of five of the 16 children's centres in Islington to be part of a primary school. The other centres are a combination of stand-alone settings and partnership arrangements with private and voluntary providers.

Where children's centres have been located within a school, the centre remit includes the reception and nursery provision, as well as provision for children under 3, plus access to stay and play sessions, family support, health advice and services for pre- and post-natal parents as well as support relating to routes into training and employment. Most offer a range of courses with crèche facilities, courses such as parenting skills, childcare with education, English as an additional language, and steps into employment.

Golden Lane Children's Centre is now at a very promising juncture of its development. Because it is based within a school it is very well placed to meet the government's requirements for an integrated service, as outlined in the extended schools prospectus agenda (DfES, 2005) which states a comprehensive range of services including the following:

- a varied range of activities including study support, sport and music clubs, combined with childcare in primary schools
- parenting and family support
- swift and easy access to targeted and specialist services
- community access to facilities including adult and family learning, ICT and sports grounds.

The success of the campus so far has largely been due to partnership working and a shared commitment to children and families. In order for this community campus to realize its potential there is much hard work, dedication, enthusiasm, organic growth and structural redevelopment that needs to take place in order to shape the identity and endless possibility that the campus brings to bear. We have just begun an exciting journey, a journey that needs to involve all stakeholders in its developing success. This development cannot be imposed but rather needs to evolve from the structures in and around the campus.

The challenges and issues facing children's centres

There are numerous challenges when dealing with the task of running an effective children's centre and these include staffing, structures and budgets and time.

Staffing

There are significant challenges in providing an integrated service of high quality as well as one that is flexible and responsive to the needs of working and/or studying parents. An effective service requires a highly qualified workforce (Sylva et al., 2004). The EPPE findings, described in more detail in Chapter 4, indicate that the quality of staff is important not only at the practitioner level but also within the realms of leadership. Heads of children's centres and members of the leadership team need to have a wealth of understanding of young children's learning based on solid practice. Without having either a head or another senior member of staff who is able to lead in this area, the quality of care and education is likely to be compromised and, consequently so is the impact of the service. (See also Chapter 15.)

There are many demands made on the heads of children's centres. Centres require someone who is able to assess complex issues, manage multidisciplinary teams, deal with budgets, establish effective partnerships as well as recognize the need for effective analytical structures. Unfortunately in some local authorities heads of centres (or, as they are sometimes unfortunately termed, 'managers') have no more than an NVQ level 3 qualification which, in my opinion, is creating structures that are likely to fail. Additionally where the extent of 'teacher' input is negligible there is again a lack of understanding and recognition that high-quality care and education requires *a multi-skilled workforce* including teachers. The role of the teacher is just as important as having highly skilled professionals from health, social care and employment.

There is still a great deal of work in supporting children's centres and ensuring that they have staff who are appropriately trained and able to provide a high quality provision. The National College of School Leadership have contributed to the skills of leadership team through the implementation of the National Professional Qualification of Integrated Centre Leadership (NPQICL). This qualification supports participants in developing skills around the broad area of inter-agency working combined with the necessity for developing a shared ethos with all its partners. The implementation of the NPQICL is a step in the right direction, and is to be welcomed. However, there is still a substantial amount of work required in developing centres leaders' understanding and ability to effectively assess how services can address the overarching objective of reducing poverty. There is also a need to develop a teaching workforce that has a greater understanding of what high-quality practice looks like within a multi-agency context.

Structures and budgets

Structures and budgets are crucial features in the development of any organization. Detailed thinking needs to be given to ensure that the budget reflects the
necessary staffing structures, structures which go beyond the simple staffing
ratios as identified under the Children's Act (2004) and include time for daily
opportunities for reflection, assessment and planning. Time is also needed for
teams of multidisciplinary professionals to establish relationships, evolve a
shared ethos and develop opportunities to jointly evaluate the impact of services. Having time for these tasks is recognized as essential to good quality early
childhood provision and it should not be acceptable to ignore this when offering provision that runs from 8 a.m. to 6 p.m. for 48 weeks of the year. It is important that local authorities create structures in their children's centres that enable
staff to have time to meet and reflect, otherwise there is the clear danger that
the impact of children's centres will be impaired.

Children's centres in schools

It is exciting and encouraging that there are a number of children's centres
being attached to infant and primary schools. Such initiatives should be praised
as models which, in principle, promote a seamless provision of services from
birth to 11 years of age. However, the pace of development has not provided
time to consider the implications and there is now an urgent need to consider
how heads of children's centres fit within a school model. Where does the head
of centre sit in relation to the head teacher? Should it be assumed that the head
of centre is line managed by the head teacher? Or are there any alternative
models, for example, the scope for a distributed leadership model?

Governance is key to all of this. It would be useful to examine alternative
models of leadership as opposed to merely accepting the current model as the
only option. It is an area that needs further consideration, consideration which
needs to take place at a national level to ensure this promising and exciting venture of children's centres is 'structured' in a way that enhances its effectiveness.

Finding enough time

With such a rapidly expanding workforce and a crucial need for partnership
working there are huge time implications for the children's centre staff team.
Team meetings are no longer confined to discussion of the curriculum but now
require time for developing an understanding of the roles of a range of disciplines and exploring ways of working effectively together to develop a shared
ethos. Providing time for such issues is, of course, difficult with a limited structure of five training days a year and weekly staff meetings; consequently, there
is the need to consider additional strategies. This may mean that the centre

opens late once a week to facilitate this urgent need for colleagues to have time together, or to have monthly development mornings, where again the centre. Clearly, such strategies need to be balanced with the needs of working and studying parents. However, my view is that such additional structures are very much needed to enable the organization to be as effective as it can be.

What makes a successful children's centre?

This is a difficult question to answer, although there are some findings from Ofsted and the EPPE research which may provide some indicators of success. *Leading to Excellence* (Ofsted, 2008), for example, noted that those organizations which provide high-quality care and education are those which hold children at the core of what they do and where there is a continuous focus to excel. Similarly EPPE (Siraj-Blatchford et al., 2003) noted that the most effective institutions were those which promoted and developed a shared ethos across all stakeholders. In light of the above, I would like to share what I have found to be particularly effective for children and families at Fortune Park and now Golden Lane Children's Centre as key elements to our success.

- *Commitment to excellence*. This drive to provide the highest possible service is crucial in enabling the organization to make a significant difference to all concerned – children, families, our partners, the local community and, of course, the staff team.
- *Partnership working*. The very nature of children's centres is the recognition that to effectively meet the needs of children and families requires a multidisciplinary approach. Consequently, children's centres must have that shared understanding that all relevant disciplines have a significant part to play in enhancing the outcomes for children and families.
- *Shared ethos*. A commitment to excellence and a belief in partnership working is not sufficient without the development of a team which embraces and owns both a shared ethos and shared objectives. The achievement of a shared ethos is one that requires time, passion and collective ownership.
- *Flexibility*. Recognizing that services may change according to the needs of the local community and having structures that will accommodate such demands. Embracing challenge with a 'have a go attitude', and a willingness to develop new structures, and initiatives. Such attributes are crucial to a children's centre.

Conclusion

Children's centres have evolved through a number of initiatives, but perhaps most important has been the early excellence agenda, Sure Start Local

Programme and the findings from the Laming Report (DH/DfES/HO, 2003) which developed into the *Every Child Matters* (DfES, 2003) framework and most have most recently been encapsulated within *The Children's Plan* (DCSF, 2007).

We are now at the stage where a seamless provision of multidisciplinary services are considered key to supporting all children and families, but of utmost importance to those in greatest need.

Given the relative newness of children's centres, there is much to be done, in particular concerning staff training, sustainability, governance and partnership working. While it has been recognized that the National College of School Leadership has made a significant contribution to developing leaders with the NPQICL, the level of rigour attached to the training of teachers, family support workers and early years practitioners does require further scrutiny, as does the newly developed Early Years Professional Status (see Chapter 14). The issue of leadership structures clearly needs to be addressed to ensure effective continuity of both partnership working and service delivery.

Budgets and sustainability are always going to be contentious and, of course, service users will inevitably state the case for more. What clearly is needed is a comprehensive evaluation of how funding is allocated in accordance to what is asked, both in relation to the strategic thinking and the practical application.

Children's centres by their very nature require a holistic approach and as such it is important to note that all disciplines involved with children and families contribute to their success. In light of these points it is perhaps not surprising that I have argued that a successful children's centre is one that has a *passion for excellence, a commitment to partnership working, a shared ethos and a flexible approach.*

While there are many challenges, the potential for children's centres is both exciting and substantially beneficial to all concerned, especially for families and children.

 Points for discussion

- Is there a need to undertake a rigorous national evaluation of children's centres to ensure not only their sustainability but also their effectiveness?

- How do we know that the funding allocation to children's centre is sufficient to address their core objectives?

- Does a potential change of government threaten the long-term future of children's centres? Are there actions needed to be taken now to prevent this possible eventuality?

Further reading

Department for Children, Schools and Families (DCSF) (2007) *The Children's Plan: Building Brighter Futures*. London: DCSF. Sets out the government's ambitions for improving children and young people's lives over the next decade and how they intend to achieve them.

Deparment for Education and Skills (DfES) (2006) *Sure Start Children's Centres Practice Guidance*. London: DfES. Provides an effective overview of the purpose and role of children's centres within a multidisciplinary context.

Department of Health (2007) *Delivering Health Services through Sure Start Children's Centres*. London: DH. Highlights the value of children's centres particularly within the context of working with health professionals and why such partnerships are so important to addressing the needs of children and families.

Siraj-Blatchford, I. and Manni, L. (2006) *Effective Leadership in the Early Years Sector (ELEYS) Study*. London: Institute of Education. Highlights common characteristics associated with effective leadership within the early years.

Whalley, M. (2006) *Children's Centres: The New Frontier for the Welfare State and the Education System?* Nottingham: NCSL. Outlines both the complexity and importance of children's centres as well as exploring issues relating to leadership.

Note

1 This is one of one of six areas that have grown out of the Children's and Young People's Partnership (CYPP), established as a result of the Children's Act (2004), which places a duty on councils to promote co-operation between named partners to improve the well-being of children.

References

Cambridge Education Associates (CEA) (2005) *What's Happening to Islington's Special Schools*. Policy statement. London: CEA.

Department for Children, Schools and Families (DCSF) (2007) *The Children's Plan. Building Brighter Futures*. Norwich: TSO.

Department for Children, Schools and Families (DCSF) (2008) *Childcare and Early Years Providers Survey 2007*. London: DfES.

Department for Education and Skills (DfES) (1997) *Early Excellence Centres*. www.surestart.gov.uk/surestartservices/settings/early excellence centres

Department for Education and Skills (DfES) (1999) *Sure Start Local Programmes*. www.surestart.gov.uk/surestartservices/settings/Surestartlocalprogrammes

Department for Education and Skills (DfES) (2002) *Delivering for Children and Families*. London: DfES.

Department for Education and Skills (DfES) (2003) *Every Child Matters*. Norwich: TSO.

Department for Education and Skills (DfES) (2005) *Extended Schools: Access to Opportunities and Services for All. A Prospectus*. London: DfES.

Department for Education and Skills (DfES) (2006) *Choice for Parents, the Best Start for Children: Making it Happen – An Action Plan for the Ten Year Strategy: Sure Start, Children's Centres, Extended Schools and Childcare*. London: DfES.

Department of Health, Department for Education and Skills and the Home Office (DH/DfES/HO) (2003) *Keeping Children Safe. The Government's Response to the Victoria Climbié Inquiry Report and Joint Chief Inspectors' Report Safeguarding Children*, CM 5861, September.

Her Majesty's Treasury (HMT) (2004) *Choice for Parents, the Best Start for Children: A Ten Year Strategy for Childcare*. London: TSO.

Office for Standards in Education, Children's Services and Skills (Ofsted) (2008) *Leading to Excellence: A Review of Childcare and Education (2005–2008) with a Focus on Organisation, Leadership and Management*. London: Ofsted.

Siraj-Blatchford, I., Sylva, K., Taggart, B., Sammons, P., Melhuish, E. and Elliott, E. (2003) *Effective Provision of Pre-School Education Project. Technical Paper 10. Intensive Case Studies of Practice Across the Foundation Stage*. London: DfEE/Institute of Education.

Sylva, K., Melhuish, E., Sammons P., Siraj-Blatchford, I. and Taggart, B. (2004) *The Effective Provision of Pre-School Education (EPPE) Project: Technical Paper 12. Final Report*. London: DfES/Institute of Education.

CHAPTER 10

THE ROLE OF HEALTH IN EARLY YEARS SERVICES

Kate Billingham and Jacqueline Barnes

Chapter Contents

- The role of health in early years services
- Understanding children's health
- Health services in the early years
- Early years health services today
- Sure Start: working together with health in the early years

---

The purpose of early years services (EYS) is to offer children and parents a range of services and programmes that will help children to achieve their potential and, for some, to overcome the impact of early disadvantage. A child's health is integral to their development, both as an influence on early development and as an outcome, and is consequently a core function and responsibility of everyone who works in early years services. The fact that health cannot be separated from the overall well-being of children is acknowledged by the fact that 'be healthy' is one of the five outcomes of *Every Child Matters* (DfES, 2004).

This chapter provides an overview of health in EYS exploring the potential role of health services as part of the range of services available for families with young children and describing the historical context for today's child health services. We draw on our experience of Sure Start children's centres, the Child

Health Promotion Programme (CHPP) and the Family-Nurse Partnership programme to suggest how early years services can most effectively protect and promote the health of children.

The role of health in early years services

It is parents who promote and protect their children's health, with services offering guidance, support and care when needed. Of those services, health has a leading role in preventing ill health and promoting good health in childhood, across the physical and psychological aspects of health and well-being. As the universal first point of contact for mothers and fathers to be and for new parents, the services provided by midwives, health visitors and general practice make up a core part of early years services. National Health Service (NHS) general practices, community health services and hospitals are also responsible for providing children and families with care and treatment for acute and long term conditions. However, because health is a broad concept that is influenced by many different factors, responsibility for health goes beyond the health service, and early years services have a number of key health roles.

Protecting and promoting the health of children

All practitioners working with young children and their families, whether or not they have a health title or role, have a responsibility to proactively protect and promote children's health and to know what to do when a child is unwell. The 'health work' of early years services ranges from deciding what snacks and drinks will help meet each child's 'five a day' and prevent dental decay, to making sure children are safe and protected against accidents, that toileting and hand-washing habits prevent the spread of communicable diseases, knowing what first aid to give and what good health advice to offer parents. Because of the influence of wider social factors on child health the work of early years services will also extend to giving advice on benefits, housing and employment or supporting a parent with relationship problems or difficult life events.

Integrating health-led services within early years services

As well as promoting and protecting the health of children in their care and supporting parents to do likewise, early years services are increasingly becoming the location for the delivery of health services. *Every Child Matters* (DfES, 2003) made the integration of children's services a priority for front-line services supported by joint working at a strategic level. Integration is seen as key for improving outcomes for children through more integrated and responsive services centred around Sure Start children's centres.

Contributing to health services provided outside early years settings

Most children's and families' contacts with health services take place outside early years setting in general practice, accident and emergency departments, walk-in centres and community health services. Nonetheless staff working in early years services have much to offer to these health services. Their expertise in working with young children and their knowledge of individual children and their families can provide useful information to support decision-making by health professionals. In addition they play a role in supporting parents to access health services and contribute to a treatment or care plan that may be in place for a child with health or behaviour problems or developmental delay. As a result staff in early years services need to be familiar with wider health services beyond those co-located in their early years setting.

Understanding children's health

Definition of health

Throughout this chapter we define health in its broadest sense to include physical, social and emotional health and well-being, each of which is interdependent and overlapping.

The 'be healthy' outcome in *Every Child Matters* is defined as 'being physically healthy, mentally and emotionally healthy, sexually healthy, healthy lifestyles, choosing not to take illegal drugs' with parents, carers and families promoting healthy choices (DfES, 2004: 9).

Children's health today

The patterns of child health and the causes of ill health change over time as societies develop and science advances (Blair et al., 2003). The health of children has improved dramatically in the past 100 years; today child mortality in the UK is fortunately a rare event. In 1911 more than one child in 10 died before their first birthday, after the Second World War one child in 20 died in infancy and today it is five in every 1,000.

The history of child health shows that these improvements were more to do with improvements in the social and physical environment than health-care interventions. Better housing, nutrition, education, water and sewage treatment has made most difference. It is only recently that public health programmes and medical treatments have played a role in improving health of children through immunizations, antibiotics and advances in medical care and treatment (Blair et al., 2003).

Today in the UK the public health priorities for children are:

• Obesity: rates for 2–10 year-olds have risen by more than 50 per cent from 1995 to 2006. If no action is taken it is estimated that by 2050 25 per cent of children will be obese and 30 per cent will be overweight (Cross-Government Obesity Unit, 2008).

- Inequalities in infant mortality: while the overall rate in infant mortality has fallen inequalities remain with the gap between 'routine and manual groups' (5.9 deaths/1,000 live births) and the population as a whole (4.9/1,000 live births) increasing (DH, 2007).
- Psychological health: the prevalence of mental health problems in children has increased since the 1970s and in 2004 it was estimated that 10 per cent of children between 5 and 15 in the UK had a clinically diagnosed mental health disorder (ONS, 1999).
- Accidents remain the major cause of death after infancy and socio-economic inequalities are particularly marked (Blair et al., 2003).
- Chronic illnesses are increasing among children and while some of this may be explained by better reporting and changing expectations, real increases have been seen in asthma and diabetes (Blair et al., 2003).

Inequalities in health

Good health in childhood is not evenly distributed and inequalities in child health persist in the UK. International comparisons and differences within the UK population show continuing inequalities in child health and well-being associated with socio-economic factors and inequalities in society as a whole (Blair et al., 2003). According to UNICEF, child well-being in the UK is lower than in 20 other industrialized countries (UNICEF, 2008). Within the UK some groups are more vulnerable than others, in particular children born to teenage mothers and to women born in some developing countries. For example, the infant mortality rate in the UK for infants of mothers born in Pakistan is double the rate of UK-born mothers. The infant mortality rate for babies born to mothers under 20 is 60 per cent greater than for babies born to older mothers (DH, 2007).

Socio-economic status is strongly associated with health outcomes for children. In recent years reductions in poverty, high employment, better educational attainment and increased welfare provision has improved the conditions for many families. However, some children and families are being left behind (HMG, 2006). The most vulnerable families still experience profound exclusion, poor health and well-being, and diminished life chances.

Factors influencing child health and well-being

Pregnancy and the first years of life are when humans are most vulnerable and highly susceptible. A useful way of understanding this is to take what Bronfenbrenner (1979) describes as an ecological system of direct and indirect factors impacting on the child from the care provided by the immediate family through to the values and laws of a society. Taking an ecological approach is helpful because it recognizes the importance of the very wide range of services, relationships and societal influences that impact on health and the relatively minor role that health services play in the health and well-being of children. It also enables us to address the factors linked to inequalities in health such as poverty, poor housing and unemployment and highlights the importance of thinking about the whole family context when planning for child health services.

Neurological development and genetics

Our expanding knowledge of how the brain develops and of genetics are having a profound influence on the understanding of child development and parenting. Early attachment and the quality of early relationships impact on how the neural pathways of the brain are pruned and shaped (Cozolino, 2006; Gerhardt, 2004).

We have always known that pregnancy is a key time for the developing child. New knowledge on the impact of toxic substances, such as tobacco, alcohol and stress in pregnancy on the development of the brain and long-term cognitive and psychological well-being has made this time more important than ever.

While there are genetic differences between children, research suggest that genes are not necessarily a fixed blueprint determining who we are and how we behave. Scientists suggest that how genes are expressed may be influenced by the environment in which the unborn child is growing and is born into (Graham, 2007; Rutter, 2007). It is early days and we must be cautious about how we interpret the research but it is clear that this area of scientific discovery will change how we understand the development of children and what and when services should be offered.

Relationship between child and adult health

Health in childhood matters not only for the child but in terms of their future adult life. From conception onwards experiences leave 'lasting memories on children's body system and therefore on their future health' (Graham, 2007, citing Barker, 1998). It is thought that adult health is influenced by what happens in the womb. One hypothesis suggests that poor maternal nutrition and foetal health puts the child at greater risk of long-term ill health in adult life such as heart disease and diabetes (Barker, 1998). Thus, ensuring the health and well-being of the mother-to-be is as, if not more, important that maintaining a range of services for infants and young children.

Summary

The health of children is shaped from conception by the complex interrelation-ship of biological, social and psychological factors. This means that early years services need to think broadly in their health work with children and families to include both social factors such as income, jobs and housing as well as individual and family factors such as health behaviours, child care practices and relationships in a family.

Health services in the early years

The historical role of health in young children's services

Child health services have historically been separate from not only the hospital-dominated NHS and maternity services but also from children's social and educational services. Recent policy is aiming to end this separation through the development of Sure Start children's centres. This section summarizes the historical context for the role of health in early years services.

In the early years of the National Health Service, from 1945 to about 1958, there was a tripartite division in health between hospital services, primary health care services, and those under the control of the Medical Officer of Health (MoH), including provision for young children. This pattern continued relatively unchanged until 1974, preventive health care for babies and children staying completely separate from the NHS and provided by the local authority. In 1974, the management of child health clinics and school health was transferred to the health authority (Melhuish and Hall, 2007).

After the 1997 election there has been a gradual but inexorable intertwining of health services for young children (and their parents) with other early years services. The Labour leadership promoted a change of focus typified by connectedness between previously separate departments responsible for health, education, childcare, social services, housing, employment and family support (Anning and Hall, 2008). It was recommended that there was a change of approach to the design and delivery of services, which should be jointly planned by all relevant bodies (HMT, 1998). Following this, in 1999 the Sure Start Unit was established to co-ordinate all departments responsible for services for young children (defined as up to 4 years of age), with a particular focus on bringing together the Department of Health and the Department for Education and Skills (Anning and Hall, 2008). Sure Start Local Programmes (SSLPs) aimed to bring joined-up primary and community health care, advice about child health and development, childcare, play, early education and parental support for all families with a child under the age of 4 years.

By 2002, to build on the idea of SSLPs, the concept of Sure Start children's centres was developed. These bring together health practitioners who focus on maternal and child health (for example, midwives, health visitors, speech therapists) but also offer a range of other services for young children, such as childcare, early education, play opportunities, child protection and family support.

The *National Service Framework for Children, Young People and Maternity Services* (DH/DfES, 2004) was another a major step in the integration of health with other early years services in that it dealt with young people and maternity services together, emphasizing preventive services and setting out standards for all organizations providing services to children and their delivery partners, and set a standard for the CHPP.

Early years health services today

In the past 10 years there has been a significant reorientation in terms of where health is positioned in relation to pregnant women, infants and young children. This is resulting in:

- the integration of health services within Sure Start children's centres
- a recognition of the wider health contribution made by early years services
- a greater emphasis on prevention and health promotion and the reduction of inequalities in health and well-being outcomes for children.

There are two programmes that exemplify these policy changes.

The Child Health Promotion Programme

The CHPP is the universal schedule of screening tests, health and development reviews, immunizations and health promotion that is offered to all parents from pregnancy to adulthood (DH, 2008). The purpose of the programme is to identify and address health and development problems early, to protect children against serious communicable diseases and guide parents to promote their children's health and well-being. In the first five years there are screening tests for a number of diseases and abnormalities including: phenylketonuria, cystic fibrosis, heart defects, deafness, undescended testes in boys and hip dislocation. Universal health and development reviews are carried out at key intervals including around 2 weeks after birth, before the first birthday, between 2 and 2½ years and at school entry. The immunization programme provides protection against serious communicable diseases such as diphtheria, measles, whooping cough, polio, tetanus and meningitis.

The Healthy Child Programme (HCP) previously know as the CHPP has been the core preventive programme for many years. It has a strong evidence base (Hall and Elliman, 2006) and has been adapted over the years to keep pace with new research and expert consensus. Traditionally it has been the territory of the NHS in isolation from wider children's services but recent years have seen some major changes in the programme, culminating in the updated CHPP for pregnancy and the first years of life (DH, 2008).

Recent changes to the Healthy Child Programme

- The inclusion of a 'progressive universal' model, that is, a universal core programme with additional evidence based preventive services and programmes for children and families socially, emotionally or physically disadvantaged
- Emphasis on promoting child health in pregnancy
- Focus on public health priorities such as obesity prevention, breast feeding and accident prevention
- Recognizing the importance of early attachment and positive parenting and relationships within families
- Giving fathers an equal role in the Healthy Child Programme
- Delivering the programme through children's centres as well as general practices
- Use of new technologies such as the Internet
- Giving the health visitor the lead role with responsibility for the overall delivery of the Healthy Child Programme in terms of quality, coverage and outcomes

---

The Family–Nurse Partnership programme (FNP)

One of the challenges for preventive services in the first years of life is to find programmes that are known to work for the most disadvantaged children and families. One such programme is the Family–Nurse Partnership programme (known as the Nurse–Family Partnership in the USA). This intensive, home-visiting preventive programme for vulnerable first-time young parents is delivered by specially trained nurses from early pregnancy through until the child is 2 years old. The programme has been developed in the USA over the past 30 years where three large-scale research trials demonstrated significant and consistent short- and long-term benefits for children and their parents (Olds, 2006). The programme goals are to improve antenatal health, child health and development, and economic self-sufficiency. The benefits are greatest where the mother has low psychological resources. It takes a different approach to traditional preventive health services for children in the UK in that it is a manualized, highly structured intensive programme. The nurses, mainly drawn from health visiting and midwifery, use activities and materials that help the parents to learn, using a strengths-based, future-orientated approach and methods that guide parents to make changes in how they care for themselves and their child. The programme has been tested in England since 2007 and the future of the programme in England will depend on the outcomes of research.

These two programmes are both health led but delivered in the context of wider early years services where their impact is enhanced by their links to other services provided in Sure Start children's centres and the health work carried out by other early years staff.

Sure Start: working together with health in the early years

The establishment of Sure Start in the late 1990s brought significant changes to early years provision. At the heart of this new service was the integration of health with other services in Sure Start Local Programmes, and the evaluation of these early programmes provides useful learning on how to work together more effectively for children and families.

Lessons from Sure Start

One of the groundbreaking aspects of the area-based Sure Start Local Programmes (SSLPs) was that they would typify 'joined-up' services for the early years, bringing together health, childcare and play, early education and parental support. To achieve this, each was required to create a partnership board consisting of local stakeholders from the statutory and voluntary agencies and including local community members such as parents. Boards received funding directly from central government with power to decide how it would be spent in the context of five core services: outreach and home visiting; support for parents and families; support for good quality play, learning and childcare; primary and community healthcare, and advice on child health and development and family health; and support for people with special needs (Melhuish and Hall, 2007). Health was represented on all but a tiny proportion of the partnership boards (Tunstill et al., 2002) but was the lead agency in only a small proportion (13 per cent) (Meadows, 2006).

The national evaluation of the early impact on children and parents of living in an SSLP area identified the importance of integrating health services with other early years services. Programmes that were more proficient in the identification of users had greater positive impacts on child development at 36 months old. Health-led programmes were better positioned to identify families with young children, because of easy access to birth records (from health services). When health was not the lead agency, information sharing was often problematic, with health the most unwilling to share information about families with outreach staff, despite the agenda of the SSLP to visit each baby born in the local area before they were 2 months old (Ball et al., 2006).

Programmes with a higher proportion of health-related staff had a greater improvement in observed maternal acceptance of child behaviour (NESS, 2005). Also, as health practitioners already had established systems for visiting families with young children prior to Sure Start, they could probably 'hit the ground running'. This is reflected by the fact that they had a significantly higher expenditure in their first year of operation compared with SSLPs led by other agencies (education, social services) or led by voluntary or community organizations (Meadows, 2006).

When midwives were seconded to SSLPs referrals were less problematic and, in particular when they were co-located in Sure Start centres (newly built in many areas), multidisciplinary work was more effective. Where midwives and health visitors worked together as part of an integrated team there were improvements in the continuity of care between the antenatal and post-natal periods and they were well placed to make referrals to other services such as psychiatric nurses, dieticians family support or nursery nurses (McLeish, 2008).

The national evaluation also found significant barriers to integrating services with health, providing useful pointers for future developments of Sure Start children's centres: primarily, the importance of equal partnerships. Where health took the lead they were seen as too dominant in relation to other groups, which could create barriers to an effective partnership. It was necessary to gain high-level commitment from each partner organization for smooth partnership working. The objectives of health leads such as PCTs were often identified as narrower than those of other partners. Health agencies and health professionals were perceived to be problematic as partnership members in that they had high status relative to other stakeholders and some members viewed the medical model as inappropriate for the preventive work at the core of the SSLP model of working (Tunstill and Allnock, 2007).

Local evaluations examining the role of health visiting within SSLPs also highlighted tensions and problems in sharing information between non-SSLP health visitors, with access to names of all new births, and SSLP personnel (Cordis Bright, 2003; McCallum Layton, 2002). There was uncertainty about the extent to which health visiting recognized that Sure Start offered the opportunity to work in a different way, rather than being about providing top-up monies for existing work, indicating that communication at the stage of SSLP service planning with health providers beyond the SSLP area had been insufficient.

Some of these barriers also related to providing maternity services in SSLPs (Kurtz et al., 2005). Local evaluations identified blocks in the referral process, with midwives seen as gatekeepers, when offering antenatal services that were additional to routine midwifery (Pearson and Thurstone, 2006). It was recommended that integration between health and other early years services should be facilitated by co-location in children's centres (DfES, 2006), guidance reflected in the CCHP's focus on both maternity services and those for young children (DH, 2008). However it was noted (McLeish, 2008) that midwifery has not featured in the design of all children's centres so there is no space for antenatal or post-natal clinics.

Thus, overall it appears from the Sure Start experience that there was at times an uneasy balance of power between health and other agencies, either statutory or from the third sector, in relation to enhancing services in the early years. Health agencies held some trump cards; in particular, they were in a good position to identify children and families eligible for SSLP services and the existing infrastructure meant that they could mobilize services more readily; but this did not necessarily happen unless they were a major player in the partnership. If they were this could lead to tensions with related health professionals not working within the SSLP, who had reservations about the additional funds being used for a small number of families in the SSLP area.

Supporting the integration of health in early years services

Given the historical context within which early years and health services operate, it comes as no surprise that the journey to integrated working is not always smooth. There is much to learn from the early days of Sure Start Local Programmes and many of these early difficulties are being addressed as children's centres become established in local communities. The evaluation of Sure Start and the experience of delivering the CHPP and the FNP suggest that an environment that supports integrated working includes the following features:

1   Joint planning from the beginning, making sure that all the partners are involved with an equal voice to shape how services are delivered, for whom and by whom.
2   The development of a common language and agreed framework for services.
3   Focusing on the needs of children and families and their hopes and aspirations.
4   Understanding and respecting each other's roles and core purpose. Individuals are more likely to work together with others if they feel valued and respected.
5   Recognizing the responsibilities of health services and the accountability and responsibility of health professionals.
6   Using research evidence and information to plan and deliver services and developing methods of ongoing monitoring and evaluation to ensure that services meet the needs of families, and are delivered effectively.
7   Having the infrastructure requirements in place, such as making sure there is space for health professionals to work in early years settings with the necessary equipment and privacy while also becoming true partners in the early years team.
8   Paying close attention to information technology (IT) and data management. Health professionals will need access to data from GPs and hospitals, data that require the highest level of data security. Systems should be put in place to ensure confidential data access and data entry.
9   Ensuring that multi-agency teams are run in a way that allows all early years staff to have an equal contribution.

Conclusion

The role of health in early years services is a 'work in progress'. Local services and the workforce delivering them will continue to change. New evidence will emerge and wider societal changes and new government policies will ensure that the landscape of children's services will continue to develop in the coming years. Nonetheless, the recognition that health is everybody's business in the early years and that there is a need for greater service integration will remain driving forces in the future.

In this chapter we have provided the context for health in early years services and shown how health services such as the Child Health Promotion Programme and the Family–Nurse Partnership Programme contribute to the shared goals of all who work with young children and families; to help children to achieve their potential and, for some, to overcome the impact of early disadvantage.

The importance of health to the immediate and future outcomes for children is likely to become more important as we learn more about early childhood development and the influences impacting on a child in pregnancy. This means that the role of health promotion and protection in early years services will become more important both through health services and through the health work of early years services. Moreover, the development of the Early Years Foundation Stage (DfES, 2007) provides an opportunity to link the holistic approach of the CHPP to that of early years services.

There is still much to be done to enable parents and children to have access to integrated high-quality preventive health services that respond to their individual needs and aspirations. In many parts of the country good progress has been made to make sure that health is a core element in early years services and that early years services are linked to wider health services. Key challenges remain. These include working together across general practices and Sure Start children's centres, developing the lead role of the health visitor for the CHPP and the wider health work of early years services, and implementing evidence-based preventive services and programmes within children's services. What matters to parents and children will always be access to skilled and knowledgeable practitioners who they can trust will act in the interest of their child and with whom they can build a relationship based on respect and partnership.

 Points for discussion

- Why has it in the past been challenging to integrate health with other early years services?
- Can you recall in your experience early years settings where health was well integrated?
- Why was the integration successful?
- have you noticed any greater focus on health in the early years setting you have personal experience of in the past five years?
  If so, how has this been achieved

 Further reading

Anning, A. and Ball, M. (eds) (2008) *Improving Services for Young Children. From Sure Start to Children's Centres*. London: Sage Publications. Presents the effects of Sure Start from a range of perspectives and explores the successful and problematic aspects of the programme. It sets out practical lessons learned for practitioners and policy-makers. It also maps and evaluates the progression of the programme into children's centres.

Belsky, J., Barnes, J. and Melhuish, E. (eds) (2007) *The National Evaluation of Sure Start. Does Area-based Early Intervention Work?* Bristol: Policy Press. Reviews the history of policies pertaining to child health and well-being which preceded and set the stage for Sure Start. It describes how the programmes were expected to function, how they actually operated and the impact on children, families and communities.

Blair, M., Stewart-Brown, S., Waterston, T. and Crowther, R. (2003) *Child Public Health*. Oxford: Oxford University Press. Provides a comprehensive overview of the public health of children. A useful textbook providing information on child health and how public health actions can make a difference.

Department of Health (2008) *The Child Health Promotion Programme: Pregnancy and the First Years of Life*. London: DH. This government publication sets out the content of the Child Health Promotion Programme and how it should be delivered. This is the core health service for children and relates closely to the work of EYS.

Hall, D. and Elliman, D. (2006) *Health for All Children*. Revd 4th edn. Oxford: Oxford University Press. A strength of the CHPP is that is has a well-established evidence base. This book pulls together the research and provides detailed information on what should be in a preventive child health promotion programme.

References

Anning, A. and Hall, D. (2008) 'What was Sure Start and why did it matter?', in A. Anning and M. Ball (eds), *Improving Services for Young Children. From Sure Start to Children's Centres*. London: Sage Publications. pp. 3–15.

Ball, M., Chrysanthou, J., Garbers, C., Goldthorpe, J., Morley, A. and Niven, L. (2006) *Outreach and Home Visiting Services in Sure Start Local Programmes*. Sure Start Report 17. London: DfES.

Barker, D. (1998) *Mothers, Babies and Health in Later Life*. Edinburgh: Churchill Livingstone.

Blair, M., Stewart-Brown, S., Waterston, T. and Crowther, R. (2003) *Child Public Health*. Oxford: Oxford University Press.

Bronfenbrenner, U. (1979) *The Ecology of Human Development*. Cambridge, MA: Harvard University Press.

Cordis Bright (2003) *Maltby Sure Start Spotlight Project Evaluation: Health Visiting*. Local evaluation report. www.ness.bbk.ac.uk/documents/findings/656.pdf (accessed 12 August 2008).

Cozolino, L. (2006) *The Neuroscience of Human Relationships*. New York: Norton.

Cross-Government Obesity Unit (2008) *Healthy Weight, Healthy Lives: A Cross-Government Strategy for England*. London: DH/DCSF.

Department for Education and Skills (DfES) (2003) *Every Child Matters*. Green Paper. London: HMSO.

Department for Education and Skills (DfES) (2004) *Every Child Matters: Change for Children*. London: HMSO.

Department for Education and Skills (DfES) (2006) *Statutory Guidance on Inter-agency Co-operation to Improve the Wellbeing of Children: Children's Trusts*. London: DfES.

Department for Education and Skills (DfES) (2007) *Early Years Foundation Stage*. Nottingham: DfES.

Department of Health (DH) (2007) *Review of Health Inequalities Infant Mortality PSA Target*. London: DH.

Department of Health (DH) (2008) *The Child Health Promotion Programme: Pregnancy and the First Years of Life*. London: DH.

Department of Health and Department for Education and Skills (DH/DfES) (2004) *National Service Framework for Children, Young People and Maternity Services: Core Standards*. London: DH.

Gerhardt, S. (2004) *Why Love Matters: How Affection Shapes a Baby's Brain*. London: Routledge.

Graham, H. (2007) *Unequal Lives: Health and Social Inequalities*. Maidenhead: McGraw-Hill/Open University Press.

Hall, D. and Elliman, D. (2006) *Health for All Children*. Revd 4th edn. Oxford: Oxford University Press.

Her Majesty's Government (HMG) (2006) *Reaching Out: An Action Plan for Social Exclusion*. London: Cabinet Office.

HM Treasury (HMT) (1998) *Comprehensive Spending Review: Cross Departmental Review of Provision for Young Children,* Chapter 21. London: The Stationery Office. www.archive.official-documents.co.uk/document/cm40/4011/401122.htm

Kurtz, Z., McLeish, J., Arora, A. and Ball, M. (2005) *Maternity Services in Sure Start Local Programmes.* Sure Start Report 12. London: DfES.

McCallum Layton (2002) *Survey of Health Visitors. Seacroft Sure Start*. Local evaluation report. www.ness.bbk.ac.uk/documents/findings/118.pdf (accessed 12 August 2008).

McLeish, J. (2008) 'Maternity services', in A. Anning and M. Ball (eds), *Improving Services for Young Children. From Sure Start to Children's Centres.* London: Sage Publications. pp. 79–92.

Meadows, P. (2006) *Cost Effectiveness of Implementing Sure Start Local Programmes: An Interim Report*. Sure Start Report 15. London: DfES.

Melhuish, E. and Hall, D. (2007) 'The policy background to Sure Start', in J. Belsky, J. Barnes and E. Melhuish (eds), *The National Evaluation of Sure Start. Does Area-based Early Intervention Work?* Bristol: Policy Press. pp. 3–21.

National Evaluation of Sure Start (NESS) (2005) *Variations in Sure Start Local Programmes' Effectiveness: Early Preliminary Findings*. Sure Start Report 14. London: DfES.

Olds, D. (2006) 'The Nurse–Family Partnership: an evidence based preventive intervention', *Infant Mental Health Journal*, 27: 2–25.

Office of National Statistics (ONS) (1999) *The Mental Health of Children and Adolescents in Great Britain*. London: Office of National Statistics.

Pearson, C. and Thurston, M. (2006) 'Understanding mothers' engagement with antenatal parent education services: a critical analysis of a local Sure Start service', *Children & Society*, 20(5): 348–59.

Rutter, M. (2007) *Genes and Behaviour: Nature–Nuture Interplay Explained*. Oxford: Blackwell.

Tunstill, J. and Allnock, D. (2007) 'Sure Start Local Programmes: an overview of the implementation task', in J. Belsky, J. Barnes and E. Melhuish (eds), *The National Evaluation of Sure Start. Does Area-based Early Intervention work?* Bristol: Policy Press. pp. 79–95.

Tunstill, J., Allnock, D., Meadows, P. and McLeod, A. (2002) *Early Experiences of Implementing Sure Start.* Sure Start Report 1. London: DfES.

United Nations Children's Fund (UNICEF) (2008) *The State of the World's Children*. New York: UNICEF.

CHAPTER 11

DIVERSITY, INCLUSION AND LEARNING IN THE EARLY YEARS

Iram Siraj-Blatchford

Chapter Contents

- Multiple identities
- Diversity and achievement
- Diversity and learning
- Promoting positive self-esteem
- Social competence
- Involving parents

In modern, diverse societies, and a world that increasingly recognizes the realities of global interdependence, it is essential that children learn social competence to respect other groups and individuals, regardless of difference. This learning must begin in the earliest years of a child's education. In this chapter I identify groups who are often disadvantaged due to the poor understanding that some early years staff have of them. I argue that there is a need to challenge the hidden assumptions which oppress particular individuals and groups. While most early childhood settings appear to be calm and friendly places on the surface, I argue that there may be a great deal of underlying inequality. This may occur through the implementation of differential policies, adult interactions, the use of displays, or through variations (or lack of variation) in the planning, curriculum or programme that the staff offer to individuals or groups. These are especially important issues to be considered because they concern the early socialization of *all* children. In the early years children are vulnerable and every adult has the power to affect each child's future actions and behaviour, as well as their intentions, learning outcomes and beliefs.

Children can be disadvantaged on the grounds of diversity in ethnic background, language, gender and socio-economic class in both intentional and unintentional ways. Children with special educational needs are also commonly disadvantaged in early childhood and this is an important area of equity education, but beyond the scope of this chapter (though see Chapter 12). The structures through which social inequality can be perpetuated and measured are related to aspects such as employment, housing or education. For instance, we know that women earn less than men as a group, and that working-class people live in poorer homes and have relatively poor nutrition, health and education. It was in response to these grim social realities that the Sure Start programme was introduced in the UK, which has been developed to support poor families and children under 4, and this remit is now extended to the 3,500 children's centres which will be up and running by 2010.

Although I am concerned with the structural inequalities which create an over-representation of some groups in disadvantaged conditions, I have cautioned elsewhere against the assumption that all members of a structurally oppressed group (for example, all females) are necessarily oppressed by those members of a structurally dominant group (for example, all males). Because of the interplay between social class, gender, ethnicity and disability, our social experience and identities are multifaceted. I therefore argue that children can hold contradictory individual positions with respect to the structural position that their 'group' holds in society. Interactional contexts are also often highly significant.

Multiple identities

Identity formation is a complex process that is never completed. The effects of gender, class and other formative categories overlap, often in very complicated ways, to shape an individual's identity. While I do not attempt to discuss this complexity in detail , it is important for practitioners to be aware of the nature of shifting and changing identities. No group of children or any individual should be treated as having a homogeneous experience with others of their 'type'.

A number of publications related to the development of children's personal, social and emotional education provide very useful strategies for supporting the positive development of children's personal identities (Roberts, 1998), yet few writers relate this work specifically to ethnicity, language, gender or class.

There is now a great deal of research evidence of racial, gender and class inequality at a structural level in education (MacPherson, 1999). Concerning racial identity, culture and 'agency' (the interactions between individuals and groups) there is only an emerging literature, and most of this is about adolescent school children. This is particularly interesting because issues of gender and class identities have received more attention over the years, but again with regard to older children.

Working-class and minority ethnic children's poor academic performance has been well documented, as has girls' performance in particular subjects (Lloyd, 1987). The link between racism, sexism, class prejudice and underachievement has also been thoroughly established (Ladson-Billings and Gillborn, 2004). However, if those who work with young children are able to undermine children's self-esteem (however unintentional this might be) through negative beliefs about children's ability due to their gender, religion, socio-economic status, language or ethnicity, then we have to evaluate these actions very carefully.

A child may be classed, gendered or 'racialized' (language status is also important here) in more than one way. Stuart Hall (1992), for example, discusses not only the discourses of identity between groups but also those of difference *within* ethnic groups. In the very act of identifying ourselves as one thing, we simultaneously distance ourselves from something else. In terms of race and ethnicity, Hall argues that there are often contradictions within these categories as well as between these and other categories such as sexuality, class, dis/ability. The way we perceive identities is very much shaped by how they are produced and taken up through the *practices* of representation (Grossberg, 1994).

Making use of the metaphor of a kaleidoscope in understanding identity based on a range of inequalities, Bailey and Hall (1992) argue that there will be individual differences within any identity-forming category, such as race, language, gender and social class. For instance, in Britain, an Indian woman who is a first-generation immigrant, and working class, will have a different identity to her daughter who is second-generation British-Indian, and has become a teacher. Their experience will vary because of how others perceive the combination of ethnic background in relation to their gender, socio-economic status, dress, language, even age and so forth. Mother and daughter will certainly not be treated by others in the same way but they might have some shared experiences.

Staff also need to find resources and a shared language with which to work with dual-heritage children and their parents to support a strong identity. But it would be even better if staff worked with all children to make them aware that they all have an ethnic/racial identity and that they all have a linguistic, gendered, cultural and diverse identity. Surely this is the way forward? In being sure of one's own identity as multifaceted, it must be easier for children to accept that others are exactly the same – even when the combinations are different!

In their early childhood, children inevitably identify closely with a range of individuals and groups; from an early age they develop multiple commitments and solidarities. In addition to the 'sense of cultural belonging' that they develop in terms of their language and faith group, their gender and social class, educationalists support children in progressively accepting the social and moral responsibilities, and the community involvement associated with national and international (global) citizenship.

The UK has never been a monocultural society, and calls for the development of any single 'national' identity have therefore always been misplaced. Citizenship, just like identity, must be recognized as a multifaceted phenomenon. Contradictions and controversies are an inevitable consequence of diversity. They are also grist to the mill of progress and creativity. In any event, democracy requires something more than simply an orientation towards common values. From the earliest years we should be preparing children to participate, critically engage and constructively contribute to local, national and global society. An appropriate aim may be to develop the sort of 'cosmopolitan citizenship' that has been identified by Osler and Starkey (2005). In doing so, we should also recognize that:

> Cosmopolitan citizenship does not mean asking individuals to reject their national citizenship or to accord it a lower status. Education for cosmopolitan citizenship is about enabling learners to make connections between their immediate contexts and the national and global contexts. It is not an add-on but rather it encompasses citizenship learning as a whole. It implies a broader understanding of national identity. It also requires recognition that British identity, for example, may be experienced differently by different people. (Osler and Starkey, 2005: 27)

As the Advisory Group on Citizenship (DES, 1998: 216) suggested: 'The ethos, organization, structures and daily practices of schools have a considerable impact on the effectiveness of citizenship education.' A few early childhood settings, particularly those influenced by Dewey (O'Brien, 2002), Frinet (Starkey, 1997) and Niza (Folque and Siraj-Blatchford, 2003), are already providing young children with significant opportunities to learn how to participate. A good deal more could be achieved in this direction.

The sexism, racism and other inequalities in our society explain why at a structural level certain groups of people have less power while others have more. But at the level of interaction and agency we should be critically aware of the danger of stereotyping and should focus on individuals. This is not to suggest that we should ignore structure; far from it. We need to engage in developing the awareness of children and staff through policies and practices, which explain and counter group inequalities. I will turn to the point of practice later. What I am suggesting is that educators need to work from a number of standpoints to empower fully the children in their care. Children need to be educated to deal confidently and fairly with each other and with others in an unjust society; in this way our values will be reflected in our children (Siraj-Blatchford and Clarke, 2000).

The experiences and values of children can come from parents' views, media images, and the child's own perceptions of the way people in their own image are seen and treated. In the absence of strong and positive role models children may be left with a negative or a positive perception of people like themselves. This bias can start from birth. In the Effective Provision for Pre-school Education (EPPE) project, the largest project on early years education in the UK, we have found some marked differences in equity issues. For instance, we know that most providers create a poor environment for children in terms of diversity (Sylva et al., 1999) with the exception of combined centres and some nursery schools (see also Chapter 4 and Siraj-Blatchford et al., 2003). The EPPE study also found that the provisions for diversity were associated with as many as five of the nine attainment outcomes measured. This was higher than for any of the other Early Childhood Environmental Rating Scale sub-scales that were applied to evaluate the quality of the learning environment that was offered. Effective Provision for Pre-school Education showed that minority ethnic workers were better represented in social services-type day care and combined centres, and very few were employed in other sectors (Taggart et al., 2000). Managers and staff in settings need to be challenged by such data and think about how this has come about and, indeed, how it might be changed.

Many parents and staff conclude from children's behaviour that they are naturally different, without considering their own contribution to the children's socialization, or considering the impact of role-modelling. Difference, apart from physiology is therefore a matter of social learning. This has implications for practice and the kinds of activities that we should make sure all children have access to, regardless of their gendered or other previous experiences.

Diversity and achievement

Cultural identity should be seen as a significant area of concern for curriculum development and values education. All children and adults identify with classed, gendered and racialized groups (as well as other groups) but what is especially significant is that some cultural identities are seen as less 'academic' than others (often by the staff and children). We know that children can hold views about their 'masterful' or 'helpless' attributes as learners (Dweck and Leggett, 1988). Dweck and Leggett (1988) therefore emphasize the importance of developing 'mastery' learning dispositions in children. There is evidence that children who experience education through taking some responsibility for their actions and learning become more effective learners. They are learning not only the content of the curriculum, but also the processes by which learning takes place (Siraj-Blatchford and Clarke, 2000). Roberts (1998) argues that the important area of personal and social education should be treated as a curriculum area worthy of separate activities, planning and assessment.

The 'helpless' views adopted by some children can be related to particular areas of learning and can lead to underachievement in a particular area of the curriculum. Children construct their identities in association with their perceived cultural heritage. Recently we have heard a good deal in educational debates about (working-class) boys' underachievement. The results from the school league tables suggest that some boys do underachieve in terms of basic literacy, but it is important to note that this is only certain groups of boys and not all boys. In the UK, working-class white boys and African-Caribbean boys are particularly vulnerable (Siraj-Blatchford, 1998). Similarly, children from some minority ethnic groups perform poorly in significant areas of the curriculum while other minority ethnic groups achieve particularly highly (Gillborn and Gipps, 1997).

It is apparent that certain confounding identities, for instance, white/working class/male, can lead to lower outcomes (in the UK and some other societies) because of expectations held by the children and adults. In asserting their masculinity, white working-class boys might choose gross-motor construction activities over reading or pre-reading activities. Similarly, some girls may identify more strongly with home-corner play and favour nurturing activities over construction choices. Class, gender and ethnicity are all complicit here and the permutations are not simple, but they do exist and do lead to underachievement. The answer is to avoid stereotyping children's identities but also requires educators to take an active role in planning for, supporting and developing individual children's identities as masterful learners of a broad and balanced curriculum (Siraj-Blatchford, 1998). As previously suggested, in the active construction of their identities, children distance themselves from 'others'.

Diversity and learning

Children need to be in a state of emotional well-being, feel secure and have a positive self-identity and self-esteem. The curriculum must be experiential, social/interactional and instructive and children need to be cognitively engaged (Siraj-Blatchford and Clarke, 2000).

It is widely recognized that an integrated, holistic and developmental approach is needed to learning, teaching and care with children from birth to 7. They learn not only from what we intend to teach but from all their experiences. For example, if girls and boys, or children from traveller families, are treated differently or in a particular manner from other people, then children will learn about the difference as part of their world view. To deny this effect is to deny that children are influenced by their socialization. The need for emotional, social, physical, moral, aesthetic and mental well-being all go hand in hand. This is also true of our youngest children, hence the references to equal opportunities in the *Early Years Foundation Stage* (DCSF, 2007).

The early years curriculum should therefore incorporate work on children's awareness of similarities and differences, and help them to see this as 'normal'. Some children can be limited in their development by their view that there are people around them who do not value them because of who they are. This would suggest that early years staff need to offer *all* children guidance and support in developing positive attitudes towards all people. A focus on similarities is as important as dealing with human differences. The early years are an appropriate time to develop this work with young children.

Children in all types of early childhood settings might have similar experiences. Students, teachers, childminders and playgroup workers have often asked how they can deal with class, gender and ethnic prejudice. It would be a great mistake to assume that this is only a 'problem' in largely multi-ethnic settings. Strategies which allow children to discuss, understand and deal with oppressive behaviour aimed at particular groups, such as minority ethnic children, girls, the disabled and younger children, are essential in all settings. I suggest that educators should always make opportunities for stressing similarities as well as differences.

Promoting positive self-esteem

Early childhood educators have an instrumental role to play in this development. Staff need to help children learn to guide their own behaviour in a way that shows respect and caring for themselves, other children and adults, and their immediate and the outside environment. Values education goes hand in hand with good behaviour management practices. The way that adults and children relate to each other in any setting is an indication of the ethos of that setting. To create a positive ethos for equity practices, staff in every setting will need to explore what the ethos in their setting feels like to the users, for example, parents, children and staff. Staff need to explore what behaviours, procedures and structures create the ethos, which aspects of the existing provision are positive and which are negative, and who is responsible for change.

Children need help from the adults around them in learning how to care for each other and to share things. To help the children in this respect, the educator must have the trust of the children and their parents. Young children's capacity to reflect and see things from another person's point of view is not fully developed. Most small children find it difficult to see another person's view as equally important. Children need a lot of adult guidance to appreciate the views and feelings of others. This can be learnt from a very early age. In her research on the relationship between mothers and their babies, and relationships between very young siblings, Dunn (1987: 38) suggests that mothers who talk to their children about 'feeling states' have children who themselves 'become particularly articulate about and interested in feeling states'. Consideration for others has to be learnt.

Of course educators cannot expect children to behave in this way if they do not practise the same behaviour themselves. If children see us showing kindness, patience, love, empathy, respect and care for others, they are more likely to want to emulate such behaviour. For many educators the experience of working actively with children in this way may be underdeveloped, especially when it comes to dealing with incidents of sexism or racism. Each setting, as part of their equity policy, will need to discuss the issue of harassment and devise procedures for dealing with it:

Short-term action

- If you hear sexist, racist or other remarks against another person because of ethnicity, class or disabilty you should not ignore it or you will be condoning the behaviour and therefore complying with the remarks.
- As a 'significant' other in the child's life, she or he is likely to learn from your value position. Explain clearly why the remarks made were wrong and hurtful or offensive, and ask the abused child how she or he felt so that both children can begin to think actively about the incident.
- Do not attack the child who has made the offending remarks in a personal manner or imply that the child as a person is wrong, only that what was said is wrong.
- Explain in appropriate terms to the abuser why the comment was wrong, and give both children the correct information.
- Support and physically comfort the abused child, making sure that she knows that you support her identity and that of her group, and spend some time working with her on the activity she is engaged with.
- At some point during the same day, work with the child who made the offending remarks to ensure that she knows that you continue to value her as a person.

Long-term action

- Target the parents of children who make offensive discriminatory comments, to ensure that they understand your policy for equality and that you will not accept abuse against any child. Point out how this damages their child.
- Develop topics and read stories which raise issues of similarities and differences in language, gender and ethnicity, and encourage the children to talk about their understandings and feelings.
- Create the kind of ethos that promotes and values diverse images and contributions to society.
- Involve parents and children (depending on the age of the children) in decision-making processes, particularly during the development of a policy on equality.

- Talk through your equality policy with all parents as and when children enter the setting, along with the other information parents need.
- Develop appropriate teaching and learning strategies for children who are acquiring English so that they do not get bored, frustrated and driven to poor behaviour patterns (adapted from Siraj-Blatchford, 1994).

A positive self-concept is necessary for healthy development and learning.

Social competence

One of the most important challenges for early childhood workers is to help children develop the skills to interact with others. Developing the social skills that assist children to get along with their peers and adults will have a significant impact on their lives. Even at this level, language is a major tool. Social skills involve the strategies we use when interacting with others. They cover awareness of the feelings of others. Social skills are used to enter and maintain interactions, to engage others in conversation, to maintain friendships and to cope with conflict. Non-verbal skills involve smiling, nodding, eye contact and the development of listening skills. All of these non-verbal strategies form foundations for language interactions.

All babies and toddlers in childcare and nursery settings need opportunities for warm interactions with adults. Young children need consistency in the care provided, and those children who come from language backgrounds other than English need support on a consistent basis from staff who speak their first or home languages. The children need to receive messages that say they are important to their caregivers. They need to develop a feeling of trust in their new environment. Staff need to respect all the children in their care. This means taking particular care to understand and acknowledge the different cultural and socio-economic backgrounds of the children and to make special efforts to work with families to assist the children to settle into a new environment (Siraj-Blatchford and Clarke, 2000).

Boys and girls can have different language experiences within the same household. Dunn (1987) studied the relationship between mothers' conversation styles with their children aged 18–24 months. She states:

> The analysis also showed marked and consistent differences in the frequency of such conversations in families with girls and with boys. Mothers talked more to 18-month-old daughters about feeling states than they did to their 18-month-old sons. By 24 months the daughters themselves talked more about feeling states than did the sons. (Dunn, 1987: 37)

In multicultural or diverse societies there is a great variety of family values and traditions and it is important that children are brought up to balance the tensions and handle the adjustments of being reared in one way and being educated in another. Children need to become socialized into the new practices and society. Early childhood staff need to be patient, caring, tolerant and flexible, and need to be able to communicate effectively with parents and other staff about their work.

The EYFS provides children with a range of first-hand experiences that promote equality and interactive learning, foster children's self-esteem and support individual children in their construction of knowledge. They also recognize the key role of play in young children's development and learning. Central to this is the role of the early childhood staff in establishing the learning environment, structuring interactions and supporting learners in their development.

Young, developing children do not compartmentalize their learning, so an integrated environment suitable for the development of cognitive, social, emotional, aesthetic, linguistic/communicative and physical dimensions needs to be created. Therefore, the approaches highlighted in this chapter must go across the whole of the curriculum.

All children have the right to an early childhood curriculum that supports and affirms their gender, cultural and linguistic identities and backgrounds. From an early age, young children are beginning to construct their identity and self-concept, and this early development is influenced by the way that others view them and respond to them and their family. Within today's society, the prejudice and racist attitudes displayed towards children and families can influence their attitudes towards themselves and others (MacPherson, 1999). Early childhood educators need to examine their own values, attitudes and prejudices, and learn to deal with them in positive ways.

A culturally responsive curriculum and staff who understand and respect the cultural and linguistic backgrounds of the children in their care can make a difference. Children can grow up with the ability to retain their home language and culture, and to have pride in their gender and class identity as well as adapting to the new cultures and languages of any early childhood setting they enter.

Any curriculum for children in the early years should:

- foster children's self-esteem
- acknowledge the cultural and linguistic backgrounds of all children
- actively maintain and develop the children's first or home languages
- promote the learning of English as an additional language
- value bilingualism as an asset
- value what boys and girls can do equally
- support families in their efforts to maintain their languages and culture
- foster an awareness of diversity in class, gender, ability and culture
- promote respect for similarity and difference
- challenge bias and prejudice
- promote a sense of fairness and justice
- promote principles of inclusion and equity
- support the participation of the parents in the children's learning (Siraj-Blatchford and Clarke, 2000).

All those working with young children can discuss with parents and community members issues which concern both parents and staff. The following list covers some of the aspects of family and community life which should be explored and so enhance understanding:

- family history
- religious beliefs and practices (including important cultural events)
- children's everyday life at home
- language practices
- parents' theories about learning
- parents' views on schooling and early education
- community events and contacts.

Involving parents

Reference has already been made to the data that were collected in the EPPE project (Siraj-Blatchford, 2004) on early years provisions for 'diversity'. The EPPE project also looked particularly closely at the quality of the early home learning environment (HLE) (Melhuish et al., 2001) that was provided by parents. Although the parents' socio-economic status and levels of education were found to be related to child outcomes, the quality of the home learning environment was found to be even more important. At the age of 3 years and onwards a strong association was found between poor cognitive attainment and less stimulating HLEs. By comparison there was only a moderate, positive association between the HLE and parents' social class and qualifications. For example, the children of parents who reported that they regularly taught/played with the alphabet had pre-reading scores 4.5 points higher than children whose parents did not teach/play with the alphabet. This could be compared to the impact of social class where the difference between the lowest class (IV and V) and the highest (I) was only 2.4 points. In other words, EPPE found that it is what parents did that is more important than who they were (Melhuish et al., 2001).

Research on pre-school education in five countries evaluated by Sylva and Siraj-Blatchford (1995) for the United Nations Educational, Scientific, and Cultural Organization (UNESCO) also considered the links between home and school. The authors report the importance of involving parents and the local community in the construction and implementation of the curriculum. When they begin school or early childhood education, children and their parents 'bring to the school a wealth of cultural, linguistic and economic experience which the school can call upon' (Sylva and Siraj-Blatchford, 1995: 37). 'It therefore becomes the responsibility of the teacher to localise the curriculum and to enlist the support of the local community and families in framing school policy and practice and making the school and educational materials familiar and relevant to the children's experience'.

Parents need to be given information about the curriculum and learning outcomes, and about the achievement of their children. They may also require support in improving their home learning environment. Early years practitioners will need to establish a dialogue with parents that is meaningful to them. Observations of children can be exchanged between staff and parents. To achieve values of true inclusiveness, everyone has to be part of the process of education and care.

 Points for discussion

- When was the last time an audit of equity issues (special educational needs, gender and racial equality and so on) conducted in your setting and what were the outcomes?

- How can the English *Early Years Foundation Stage* (DCSF, 2007) and the Welsh *Foundation Phase* (DCELLS, 2006) be truly inclusive to all children – and their parents?

- How are parents involved in informing your inclusive practice and how do they remain partners in its implementation?

 Further reading

Department for Children, Families and Schools (2008) *Early Years Foundation Stage.* Nottingham: DfES Publications. Also online at: http://www.standards.dcsf.gov.uk/eyfs/ The sections in the EYFS which relate to relationships and identity are very helpful; please also look at the material provided on the DVD relating to promoting diversity and equality through the curriculum.

Dunn, J. (1987) 'Understanding feelings: the early stages', in J. Bruner and H. Haste (eds), *Making Sense: The Child's Construction of the World*. London: Routledge. pp. 26–40. This chapter illustrates early socialisation which is strongly, but inadvertently, gendered by mothers of children before age 2.

Osler, A. and Starkey, H. (2005) 'Learning for cosmopolitan citizenship', *Ad-Lib*, University of Cambridge Institute of Continuing Education, Issue 28. www.Cont-Ed.Cam.Ac.Uk/BOCE/Adlib28/Article1.html A nice argument is presented here for the acceptance of multiple identities. As cosmopolitan citizens, all of us are freed from the pressure to conform to one single identity.

Siraj-Blatchford, I. (2004) 'Educational disadvantage in the early years: how do we overcome it? Some lessons from research', *European Early Childhood Education Research Journal*, 12(2): 5–20. This paper brings together key information on how to support young children's learning, especially those children who may suffer disadvantage due to their ethnicity, gender or social class. It provides robust evidence for why we should change practice.

Siraj-Blatchford, I. and Clarke, P. (2000) *Supporting Identity, Diversity and Language in the Early Years*. Buckingham: Open University Press. A very practical book which brings together theory, practice and policy to help promote equality at centre level for children from birth to 7. All chapters offer staff activities and strategies for supporting self-reflection and better practice in terms of language development, assessment and involving and supporting parents.

References

Bailey, D. and Hall, S. (eds) (1992) 'Critical decade: Black British photography in the 80s', *Ten. 8*, 2: 3.

Department for Children, Education, Lifelong Learning and Skills (DCELLS) (2006) *The Foundation Phase in Wales 3–7*. Cardiff: National Assembly for Wales.

Department for Children, Schools and Families (DCSF) (2007) *Early Years Foundation Stage*. Nottingham, DfES Publications. Also online at: www.standards.dcsf.gov.uk/eyfs/

Department for Education and Science (DES) (1998) *Education for Citizenship and the Teaching of Democracy in Schools*. The Crick Report. London: QCA.

Dunn, J. (1987) 'Understanding feelings: the early stages', in J. Bruner and H. Haste (eds), *Making Sense: The Child's Construction of the World*. London: Routledge. pp. 26–40.

Dweck, C.S. and Leggett, E. (1988) 'A social-cognitive approach to motivation and personality', *Psychological Review*, 95(2): 256–73.

Folque, M. and Siraj-Blatchford, I. (2003) 'Children and pedagogues learning together in the early years: the collaborative process of the Portuguese MEM pedagogy', European Early Childhood Educational Research Association Conference, 3–6 September, University of Strathclyde.

Gillborn, D. and Gipps, C. (1997) *Recent Research on the Achievements of Minority Ethnic Pupils*. London: HMSO.

Grossberg, L. (1994) 'Introduction: bringing it all back home – pedagogy and cultural studies', in H.A. Giroux and P. McLaren (eds), *Between Borders: Pedagogy and the Politics of Cultural Studies*. London: Routledge. pp. 1–28.

Hall, S. (1992) 'Race, culture and communications: looking backward and forward in cultural studies', *Rethinking Marxism*, 5: 10–18.

Ladson-Billings, G. and Gillborn, D. (2004) *The Routledge Falmer Reader in Multicultural Education*. London: RoutledgeFalmer.

Lloyd, B. (1987) 'Social representations of gender', in J. Bruner and H. Haste (eds), *Making Sense: The Child's Construction of the World*. London: Routledge. pp. 147–62.

MacPherson, W. (1999) *Report of the Stephen Lawrence Enquiry*. London: HMSO.

Melhuish, E., Sylva, K., Sammons, P., Siraj-Blatchford, I. and Taggart, B. (2001) *The Effective Provision of Pre-School Education (EPPE) Project: Technical Paper 7 – Social/Behavioural and Cognitive Development at 3–4 Years in Relation to Family Background*. London: DfEE/Institute of Education, University of London.

O'Brien, L. (2002) 'A Response To "Dewey and Vygotsky: Society, Experience, and Inquiry in Educational Practice"', *Educational Researcher*, 31(5): 21–3.

Osler, A. and Starkey, H. (2005) 'Learning for cosmopolitan citizenship', *Ad-Lib*, University of Cambridge Institute of Continuing Education, Issue 28. www.Cont-Ed.Cam.Ac.Uk/BOCE/Adlib28/Article1.html.

Roberts, R. (1998) 'Thinking about me and them: personal and social development', in I. Siraj-Blatchford (ed.), *A Curriculum Development Handbook for Early Childhood Educators*. Stoke-on-Trent: Trentham. pp. 155–74.

Siraj-Blatchford, I. (1994) *The Early Years: Laying the Foundations for Racial Equality*. Stoke-on-Trent: Trentham.

Siraj-Blatchford, I. (ed.) (1998) *A Curriculum Development Handbook for Early Childhood Educators*. Stoke-on-Trent: Trentham.

Siraj-Blatchford, I. (2004) 'Educational disadvantage in the early years: how do we overcome it? Some lessons from research', *European Early Childhood Education Research Journal*, 12(2): 5–20.

Siraj-Blatchford, I. and Clarke, P. (2000) *Supporting Identity, Diversity and Language in the Early Years*. Buckingham: Open University Press.

Siraj-Blatchford, I., Sylva, K., Taggart, B., Sammons, P., Melhuish, E. and Elliot, E. (2003) *Technical Paper 10 – Case Studies of Practice across the Foundation Stage*. London: DfEE and Institute of Education, University of London.

Starkey, H. (1997) 'Freinet and citizenship education, pleasure of learning et Travail Coopératif: Les méthodes éducatives et la philosophie pratique de Célestin Freinet', Séminaire International a L'alliance Francaise De Londres, June.

Sylva, K. and Siraj-Blatchford, I. (1995) *The Early Learning Experiences of Children 0–6: Strengthening Primary Education through Bridging the Gap between Home and School*. Paris: UNESCO.

Sylva, K., Siraj-Blatchford, I., Melhuish, E., Sammons. P. and Taggart, B. (1999) *Effective Provision for Pre-school Education Project, Technical Paper 6*. London: DfEE and Institute of Education, University of London.

Taggart, B., Sylva. K., Siraj-Blatchford, I., Melhuish, E. and Sammons, P. (2000) *Effective Provision for Pre-school Education Project, Technical Paper 5*. London: DfEE and Institute of Education, University of London.

CHAPTER 12

MEETING SPECIAL NEEDS IN THE EARLY YEARS: AN INCLUSIVE APPROACH

Mary Robinson[1]

Chapter Contents

- Contextualizing and realigning special needs in the early years
- Placing special needs in the early years on the educational and social agenda
- Promoting partnership with parents in special needs and early years
- Collective responsibility for children with special needs in the early years
- Inclusion in the early years
- Judging quality and effectiveness of provision for young children with special needs
- Case study

Contextualizing and realigning special needs in the early years

Recent developments have done much to erode the hitherto disparate world of special needs and mainstream early years provision. Historically, and until recently, the domains of early years and special needs were largely separate – this proposition was examined in Wolfendale (2000) and realignment was proposed. A similar philosophy was expounded by Ruth Wilson (2003) who points out that, traditionally, early childhood education and special education have followed separate and differing paths and that the contemporary merging of these disciplines is to be welcomed by all early years practitioners.

These sentiments accord with

- the overarching outcomes for children framework which is a universal and inclusive set of goals towards which children's services, in partnership with parents, strive to achieve
- moves to ensure that children's centres are accessible for all young children
- extended schools – the prospectus for extended schools states 'children with disabilities or SEN must be able to access the new services' (DfES, 2005a: 8)
- the *Early Years Foundation Stage* (DfES, 2007)

Underpinning such inclusive approaches is a core philosophy which states that all children have primary and secondary needs, most attain competence in key cognitive, physical, affective, social, linguistic areas of development, and for those children whose life-path contains learning and developmental challenges (vulnerable children and those with special needs and disabilities), it is society's responsibility to offer them and their families maximum support and resources to surmount and cope with these challenges (Abbott and Langston, 2005). This philosophy informs the rest of the chapter.

Placing special needs in the early years on the educational and social agenda

Significant landmarks with reference to special needs in the early years since the seminal and influential Warnock Report (1978) have included the

- 1981 Education Act on special educational needs
- 1993 Education Act, Part 3 (which subsumed the 1981 Education Act)
- 1994 SEN Code of Practice (replaced by the 2001 SEN Code of Practice, see below)
- special educational needs (SEN) Programme of Action (DfEE, 1998) outlining plans by the newly elected Labour government
- SEN Tribunal, now called the SEN and Disability Tribunal (SENDIST)
- Early Years Development and Childcare Plans/Partnerships
- creation of Sure Start and the transition from Sure Start Local Programmes to locally funded Children's Centres
- *Early Years Foundation Stage* (DfES, 2007) with its emphasis on providing access and meeting the needs of all children.

In the new millennium the special needs/early years profile has continued to rise, with the landmarks listed above acting as building blocks for recent and current developments, several of the most important of which are highlighted below to illustrate practice as well as the growing and pervasive ideology that meeting children's special needs is an indivisible part of a children's services agenda, applicable to all children.

SEN legislation and guidance

The 2001 SEN Code of Practice (DfES, 2001) replaced the 1994 SEN Code of Practice and goes hand in hand with the 2001 SEN and Disability Act (SENDA) which replaced the 1993 Education Act in respect of special needs.

Chapter 4 of the 2001 SEN Code of Practice deals with identification, assessment and provision in early years education settings, all of which are expected to have regard to the Code of Practice. They are also expected to identify a member of staff to act as the special educational needs coordinator (SENCO) – a post that can be shared between individual childminders, or playgroups and the co-ordinator of that network. The responsibilities vary from liaising with parents and professionals to organizing a child's individual education programme (DfES, 2001: 34, para. 4.15).

The Code outlines two action points: Early Years Action and Early Years Action Plus. This approach is described as a 'graduated response so as to be able to provide specific help to individual young children' (2001: 33, para. 4.10) and 'once practitioners have identified that a child has SEN ... the provider should intervene through Early Years Action' (2001: 33, para. 4.11) and if further advice and support are needed, then Early Years Action Plus is triggered, leading to statutory assessment.

In 2004 the government's vision of meeting SEN in the early years and beyond was set out in the publication *Removing Barriers to Achievement* (DfES, 2004a). This outlines how children with special needs and disabilities would be afforded the opportunity to succeed. Building on the proposals for the reform of children's services in *Every Child Matters* (DfES, 2003a), it set the agenda for improvement and action at national and local level. A central aim of the strategy was to embed SEN and disability in mainstream policy and practice by focusing on improving outcomes for (all) children and young people.

Sure Start children's centres

A cornerstone of the present government's drive to tackle child poverty, social inclusion and early learning is the ambitious, long-term early years Sure Start programme. The programme aims are to improve the health, well-being and therefore life-chances of children before and after birth, offering services such as family support, advice on parenting, increased and better access to health care and other services. Children's Minister, Beverley Hughes, described Sure Start as 'a journey (never an end) ... to transform local services for under fives and their families' (DCSF, 2008a).

A key difference of the Sure Start programme which distinguished it from what had gone before is that the programmes are area based, seeing all children as the target of intervention. This provides the opportunity for identification of special educational needs and limits the possible stigma attached to recognition of needs at an early stage. The success of early Sure Start Local Programmes and initiatives such as early excellence centres and neighbourhood nurseries between 1999 and 2003 led to the recommendation for the development of children's centres which offered a number of services to children and families. (For further discussion of children's centres see Chapter 9.)

Each children's centre has to make a clear statement on special needs and there is a commitment to early identification and social inclusion. They are required to set out:

- the different provision and services available to young children with SEN and their families
- arrangements made by existing service providers for early identification, assessment and support for young children with SEN
- details of specialist provision and services.

Outcomes for children: linking philosophy to practice

Five core 'outcomes' for children were first identified in the Green Paper *Every Child Matters* (DfES, 2003a) and these were subsequently given expression in *Every Child Matters: Change for Children*, (DfES, 2004b).

The five outcomes for children represent the conceptual-philosophical framework within which practitioners and policy-makers now operate. The link between the outcomes for children as first espoused in *Every Child Matters* (DfES, 2003a) and their relevance to children with special needs is expressed within the government's strategy document for SEN, *Removing Barriers to Achievement* (DfES, 2004a).

The proposed integration of services for all children, including those with special educational needs was the focus of the Childcare Act 2006, which gave statutory support to the implementation of the aims set out in *Choice for Parents, the Best Start for Children: A Ten Year Strategy for Childcare* (HMT, 2004).

This brief historical account of early years and special needs in wider contexts indicates clearly that the profile has risen on the educational and social agenda, in tandem with an evolving, inclusive ideology which itself drives a moral imperative to ensure that:

- special needs and disabilities are identified as early as possible in a child's life
- appropriate intervention is in place to meet these identified needs so that they are not overlooked nor neglected in a system where every child matters.

This chapter goes on to single out a number of related areas of significance to early years and special needs.

Promoting partnership with parents in special needs and early years

Paralleling the rising profile of early years/special needs, the involvement of parents and carers in their children's development, learning and education has commensurately increased over the years, as a number of texts have chronicled (see, for example, Edwards, 2002; Hallgarten, 2000; Moran et al., 2004; Qinton, 2004; Wolfendale and Bastiani, 2000; Wolfendale and Einzig, 1999).

The involvement of parents in the area of special needs has been particularly active over the years. Some of the landmark developments in this area include:

- a chapter devoted to partnership with parents contained in the 1978 Warnock Report on special educational needs
- a number of parental rights to be involved in (SEN) statutory assessment being enshrined in special needs legislation (1981, 1993 Education Acts and the 2001 Special Educational Needs and Disability Act (SENDA))
- partnership with parents principles outlined in the 1994 SEN Code of Practice and the 2001 SEN Code of Practice
- advent of local, regional and national parents' groups, lobbying for special needs/inclusive provision (Wolfendale, 1997)
- creation in 1994 of local SEN Parent Partnership Services: these were designed to provide parents with information about SEN provision and assessment procedures and to offer support during and after statutory assessment (see Wolfendale, 2002, for a national overview of developments and accounts of several local SEN PPSs).
- increased confidence through 'Every Disabled Child Matters': a campaign led by Contact a Family, Council for Disabled Children and Mencap (launched in September 2006)
- commitment to providing information, support and training for parents highlighted in *The Children's Plan* (DCSF, 2007b).

Within the *Every Child Matters* and *The Children's Plan*, parents are seen as essential partners in service provision and delivery. In the vision of extended schools (DfES, 2005a) and children's centres (DfES, 2006a) advice and information for parents and parenting support are seen as key to the realization of the outcomes for children.

A government innovation that epitomizes partnership working is Early Support (initially called the Early Support Pilot Programme), initiated in 2002 and outlined in *Together From the Start* (DfES, 2003b). This was designed to offer a co-ordinated service to families with babies and very young disabled children, key features of which include:

- the assessment of children's needs
- co-ordination of multi-agency support for families
- information and access for families
- professional knowledge and skills
- how services are reviewed and developed
- partnership working across agencies and geographical boundaries.

Between 2003 and 2006 £13 million was invested in the initiative, aimed primarily at working in partnership with voluntary organizations to share ideas on new ways of working. It was positively evaluated in 2005 (DfES, 2006b) and a commitment given to fund and support the mainstreaming and consolidation of the programme as a standard part of services provided by local authorities for children and families. Commenting in May 2007, Beverley Hughes (Minister of State for Children Young People and Families) identified Early Support as 'the Government's recommended approach to co-ordinating services'. In December 2007, about 65 per cent of local authorities were implementing Early Support.

There is an increasing evidence base for the impact and effectiveness of parental involvement (Desforges and Abouchaar, 2003; Whalley, 2007; see also Chapter 13), that goes hand in hand with the growing commitment by central and local government to *actively* involve parents in assessment and decision-making.

That parents have a wealth of first-hand experience and accumulating expertise about their children is now being acknowledged. A DCSF-commissioned survey of parental involvement in school (Peters et al., 2008) indicated increased parental involvement for parents of pupils with SEN and a higher level of satisfaction with the quality of information provided. A recently launched programme to co-ordinate multi-agency information to parents (DCSF, 2008b), recommends the extension of information media to include telephone helplines, websites and mobile phones, to more accurately target support to the sources where parents are more likely to seek information.

Collective responsibility for children with special needs in the early years

For many years practitioners subscribed in principle to the tenets of multi-agency working but there were many difficulties in practice to implementing the exhortations contained in a raft of government circulars, including the 1994 and 2001 SEN Codes of Practice. The government intention is to change the children's services landscape over time by changing working practices. Two fundamental areas of change, which have profound implications for those working with and on behalf of young children with special needs, are the *Children's Workforce Strategy* (DfES, 2005b) and the *Early Years Foundation Stage* (DfES, 2007).

The DfES consultation document on the *Children's Workforce Strategy* (DfES, 2005b) set out an ambitious medium- and long-term vision for restructuring training and working practices for the many thousands of people working with and on behalf of children, including meeting the highly specific needs of young children identified as having special needs.

The government agenda for integrating education and care has come together in the *Early Years Foundation Stage* (DfES, 2007) which, from September 2008, provides the framework for practice for all early years providers, including private sector and childminders. Within this framework the needs of children with special educational needs can be identified early. The Foundation Stage focuses on the 'unique child' and the commitment to development, inclusion, safety and well-being moves the identification of need away from the 'special' category and into the notion of fostering positive outcomes for all children.

Local authorities, via their services and providers, have a responsibility to all children to scrutinize their care and development and the identification of additional needs, and the interventions required to meet these are an extension of that scrutiny rather than a separate agenda or responsibility. The approach to early intervention is through an equal opportunities focus and allows consideration of each individual child's learning, development and care needs by:

- removing or helping to overcome barriers for children where these already exist
- being alert to the early signs of needs that could lead to later difficulties and responding quickly and appropriately, involving other agencies as necessary
- stretching and challenging all children.

Via these measures and reforms the government is intent on fostering an ethos of collective responsibility for the planning and delivery of children's services. Two fundamental areas of change are briefly mentioned below, as they will have profound implications for those working with and on behalf of young children with special needs.

Inclusion in the early years

A major change in the way that the needs of our youngest children are met has come about through the shift in educational philosophy that emphasizes including children with special educational needs within mainstream educational and care settings. This philosophy, which embraces both equality of opportunity and the valuing of difference, has followed on from the recognition of the need for universal education and a redefinition of 'education' to mean the way in which we learn to adapt to and interact with our environment (NCB, 2004). The broadening of the concept of 'education' fits well with the social model of special educational needs which places an emphasis on the person first and then considers the needs arising from the disability.

This approach contrasted with the medical model of disability, with its focus on early identification of need, high-quality diagnostic procedures and recommendations for the most appropriate placement, management and monitoring. The social model questions the implication that there is only one way in which the identified need can be met in educational terms. For parents and those supporting the child at this early stage, this is often where the first battles for inclusion are staged. Once the expectation is established that the options for the child include mainstream education with support, it becomes imperative to focus on what is needed rather than describing the deficit, and this opens the door to discussion and negotiation around what is most appropriate for the individual child. This philosophy underpins the *Early Years Foundation Stage* (EYFS) (DfES, 2007) and is enshrined in its core principles. Throughout the EYFS, stress is placed upon 'understanding each child and their family as unique, with different needs and concerns'. While age is viewed as a useful starting point for considering the needs and achievements of children, the overlap in the stages recognizes the differences that can exist in the development of children of similar ages. This overlap is intended to emphasize the fact that there can be big differences in the developmental levels of children of similar ages. At the same time age can be a cue, when taken with all other factors, to indicate that 'development may be atypical and that a child may need extra support' (DCSF, 2007b).

The placement of children with special educational needs depends on local as well as national agreements and practices. The DCSF's guidance indicates the assumption of mainstream education, with any other alternative needing justification and discussion (DfES, 2001). Even where it is agreed that segregated education may be the appropriate long-term option, many parents request an inclusive early years experience for their child. One of the reasons given for the success of inclusion in the early years is the flexibility of the early years curriculum with its emphasis on play, exploration and the sensory aspects of learning (QCA, 2000). The value of this guidance and the necessity of ensuring the maintenance of the core principles of *Birth to Three Matters* (DfES, 2002) was recognized in their incorporation into the *Early Years Foundations Stage* (DfES, 2007). The focus on social and emotional development and the acquisition of play skills highlights the importance of peer group interaction and the discovery of what is shared rather that what discriminates between children.

The inclusion of children at this early stage has a pragmatic as well as a philosophical impact on both parents and providers. Parents are likely to take a wider view of 'education' and see their child in terms of developing abilities, rather than disabilities; staff are empowered by experiencing how well many such children manage the mainstream environment and flourish within it; and society's expectations shift with each positive experience. While special schools are likely to continue to be necessary for some children and popular with some parents, the automatic assumption of special schooling has been replaced by a consideration of what is best for each child and this is most evident at the point of diagnosis within early years.

Judging quality and effectiveness of provision for young children with special needs

Service providers are held accountable for the quality of their provision in a number of ways, but chiefly via inspection and report. The way in which Ofsted carries out inspections of childcare and nursery provision changed quite radically in 2005 (Ofsted, 2005a). A key aspect of this change was to allow for inspectors to assess performance and quality against a set of 14 Standards, one of which (Standard 10) is 'special needs, including SEN and disabilities'. This Standard ensured that SEN is embedded within an inclusive framework.

Since September 2008 early years settings are inspected by Ofsted under sections 49 and 50 of the Childcare Act (2006) with regard to the Statutory Framework for the *Early Years Foundation Stage* document (DfES, 2007). See also Chapter 5.

Local authorities are also subject to inspection regarding their provision for all children, including 'children and young people who are vulnerable, such as those looked after by the council and/or those with learning difficulties or disabilities' (Ofsted, 2005b: 2). Under the new arrangements for Joint Area Reviews (JARs) of Children's Services, Ofsted (2007) outlines how all JARs will cover investigations on safeguarding looked after children and children and young people with learning difficulties and or disabilities.

In its review of childcare and early education, based on inspections in early years settings during the period 2005–08, Ofsted (2008) reported that the quality of childcare and early education has improved year on year, with 97 per cent of settings now achieving satisfactory or better. The report also confirmed that there is a higher proportion of good or outstanding in day care and early education than ever before and in almost half of JARs the provision made for SEN in the early years was a key strength.

Another means of exploring quality is to search for evidence that provision 'works', that is, meets young children's developmental and learning needs by offering sound, proven practice. A performance and evidence-based approach to service delivery is increasingly taking hold, on pedagogical as well as ethical grounds, as Macdonald and Roberts stated: 'Children and their families have a right to expect that our interventions in their lives will be based on the best available knowledge' (1995: 3).

Bodies of knowledge about 'what works' and what is good or best practice in early years and special needs services are beginning to accumulate (see McNeish et al., 2002, Thomas and Pring, 2004, and Hammersley, 2007 for a broader introduction to evidence-based practice in education). The DfES has drawn upon the findings of the longitudinal Effective Provision of Pre-School Education (EPPE) study (see Chapter 4) which includes SEN as one of its main areas of study (Sammons et al., 2002; Taggart et al., 2003). Schneider et al. (2007) have extracted some of the lessons from Sure Start that inform health, social care and education.

These studies provide a sound empirical basis for organizing and operating provision for young children with special needs, and such investigations act as a powerful model of research evidence informing practice.

 ## Case study 12.1: Max

Max (not his real name) lives in an Outer London borough where services are organized in three area-based Children's Resource Centres.

Max is one of twins, born at 34 weeks gestation and suffering from cerebral palsy as a result of birth trauma. Both babies were in the special care baby unit initially and Max remained there for a total of two months, experiencing breathing difficulties and kidney problems. On discharge from hospital Max made good progress, but parents noted delay in developing skills in comparison with his brother, particularly in the area of physical development.

Early support

Max was diagnosed as having quadriplegic cerebral palsy at the age of 12 months and his parents decided that his mother would delay her planned return to work for a year in order to focus on securing the support Max would need and selecting the most appropriate setting for his pre-school care and education. The paediatrician at the local Child Development Centre referred him to the pre-school liaison group (PSLG) at the age of 16 months. The PSLG is a multidisciplinary group which meets every two weeks to consider new referrals and to discuss issues of continuing support for children in the pre-school age range. Established to co-ordinate early response to the identification of difficulty and to ensure that intervention is planned effectively, this group incorporated the principles of Early Support and considered Max's needs in terms of development, care and early education. It was agreed that the pre-school home visiting team (PSHV) would be involved and that a member of this team would act as his key worker.

Pre-school experience

From the age of 18 months to 2 years, the key worker visited the family at home on a two-weekly basis, working with his parents to establish play skills for both boys and foster exploration for Max that took account of his limited mobility. She also worked with the family to ensure that other services, for example, speech and language therapy, physiotherapy and occupational therapy were co-ordinated and used in such a way that family life was not totally dominated by clinic appointments and therapy. She set up a family file (held by the parents) which contained all the key information about Max, contact details for each of the services involved and therapy and support plans from each of the services involved. At this point Max's mother felt that she could now return to work, and a place at the local children's centre for three days each week was secured. Following a few weeks of transition, the key worker role passed to the children's centre and arrangements were made for Max to have some of his appointments in this setting.

While Max (and his brother) settled happily in the children's centre, his parents found the transition to pre-school quite difficult and struggled to cope with the need for a more organized family routine and the increasing (but different) demands for independence from their children. As part of the training arranged for the centre under the EYFS preparation, staff had established family support groups where parents could meet to discuss issues such as managing their children's behaviour, fostering independence in self care skills, and so on. Both parents joined a 12-week programme and took advantage of a programme of talks by local providers on the use and possibilities of play and leisure facilities in the area.

Transition

Max's Pre-School Support Plan is established and includes advice from speech and language therapist, physiotherapist and educational psychologist. Reviews of this plan are held on a termly basis and his parents are fully involved in co-ordinating the support in the centre and at home, and keeping the centre informed of progress or difficulties. Max is fully included in all activities at his level, with support for mobility and physical access being provided as appropriate. As he is due to start at nursery in his local school, planning has already begun for transition in order to ensure that the progress made can be maintained. With a further term remaining at the centre, he will attend for an additional morning each week from the beginning of term in order to access a speech and language group. Throughout the half-term before transfer he will visit the nursery each week, and the staff from the class he will join will also visit the centre to observe him at play.

Summary comments

This case study exemplifies the benefits of joint planning and shared information in supporting children with special educational needs from the earliest involvement. It demonstrates the effectiveness of active parental involvement and the benefits of access to a mainstream educational environment and peer group. Longer-term planning is facilitated by the focus on targeting support to meet need, rather than accessing placement or support.

 Points for discussion

- How to best promote inclusive education?
- How to ensure quality early years/SEN services?
- What are the professional skills needed to work with early years and SEN?
- What are the hallmarks of good practice in working with families?

 Further reading

Department for Education and Skills (DfES) (2003) *Together from the Start*. London: DfES. This includes information about early support.

Department for Education and Skills (DfES) (2007) *The Early Years Foundation Stage*. London: DfES. With its focus on inclusion, and where the underlying philosophy and care principles are to 'understand each child and their family as unique with different needs and concerns'.

Every Disabled Child Matters website – www.edcm.org.uk is a useful site to visit.

Note

1   This is a revised version of a chapter in the fourth edition by Sheila Wolfendale and Mary Robinson.

References

Abbott, L. and Langston, A. (eds) (2005) *Birth to Three Matters*. Maidenhead: Open University Press.

Childcare Act 2006, London: The Stationery Office.

Children Act 2004, London: The Stationery Office.

Department for Children, Schools and Families (DCSF) (2007b) *The Children's Plan*. Norwich: TSO.

Department for Children, Schools and Families (DCSF) (2008a) 'News centre: report on conference for children's centre leaders'. Press notice 2008/0037. info@dcsf.gsi.gov.uk

Department for Children, Schools and Families (DCSF) (2008b) *Parent Know How: Working Together, Supporting Families*. London: DCSF.

Department for Education and Employment (DfEE) (1994) *Special Educational Needs Code of Practice.* London: HMSO.

Department for Education and Employment (DfEE) (1998) *Meeting Special Educational Needs: A Programme of Action.* London: HMSO.

Department for Education and Skills (DfES) (2001) *Special Educational Needs Code of Practice.* London: DFES.

Department for Education and Skills (DfES) (2002) *Birth to Three Matters: A Framework to Support Children in their Earliest Years.* London: DfES.

Department for Education and Skills (DfES) (2003a) *Every Child Matters.* Green Paper. Norwich: TSO.

Department for Education and Skills (DfES) (2003b) *Together From the Start.* London: DfES.

Department for Education and Skills (DfES) (2004a) *Removing Barriers to Achievement. The Government's Strategy for SEN.* Nottingham: DfES.

Department for Education and Skills (DfES) (2004b) *Every Child Matters: Change for Children.* Nottingham: DfES.

Department for Education and Skills (DfES) (2005a) *Extended Schools: Access to Opportunities and Services for All, Prospectus.* London: DfES.

Department for Education and Skills (DfES) (2005b) *Children's Workforce Strategy: Consultation Paper.* London: DfES

Department for Education and Skills (DfES) (2006a) *Sure Start Children's Centres Practice Guidance.* London: DfES.

Department for Education and Skills (DfES) (2006b) *An Evaluation of Phase 3 of Early Support.* London: DfES.

Department for Education and Skills (DfES) (2007) *Early Years Foundation Stage.* Nottingham: DfES.

Desforges, C. and Abouchaar, A. (2003) *The Impact of Parent Involvement, Parent Support and Family Education on Pupil Achievement and Adjustment, a Literature Review.* Research Report 433. London: DfES Publications.

Early Support (2007) www.earlysupport.org.uk

Edwards, R. (2002) *Children, Home and School.* London: Routledge.

Gough, D.A. (2004) 'Systematic research synthesis to inform the development of policy and practice in education', in G. Thomas and R. Pring (eds), *Evidence Based Practice.* Buckingham: Open University Press.

Hallgarten, J. (2000) *Parents Exist OK – Issues and Visions for Parent–School Relations.* London: Institute for Public Policy Research.

Hammersley, M. (ed.) (2007) *Educational Research and Evidence Based Practice.* Buckingham: Open University Press.

Her Majesty's Treasury (HMT) (2004) *Choice for Parents, the Best Start for Children: A Ten Year Strategy for Childcare.* London: TSO.

Macdonald, G. and Roberts, H. (1995) *What Works in the Early Years? Effective Intervention for Children and their Families in Health, Social Welfare, Education and Child Protection.* Barkingside: Barnardo's.

McNeish, D., Newman, T. and Roberts, H. (eds) (2002) *What Works for Children? Effective Services for Children and Families.* Buckingham: Open University Press.

Moran, P., Ghate, D. and van der Merwe, A. (2004) *What Works in Parenting Support? A Review of the International Evidence.* Research Report 574. London: DfES and Home Office, DfES Publications.

National Children's Bureau (NCB) (2004) *Spotlight Briefing.* London: NCB.

Office for Standards in Education (Ofsted) (2005a) *Every Child Matters, Framework for the Inspection of Children's Services.* London: Ofsted Publications.

Office for Standards in Education (Ofsted) (2005b) *Inspection of Children's Services*. London: Ofsted.

Office for Standards in Education, Children's Services and Skills (Ofsted) (2007) *Joint Area Review of Children's Services from April, 2007*. London: Ofsted.

Office for Standards in Education, Children's Services and Skills (Ofsted) (2008) *Early Years: Leading to Excellence*. London: Ofsted.

Peters, M., Seed, K., Goldstein A. and Coleman, N. (2008) *Parental Involvement in Children's Education 2007*. BMRB Social Research. www.dcsf.gov.uk/research

Qualification and Curriculum Authority (QCA) (2000) *Guidance for the Curriculum Foundation Stage*. London: QCA.

Quinton, D. (2004) *Supporting Parents, Messages from Research*. London: Jessica Kingsley.

Sammons, P., Taggert, B., Smees, R., Sylva, K., Melhuish, E., Siraj-Blatchford, I. and Elliot, K. (2002) *SEN across the Preschool Period*. EYTSEN Technical Paper 1. Institute of Education, University of London.

Schneider, J., Avis, M. and Leighton, P. (eds) (2007) *Supporting Children and Families: Lessons from Sure Start for Evidence-based Practice in Health, Social Care and Education*. London: Jessica Kingsley.

Special Educational Needs and Disability Act (SENDA) (2001), London: The Stationery Office.

Taggart, B, Sammons, P., Smees, R., Sylva, K., Melhuish, E., Siraj-Blatchford, I. and Elliot, K. (2003) *SEN in the Early Years: The Parents' Perspective*. EYTSEN Technical Paper 3. London: Institute of Education.

Thomas, G. and Pring, R. (eds) (2004) *Evidence-based Practice in Education*. Maidenhead: Open University Press/McGraw-Hill.

Warnock, M. (Chair) (1978) *Special Educational Needs*. Warnock Report. London: The Stationery Office.

Whalley, M. (2007) *Involving Parents in their Children's Learning*. 2nd edn. London: Sage.

Wilson, R. (2003) *Special Educational Needs in the Early Years*. 2nd edn. London: Routledge.

Wolfendale, S. (ed.) (1997) *Working with Parents after the SEN Code of Practice*. London: David Fulton.

Wolfendale, S. (2000) 'Special needs in the early years: prospects for policy and practice', *Support for Learning*, 15(4): 147–51.

Wolfendale, S. (ed.) (2002) *Parent Partnership Services for Special Educational Needs: Celebrations and Challenges*. London: David Fulton.

Wolfendale, S. and Bastiani, J. (eds) (2000) *The Contribution of Parents to School Effectiveness*. London: David Fulton.

Wolfendale, S. and Einzig, H. (eds) (1999) *Parenting Education and Support, New Opportunities*. London: David Fulton.

CHAPTER 13

WORKING WITH PARENTS

Lucy Draper and Helen Wheeler

Chapter Contents

- Why is partnership important?
- What are the benefits and challenges of working in partnership with parents?
- Thomas Coram Children's Centre and PEAL: working with parents to support children's learning
- Support for parents
- Further training for parents and practitioners

Parents are children's first and most enduring educators. When parents and practitioners work together in early years settings, the results have a positive impact on children's development and learning. (EYFS, 2007: Commitment 2.2)

We need to begin with the firm belief that all parents are interested in the development and progress of their own children. (Pen Green Centre for under Fives and Families, 2004: 15–22)

In this chapter, we draw on the work of Thomas Coram Children's Centre in London and use extracts of practice examples from PEAL (Parents, Early Years and Learning)[1] to look at the central importance of parents and practitioners working in partnership together in early years settings.

We ask 'Why is it important that we work in partnership with parents?' and 'What are the benefits and challenges of working together?' We then describe the work of Thomas Coram Children's Centre and some of the practice gathered by PEAL.

When we use the term 'parents' we are referring to all those – both male and female – who take on this role in children's lives, whether or not they are the child's biological parent. When we use the term 'practitioner', we are referring to the wide range of adults who support children's learning and development in early years settings and services, whether paid or unpaid.

Why is partnership with parents important?

It is possible to work in partnership with parents in a variety of ways. These can include parents working with staff in settings, parents as governors or on management committees, parents involved in staff recruitment, or in the design and shaping of services, parents attending workshops and courses, practitioners visiting families at home, parents running services such as toy libraries and parents sharing observations and jointly planning next steps for their child's learning with practitioners.

The principle of working in partnership with parents is now firmly established within national policy. *Every Child Matters: Change for Children* (DfES, 2004) stresses the importance of parents, carers and families in meeting the desired outcomes for children. The Sure Start Children's Centre programme recognizes the central importance of parental involvement from the start. The *Children's Centre Practice Guidance* (DfES, 2006) advocates high levels of parental involvement in governance, design and development of services, as volunteers, trainees and as partners in their children's learning. *The Children's Plan* (DCSF, 2007) emphasizes parents' support for learning as an essential foundation for positive children's outcomes.

The *Early Years Foundation Stage* (EYFS) (DfES, 2007) sets out detailed principles and commitments on working with parents as partners in children's care, learning and development. It requires settings to acknowledge parents as children's first and most enduring educators, to assign a key person to each child who should establish a warm, respectful relationship with that child and their family, establish an ongoing dialogue with parents, share information, take account of parents' own observations of their child, and offer ideas and support to extend learning and development at home.

Working in partnership: benefits for children

What parents do at home with their babies and young children has the greatest impact on social, emotional and intellectual outcomes. The Effective Provision of Pre-School Education (EPPE) study (Sylva et al., 2004) concludes: 'What parents do is more important than who parents are'. Social class, income, living conditions and parents' own education levels are clearly directly related to child development outcomes. However, the quality of the home learning environment can act as a significant modifying factor. Parents (both mothers and fathers) who engage in activities that encourage thinking and 'stretch a child's mind' as part of everyday life at home, can enhance their child's progress significantly. Children with strong home learning environments are ahead in both social and intellectual development at the age of 3, and this advantage continues as children progress through school to the age of 7. The latest evidence shows that the quality of early home learning environment continues to be a strong predictor of higher attainment at the age of 10 (Sammons et al., 2007).

Parents have a powerful effect on children's outcomes, and research shows that settings and schools that develop effective partnership with parents – a partnership that builds parents' confidence in what they do already – achieve the best intellectual and social outcomes for children. These settings:

- have designated staff with responsibility for parental partnership
- know their community well
- work hard at building trusting relationships
- work at breaking down barriers to involvement and reach out to families
- loan equipment to support learning at home
- listen to what parents say about their own child
- share information with parents regularly
- encourage parents to be active partners in decision-making (Desforges and Abouchaar, 2003; Siraj-Blatchford and Manni, 2007; Siraj-Blatchford et al., 2003; Sylva et al., 2004).

Working in partnership with parents in this way helps to build respectful relationships and to develop shared understandings for the benefit of children. In a survey of parents carried out at Thomas Coram on parents' views of their children's transitions into nursery (Draper and Khan, 2004), it was clear that their main worry was whether the nursery staff would *understand* their child in the way that the child had up until then taken for granted that they would be understood. They listed their worries:

- 'Will my child be able to go to the toilet?'
- 'Will they give extra time to the new children?'
- 'Are there any other children from my ethnic background?'
- 'Will there be someone who speaks my child's language?'
- 'He asked if they'd cook him pasta if he doesn't like the dinner!' (Draper and Khan, 2004)

It is important to children that the adults in their lives share an understanding of who they are, what matters most to them and what they are capable of. They mind very much about whether the adults they care about – first their parents and, later in their lives, their nursery workers – seem to like and respect each other. Continuity between home and setting benefits children's learning. Parents and staff who are focusing together on the child's well-being and learning are able to share insights and to understand the child more fully. This involves the practitioners going to some degree of trouble to get to know the family and in showing an interest (without being unnecessarily intrusive) in a child's home circumstances and life history to date, in their interests and achievements, hopes and fears, likes and dislikes. It also entails staff sharing with parents the details of a child's life in the nursery, and the sometimes familiar and sometimes entirely new facets of a child's personality that reveal themselves in the early years setting.

Working in partnership: benefits for parents

Parents benefit from positive relationships with staff. They enjoy sharing information about their child. They can see that the better the practitioner understands their child the happier their child is likely to be. They are also intrigued to know about what their child is doing and learning during the hours they are apart from them, and children, frustratingly, are not always able (or willing) to explain this themselves. ('*What did you do at nursery today?*' '*Played.*') Parents may also welcome a different (and less intense) perspective on the rewarding, but often challenging, experience of bringing up a child. Practitioners bring a broader view of the different developmental stages young children go through, what is 'normal' and, perhaps, what really is concerning, and parents are grateful to learn from this. They are often fascinated to find out a bit more about the ways in which early years settings provide learning opportunities and the particular ways in which their own child responds to these.

Some parents also welcome the chance to develop themselves as individuals; if they are asked to contribute their particular ideas, knowledge or skills to share with children in the setting, they will feel respected and valued. Involvement of this kind can release untapped potential – many early years practitioners have started out this way. Other parents have got involved in courses, which have led on to further and higher education. Involvement in management committees and governing bodies empowers parents and gives them a voice in their community, as well as ensuring that their perspective informs the thinking of the setting. Programmes designed to bring practitioners and parents together also bring parents together, reducing parental isolation and helping to build support networks in the wider community.

Parents may also feel encouraged to sustain involvement in learning beyond the early years. They grow in confidence in their role as educators and carers of their children. Confident parents are more likely to continue their involvement, having clearer expectations of schools and teachers and articulating these more powerfully.

Stop, look and listen is an approach used in Camden settings that encourages practitioners and parents to take time out to observe children as they play, and listen to what they say on a regular basis . The observations – called Learning Stories – are then shared and plans made in partnership to encourage children's future learning based on individual needs and interests. Parents describe the benefits of this process:

'It's made me realize how wise she is'; 'I talk more about what she is interested in now.'
'I'm more aware of what she's doing and saying now, sometimes I'm busy and I answer her but I didn't really listen to what she was saying.'
'I realize how little I used to take part.'
'I feel a lot more comfortable now, coming to talk to Joanna (practitioner), if I've got any problems it's made it a lot easier for me to talk to her.'

PEAL Practice example 'Stop! Look! Listen! Sharing observations with parents'

This and other PEAL practice examples can be viewed in full at www.peal.org.uk

Working in partnership: benefits for practitioners

Parents and practitioners need each other and have useful, complementary approaches, knowledge and skills. Parents are experts on their own individual child and their family culture, and practitioners offer expertise in children's development and learning. By combining these sets of expertise, the best opportunities can be provided for each child.

For many staff, the opportunity to work closely with parents also adds a new dimension to their work. Practitioners can sometimes assume that their own experience of family life is the only way it can be, and working with parents from diverse communities widens their views on families and family life. Differences can be shared, respected and explored. The children's life at home provides many opportunities for learning, on which the setting can build.

Common messages run through the feedback from settings where work with parents has been developed after PEAL training. Practitioners report how much they appreciate the increased knowledge about their families and children and enjoy the friendlier relationships, how they have greater awareness and understanding of some of the difficulties parents face, and develop more confidence in approaching and communicating with parents. They also say they find their work much more interesting and satisfying, as they see positive changes in both parents and children.

Clifton Children's Centre in Hull worked with parents to learn how to make and edit videos of children playing. Sessions were held on Saturdays to observe and talk about videos made at home and in the setting. This has helped develop practitioner

(Continued)

(Continued)

confidence: 'I feel a lot more confident communicating with parents. They don't seem as anxious when I approach them'. 'Learning together with parents has really helped. They saw I wasn't totally confident using the computer and this seems to have opened up relationships with some of the parents'.

PEAL practice example: 'Saturday sessions – sharing observations with video'

The challenges of partnership

Studies looking at parental involvement from the point of view of parents show that parents welcome confident and well-informed practitioners with valuable expertise but that they also want to be listened to, have their views and knowledge taken seriously, to be respected and to be treated as more equal partners in the upbringing of their children. (Moran et al., 2004; Quinton, 2004; Tunstill et al., 2005)

However, working together in partnership is not always easy for either parents or practitioners, and partnerships are not necessarily equal. Both may have anxieties about the relationship; for example, if practitioners see themselves as the experts on children's learning they may find it difficult to value the parents' views. Often, practitioners who feel confident in their work with children feel less confident in their work with parents, or with parents who are very different from them. On the other hand, parents may have negative memories of school, or may have questions about some aspect of the curriculum, but find it hard to find the courage to express this. For instance some parents may not share an understanding about how children learn through play and choose not to follow advice in the way they help their children at home.

Brooker (2002) found some Bangladeshi parents were particularly confused about how children were learning through play at school. Children at home spent time joining in adult activities rather than playing, and school was perceived as a place to work hard, not play.

In this situation, it can help if practitioners listen to what parents think and acknowledge what they are already doing at home to help their child learn. Practitioners can affirm how much children do learn as they work alongside parents at home, engaging in real activity. They could also explain their own practice in school more fully, demonstrating how children learn through play and how adults can enable and engage in that play. Ideas for play at home could be offered and modelled for parents, and loans of equipment made.

Wheeler and Connor (2009)

Family circumstances (lack of time, pressures of work, no crèche facilities for younger children) may make it difficult for parents to participate in programmes or events organized by the setting. Practitioners are often busy, and where children are transported long distances to attend, or where there is a rapid turnover of children, opportunities to build relationships can be limited. A lack of shared language (both literally or metaphorically) can make communication harder.

Settings may find it harder to work in partnership with some parents than with others. Discussions about so-called 'hard to reach' parents – within Thomas Coram and during the delivery of PEAL training – raised questions about who it was that was having the difficulty in 'reaching'. The reality is that many services are very hard for families to locate, understand and reach, and it is more appropriate to challenge services to reflect upon and adapt everyday practice in order to reach out and meet need.

Exciting work has taken place at Thomas Coram with both very young parents and with fathers, who are as keen to support their children as any other parent, but who may want to get involved in different ways. It's important for services to consider how to reach out, ask parents what would help, adapt and offer a range of flexible options. Working parents may ask for and welcome sessions offered at earlier or later times during the day. Some settings now offer Saturday sessions and meetings in response to parents' requests.

There are constant challenges to good partnership working, but no problems are insurmountable and, in the following section, we describe some of the ways in which Thomas Coram has tried to put partnership into action. We also include some examples of successful practice from other settings included in the PEAL material.

Thomas Coram Children's Centre

Thomas Coram Children's Centre, Camden, provides 106 nursery places for children aged 6 months to 5 years and a range of health, education and support services for their parents and other local families. The centre consists of the Early Childhood Centre – commonly known as the 'nursery' – and Coram Parents Centre, which provides support and training for parents, health and mental health services, as well as a drop-in centre, crèches and out-of-school childcare. There are also close links with the local Sure Start family support service. The activities in the Parents Centre are accessible to both the parents of children attending the nursery and to families in the wider community.

A successful partnership involves a two-way flow of information, and flexibility and responsiveness are vital. Thomas Coram wanted to create a centre that reflects their ethos that everyone is welcome, that parents can express their views and feelings, that diversity is valued and that the centre is seen as part of the wider community.

Working with parents to support children's learning

Thomas Coram and PEAL

The 'settling-in' process is crucial for the establishment of a good partnership between parents and practitioners. We know from attachment theory that if a child feels securely attached to their parent or carer, they will also have more confidence to be able to learn from new experiences. The Parents Centre at Thomas Coram gives the opportunity for parents and children to 'practise' small amounts of separation, without the stress that is sometimes felt when a child is starting nursery full-time and a parent perhaps needs to get back to work. In the drop-in, which parents and children attend together, a child may start by taking a few small steps away from his or her parent or, sitting on their lap, simply start to show an interest in an activity in which other children are involved. Later, parents may attend groups or classes, while the children stay in the crèche for an hour or two. In the nursery, some children will already have visited from the Parents Centre drop-in before they are offered a place, but staff's first contact with others is during weekly visitors' mornings, when prospective families come to look at the centre.

Once children are offered a nursery place, the family is invited to join an induction programme, which consists of visits to the centre, home visits by the key worker, and a settling in period. During this time, staff and parents start to get to know each other.

Part of this process is a detailed parent conference during which parents are asked to talk about their child in a semi-structured interview. The information from this covers all areas of the child's development and learning, and provides the foundation for the nursery's planning for the individual child. At the same time, parents and children are starting to make a relationship with the key worker – if they feel that they like and trust them (which often comes from feeling that the key worker has a genuine and open interest in the child), this is a sound basis for good communication in the future.

Arrival and collection times are crucial for communication between parents and practitioners, though in a nursery as large and busy as Thomas Coram, they can also be quite pressured. Sessions are organized to ensure that staff, especially key workers, are free at these important times of day to welcome families and exchange information. As well as daily informal contacts, there are regular times for parent and key worker to meet and review the progress of individual children. As part of this review, parents and key workers jointly decide the next priorities for learning and discuss how they can work together to support the child. Key workers in each base room also hold regular meetings with parents to discuss what is going on in the room and possible new developments.

Konstam Children's Centre, Camden always ensures that a member of staff is on the door to meet and welcome parents and children on entry. It is established that part of this role is to exchange messages between parents and key workers. The management team also has an 'open door' policy and parents are made welcome if they need to talk.

The Pen Green Centre for Under Fives, Northamptonshire, has a staggered entry. Families are able to arrive at the centre at any time between 8.15 and 9.45 a.m. This means there is a steadier flow of families into the nursery so there is more time to converse and exchange information and learning observations with individual parents.

> **At Gamesley Early Excellence Centre, Derbyshire**, children receive two home visits and parents take part in at least three consultation meetings that last up to an hour, with the time negotiated to suit work and childcare commitments.
>
> PEAL practice example: 'Time to talk'

Thomas Coram makes full use of video footage to share children's nursery experiences with parents; parents love to come in and talk about their children's lives in more detail. While key workers have been privileged to learn a little more about the child's family life from the home visit – perhaps seeing a child they have thought of as quiet showing confident fluency in their home language – parents watching a video of the child's day in nursery will often be struck by the ways in which their children are different in the setting – passing food around at lunchtime, for instance, might be something they have never done at home. In this way the child's two worlds are brought together, with the adults in each having a greater understanding of the child's experiences in the other.

> **At Thomas Coram** children all have 'easy to access' portfolios. These large display books include drawings, paintings, early writing, photographs, and written narratives of children's play and talk. In this way, a child's progress is made very clear and can be celebrated by child, parent and practitioner alike. The portfolios are kept out in the main nursery area, easily accessible, so that parents and children can look through them at any time. They can be taken home to share with the family, and parents can contribute their own observations.
>
> PEAL practice example: 'Sharing parents'

Attempts from the Parents Centre at Thomas Coram to engage some of the most traditionally excluded parents (for example, teenage parents and Bangladeshi fathers) have shown that a focus on the importance of what parents do to contribute to a child's success in learning can be a 'way in'.

The Born to Learn programme worked with parents of 1- to 3-year-olds and provided a series of home visits and group sessions for parents who had never attended the centre before to discuss aspects of children's learning and development. On home visits, family support workers shared observations of the children with parents and left ideas for simple play activities to continue with their children at home after a visit. Bangladeshi fathers proved to be particularly interested in information about brain development and the idea that what they did could make a significant difference to how their children learned.

At the end of the home visiting programme, families reported reading and playing more with their children. The family support workers remarked on how many parents had gained in confidence and were more prepared to try new things. Talking with parents about their children's development proved to be an effective way to open conversations and develop relationships. It also led to families being encouraged into group settings in the Parents Centre – sometimes accompanied by their family support worker at first to help them feel more confident – and they were then able to access other services.

Parents, whose interest is first caught by the question of how their children learn, have sometimes gone on to train as early years practitioners themselves. At Thomas Coram, parents have been able to enrol in the Parents Centre for an 'Introduction to Childcare' course and may then go on to undertake the accredited 'Level 2 Certificate in Childcare', which is offered in partnership with the local college. Some have even gone on to complete graduate and postgraduate training in early years.

For Thomas Coram, this also brings the opportunity to employ practitioners from among parents in the local community, with all the benefits that brings. Other parents have trained as community interpreters or outreach workers, again building on the skills and knowledge of their communities.

Support for parents

At Thomas Coram, all the work rests on an acknowledgement of the importance of parents and carers in their children's lives, and of the rewards – as well as the challenges and difficulties – involved in the parenting task. While the centre is accessible and open to all families from the local community, there are additional services available for parents who are struggling with particular difficulties or who may need additional help. These include parenting groups and access to a family psychology and psychotherapy service, which has proved both popular and helpful. It seems that because the service, though specialized, is based in a community setting, parents find it much easier and less threatening to use.

There are very wide variations in beliefs (held by both practitioners and parents) about what is 'good for children'. Thomas Coram is situated in a culturally very diverse neighbourhood, and families attending the centre speak 48 different languages. Working in effective partnership with parents from different ethnic backgrounds requires both knowledge of and respect for these differences, and a commitment to provide a service of equal quality to all their children. Parents who were not themselves educated in the UK may be unfamiliar with the British education system and possibly are less confident that it will serve their children well.

At a series of 'International Parenting' workshops, groups of parents made presentations about their home cultures, particularly in relation to pregnancy, childbirth and child-rearing. Childcare practitioners who attended these workshops found them particularly valuable and the material was published in a booklet entitled 'Sharing our Stories'.

Research in the UK has shown that black and ethnic minority parents are less likely to attend family centres or 'parenting skills' classes than white parents, even though they have similar needs for support (Butt and Box, 1998). The Parents Centre looked for particular models of parenting support that would meet the needs of all parents and have for some years been running a programme called Strengthening Families: Strengthening Communities (Steele, 2000). This has many things in common with better known models, but two of its features are unique. One is that it emphasizes the strengths in a family's cultural history and looks at ways in which parents can pass these on to their children (rather than focusing on problems). The other is that it includes discussion of a 'spiritual' component in parenting, which can mean a variety of things, from formal religious teaching to creating a moral framework for children's lives. This has been eagerly welcomed by parents, who have taken from it not only new ideas about children's learning and behaviour, but also a determination to make the local neighbourhood a safer and happier place for their children to grow up in.

Like the wider group of families, the Teenage Parent Project includes young parents from many different backgrounds, including some who are refugees from war-torn countries, as well as those who grew up in the UK. There are as many individual stories as there are individual young parents, including 16-year-old married couples, young care-leavers, and teenagers who arrived in this country pregnant having experienced severe trauma. The project has an educational focus and the young parents are given an opportunity to study, while keeping their children close by them (some in the same room, some in crèches and some given nursery places, according to their parents' wishes). Their successes have challenged the stereotype of feckless teen parents; their motivation to take part in various photographic and film projects about the lives of young parents have stemmed from their desire to put the record straight and to demonstrate their serious commitment to their children.

We have learned that it is important to provide specific services targeted at the particular needs of certain groups (such as young parents); after a while, though, they may welcome the opportunity to take part in more general activities. The same is true of fathers, whose particular needs and interests often get forgotten, even while we are talking about work with 'parents'. Designated Fathers Workers may be helpful and can provide services of special interest to men, but they will also advise on making the service overall more father-friendly.

What gets fathers[2] involved?

- Positive attitudes, welcoming fathers personally.
- Targeting publicity directly at fathers and sending personal invitations by post.
- Children giving personal invitations to fathers.
- Consulting fathers – what would they like to do?
- Emphasizing how a father's involvement will help a child's education.
- Inviting non-resident fathers to events and sending regular information to them.

- Short-term projects with fathers and children – such as ICT, outings, videos, sport.
- Asking fathers to help in practical ways that make use of their skills.
- Flexible timings that suit all work patterns.
- Holding specific fathers' groups or events.
- Ensuring displays and materials reflect images of fathers and young children (Goldman, 2005; Pre-school Learning Alliance, 2005).

Further training (for parents and practitioners)

The centre at Thomas Coram offers a number of ways in which parents can access further training. There is a well-resourced information technology room, in which a range of courses are offered as well as individual access to computers, and classes are also available in basic numeracy and literacy, first aid, English for speakers of other languages (ESOL) and return to work. Ongoing support and encouragement from staff are important as a return to study can be daunting, but, when parents are ready, there are also accredited professional training courses in childcare, interpreting and outreach. Teenage parents, whose studies may have been interrupted by the birth of their babies, are able to continue to study, while keeping their children close to hand, and are given support with their other concerns.

Parental involvement in the management of the centre

Parents may also wish to become involved in the management of early years centres. At Thomas Coram, the development of the local Sure Start programme has particularly supported parents to gain the skills and confidence necessary to contribute to the planning and delivery of services. There are five parents on the governing body, one of whom is the chair, and parents are represented on each of the subcommittees, chairing two of them. The parents' forum, which is organized and chaired by the parent governors, offers an opportunity for other parents to have their say and they also organize surveys of parents' views on key issues.

Conclusion

We have seen from both the work at Thomas Coram and other centres cited in the PEAL practice examples, how crucial it is to have a close working relationship with parents. The opportunity to be involved, especially in their own child's learning and in the management and development of the centre, must be open to all parents, and not only they, but also their children and early years practitioners, will benefit from this partnership.

Points for discussion

- Does your setting have a policy on partnership with parents? Who has been involved in devising and developing it?
- Are parents involved in all aspects of your setting?
- Do parents make and share observations on their own children's learning and development regularly?

 Further reading

Desforges, C. and Abouchaar, A. (2003) *The Impact of Parental Involvement, Parental Support and Family Education on Pupil Achievements and Adjustment: A Literature Review*. London: DfES. A thorough overview of a wide range of research showing that 'at-home good parenting' has a significant positive effect on children's achievement.

Family and Parenting Institute (2007) *Listening to Parents: A Short Guide*. London: FPI. Offers clear guidance into what works when listening to parents, with some practical ideas about how to listen to parents effectively.

Sylva, K., Melhuish, E., Sammons, P., Siraj-Blatchford, I. and Taggart, B. (2004) *The Effective Provision of Pre-School Education (EPPE) Project: Final Report*. London: DfES and Institute of Education. An important study of the impact of early learning environments on subsequent outcomes for 3,000 UK children. The children were followed from home – through a range of different pre-school experiences – and then observed in their first few years at school.

Whalley, M. and the Pen Green Team (2008) *Involving Parents in their Children's Learning*. 2nd edn. London: Paul Chapman Publishing . The story of the work of the Pen Green Centre for children and families, including detailed case studies which demonstrate how working collaboratively with parents impacts on their involvement in learning.

Wheeler, H. and Connor, J. (2009) *Parents, Early Years and Learning. Parents as Partners in the Early Years Foundation Stage: Principles into Practice*. London: NCB. A really helpful overview of the theory underpinning partnership working with parents, coupled with many vivid practice examples, some of which have been cited in this chapter.

Notes

1   PEAL was commissioned by the Department for Education and Skills (DfES) and developed by the Early Childhood Unit of the National Children's Bureau (NCB) in partnership with Coram and the London Borough of Camden. The training supports practitioners to work in partnership with parents to enhance children's early learning and development. PEAL training is available from the National Children's Bureau: ncb.org.uk
2   'Fathers' denotes all those acting as a father figure.

References

Brooker, L. (2002) *Starting School: Young Children's Learning Cultures*. Buckingham: Open University Press.

Butt, J. and Box, L. (1998) *Family Centred – a Study of the Use of Family Centres by Black Families*. London: Race Equality Unit.

Department for Children, Schools and Families (DCSF) (2007) *The Children's Plan: Building Brighter Futures*. London: DCSF.

Department for Education and Skills (DfES) (2004) *Every Child Matters: Change for Children*. Nottingham: DfES.

Department for Education and Skills (DfES) (2006) *Sure Start Children's Centres: Practice Guidance*. London: DfES.

Department for Education and Skills (DfES) (2007) *The Early Years Foundation Stage: Setting the Standards for Learning, Development and Care for Children from Birth to Five*. London: DfES. (Revised 2008.)

Desforges, C. and Abouchaar, A. (2003) *The Impact of Parental Involvement, Parental Support and Family Education on Pupil Achievements and Adjustment: A Literature Review*. Research Report 433. London: DfES.

Draper, L. and Khan, T. (2004) 'Parents' views of children's transitions from home to nursery'. Unpublished evaluation report.

Goldman, R. (2005) *Fathers' Involvement in Their Children's Education*. London: NFPI.

Moran, P., Ghate, D. and van der Merwe, A. (2004) *What Works in Parenting Support? A Review of the International Evidence*. Research Report 574. London: DfES.

PEAL (Parents and Early Learning) – see www.peal.org.uk

Pen Green Centre for Under Fives and Families (2004) 'All about ... working with parents', *Nursery World*, 3 June, Supplement: 15–22.

Pre-school Learning Alliance (2005) *Fathers Matter*. Leaflet. London: PSLA.

Quinton, D. (2004) *Supporting Parents: Messages from Research*. London: Jessica Kingsley.

Sammons, P., Sylva, K., Melhuish, E., Siraj-Blatchford, I., Taggart, B., Grabbe, Y. and Barreau, S. (2007) *Influences on Children's Attainment and Progress in Key Stage 2: Cognitive Outcomes in Year 5. Effective Pre-school and Primary Education 3–11 (EPPE 3–11)*. London: University of London, Institute of Education, DfES.

Siraj-Blatchford, I. and Manni, L. (2007) *Effective Leadership in the Early Years Sector: The ELEYS Study*. London: University of London, Institute of Education.

Siraj-Blatchford, I., Sylva, K., Taggart, B., Sammons, P., Melhuish, E. and Elliot, K. (2003) *Intensive Case Studies of Practice Across the Foundation Stage*. Technical Paper 10. London: University of London, Institute of Education, DfES.

Steele, M. (2000) *Strengthening Families: Strengthening Communities: An Inclusive Parent Programme*. London: Racial Equality Unit.

Sylva, K., Melhuish, E., Sammons, P., Siraj-Blatchford, I. and Taggart, B. (2004) *The Effective Provision of Pre-School Education (EPPE) Project: Final Report*. London: DfES and Institute of Education, University of London.

Tunstill, J., Meadows, P., Akhurst, S., Allnock, D., Chrysanthou, J., Garbers, C. and Morley, A. (2005) *Implementing Sure Start Local Programmes: An Integrated Overview of the First Four Years*. NESS Summary SF010. London: DfES.

Wheeler, H. and Connor, J. (2009) *Parents, Early Years and Learning. Parents as Partners in the Early Years Foundation Stage: Principles into Practice*. London: National Children's Bureau.

PART 3

WORKFORCE

CHAPTER 14

TRAINING AND WORKFORCE ISSUES IN THE EARLY YEARS

Sue Owen and Gill Haynes

Chapter Contents

- The current context
- Reforms under Every Child Matters
- New professionals and leaders
- Conclusion: a better future?

> Early years services for young children are critical to delivering both economic prosperity and social justice for Britain. However, average pay is £6.80 an hour, only 7 per cent of the workforce has a post secondary qualification and 98 per cent are women. (Cooke and Lawton, 2008: 6)

The early years world has now experienced over 10 years of an unprecedented political interest in the provision of care and education for young children. There have been many initiatives to improve the planning of services, the number of places available for children and the quality of those places. In terms of training, the creation of a National Qualifications Framework was central to change: raising the standard of training, making qualifications clearer and making it easier for workers to progress. All these elements need to be present if early years work is to become a career which is recognized, valued by the public and attractive to high-quality applicants.

Many of the issues which are now driving change in training, qualifications and workforce organization have been covered in other chapters of this book. They include a growing understanding, through research, of the needs of young children and their families, the continuing low status of the work and pay differentials within the sector, low levels of qualifications, high rates of turnover, the persistence of low standards in some provision, and the need to work to the government's Every Child Matters agenda, with a particular focus on its vision of an integrated children's workforce. These all present challenges that need to be addressed as part of the government's ambitious strategy to increase both the amount and quality of provision and improve outcomes for children.

In this chapter we will chart some of the developments which have led to the current situation, describe the main initiatives which are being proposed and consider how they might affect early years practice as a career.

The current context

As can be seen from Table 14.1, despite the huge changes in early years policy and the big expansion of places since 1997, some characteristics of the workforce have hardly changed at all. It is still a workforce which is overwhelmingly female and low paid, and the levels of qualifications vary considerably across the sector, with those in maintained settings registering higher levels of qualifications and pay. This underlines the fact that the early years sector is still highly divided between the maintained and the private, voluntary and independent sector. Approximately one-third of places for under 5s are in schools and the *average* pay rates shown in Table 14.1 for provision in maintained schools mask the much higher hourly rate that early years teachers command, that is, £19.60 an hour (DCSF, 2008a: 87). The qualifications structure for early years remained complex pending the full introduction of a new Qualifications and Credit Framework (to replace the National Qualifications Framework) in 2008 and the phased implementation of qualifications requirements for the *Early Years Foundation Stage*. The *Sector Learning Strategy* (Skills for Business and CWDC, 2008) identified the need to rationalize and clarify qualifications as a continuing priority, to be addressed through the new Integrated Qualifications Framework, which we will describe later in the chapter. This will be an important step towards professionalizing the workforce, as 'unclear and uncertain progression paths' (Cooke and Lawton, 2008: 6) are recognized as a key factor, which – when combined with low pay – can lead to practitioners leaving the early years world for a more coherent package elsewhere.

Some of the more long-standing initiatives in the sector have undergone changes over the past 10 years. National Vocational Qualifications (NVQs), for instance were brought in for all industries in 1992 as a radically different approach to qualifications, based on the existing competence of the candidate

Table 14.1   Characteristics of the early years and childcare workforce, 2007

Group	Women (%)	Under 25 (%)	NVQ level 3 (or above) (%)	NVQ level 6 (%)	Hourly pay (all staff)(£)	Hourly pay(non-supervi sory)(£)
Full day care/early years workers	98	31	61	3	6.90	5.90
Full day care/early years workers in children's centres	98	25	61	7	9.30	7.10
Sessional (playgroup) early years workers	99	5	52	3	7.00	6.10
Registered childminders (self-employed)	99	1	36	2	3.60 per child hour	
Early years provision in maintained schools	98	5	44	24	13.00	8.70 (Nursery nurses 10.40)

Source: Adapted from DCSF, 2008a

and his or her ability to demonstrate that competence in real-life situations, rather than on a course of training leading to an examination. They are based on sets of National Occupational Standards (NOS) to ensure that all workers cover the same range and standard of knowledge and practice, and these are reviewed regularly to keep pace with changes in the sector. National Vocational Qualifications are particularly well suited to workers with experience but no formal qualifications, and so they found a ready market among childcare workers, especially childminders and those in the voluntary sector, many of whom had entered the profession when their own children were young and might have done extensive training which was not related to formal qualifications.

However, NVQs have been criticized for low standards as funding constraints have forced some training providers and assessment centres to cut corners and move candidates through the qualifications too fast to ensure high-quality practice. These problems have surfaced even more frequently in the past few years as there have been cutbacks in further education funding and serious problems in recruiting and retaining tutors and assessors. The *Sector Learning Strategy* (Skills for Business and CWDC, 2008) identified 'improving the quality of learning' as one of the specific areas for change.

In addition, although NVQs seem so ideal for the early years workforce, the funding arrangements developed nationally have discriminated against the kind of candidates who need the qualifications most. For instance, targets set for the Learning and Skills Council (LSC), which has controlled vocational qualification funding since 2000, concentrated on young people obtaining basic skill and job qualifications at level 2 and some local authorities have found it very difficult to negotiate funding for the older, level 3, students who were needed within the expanding early years sector. In recognition of these and other issues the government introduced a new Transformation Fund as part of its response to the Children's Workforce Strategy consultation (DfES, 2006), which set out plans to raise the qualification levels of the early years workforce. This £250 million injection of cash was warmly welcomed by the sector but overall take-up was low and it was considered too bureaucratic to administer effectively, so in April 2008 it was replaced by a more flexible Graduate Leader Fund of £305 million. During the same period, the LSC introduced financial support for level 2 qualifications through a new scheme called Train to Gain, which provided funding for some parts of the sector with historically low levels of qualifications.

The level 4 NVQ, which was developed in 2000, has also suffered from set-backs and it has had little impact on the sector. This is mainly because of the creation, in 2001, of foundation degrees. These were designed to provide an accessible route into higher education for non-traditional students who, on completion, could apply to move into the later stages of a related honours degree. A sector-endorsed foundation degree was developed for early years practitioners which could be studied part-time, while people continued to work, and it has been extremely popular. The direct and clear link into the traditional higher educational sector and then, for those who want it, into teaching makes it far more attractive than an NVQ level 4 which requires the same depth and range of study but without such an obvious payback for the effort. However, new level 4 qualifications, like the Higher Professional Diploma in Early Years, are being developed to offer a bridge to foundation degrees for experienced practitioners at level 3 – since progression from level 3 to level 6 is a key aspiration for the government's early years strategy.

Another major development in the field of higher education came with changes to early childhood studies degrees. These degrees were initiated in the 1980s in an attempt to provide an integrated course of study and qualification for the early years sector which was then campaigning for higher levels of qualifications and the recognition that the traditional split between childcare and early education was counterproductive for young children. Most follow the pattern of other degrees in being three-year courses of study but many offer practice placements or allow part-time study for workplace-based students, and all are interdisciplinary, attempting to create a body of knowledge which integrates childcare and education at degree level, something which should be popular with government now that integration is so high on the agenda. However, there was criticism that they could produce graduates with no practical experience and competence, and so a nationally recognized 'practice option' has now been developed which can be inserted into the degree and taken by students with no current experience of an early years setting.

Training and qualifications for childminders has been one notable area of improvement over recent years. In the 2002–03 Childcare and Early Years Workforce Survey (quoted in DfES, 2005a) only 16 per cent of childminders had a level 3 qualification, the lowest rate of qualification in the childcare workforce. In the 2007 Childcare and Early Years Providers Survey (DCSF, 2008a), this had more than doubled to 36 per cent; and four out of five childminders reported that they had attended a preparatory training course when they first registered as a childminder, maintaining the levels reported since 2005. Nearly seven in 10 childminders had undertaken some training in the last 12 months and on average childminders had received seven days of training in the last 12 months.

These improvements owe much to the dedication of childminders themselves, which has been supported by the National Childminding Association's (NCMA's) commitment to quality and accredited training, together with the opportunities and funding offered by many local authorities. This improvement is even more impressive in light of the continuing shortcomings in the regulation for home-based childcare, which means that, despite many years of lobbying, childminders are still not required to achieve an early years qualification as a condition of registration.

The development of NCMA approved childminding networks, which was supported by government as part of the national childcare strategy, attempted to redress this situation, with a requirement to work towards level 3 qualifications as a condition of membership of the NCMA networks. In one study (Owen, 2005) over 70 per cent of networked childminders either already had a level 3 or equivalent qualification, or were working towards one. The ability to access training and qualifications was the most frequently mentioned positive aspect of networks, and childminders highlighted the following factors which had impacted on their ability to take this training:

- funding – making the training free or cheap
- accessibility – in terms of the days and hours on which it was offered
- appropriateness – having it run by people who understood the specifics of childminding practice
- planning – customizing training packages for individual needs
- peer support – providing training through a network means that childminders can take it as part of a supportive group within a culture of learning and change.

In view of the success of this approach, it is disappointing to note that less than half[1] of local authorities have taken the opportunity to raise standards and support childminding networks as a high-quality choice for parents of the free nursery education entitlement for 3- and 4-year-olds. This is despite the fact that hosting a childminding network is part of the core offer for children's centres in the 30 per cent most disadvantaged areas.

Reforms under Every Child Matters

The government created the Every Child Matters agenda in 2003 (DfES, 2004a) as a new approach which would integrate all work done with children and families on a continuum from universal services for all children to targeted work with the most vulnerable.

As part of this the Treasury took the lead in the introduction of a 10-year childcare strategy (HMT, DfES, DWP and DTI, 2004), underpinned by new legislation and, most importantly for this discussion, a workforce strategy to address the problems of the children's workforce as a whole. This included commitments that, in the long term, all managers of full day care settings will be graduates, bringing business and management skills as well as professional competence,[2] and that there will be support for more early years workers, including childminders, to gain level 3 qualifications.

> The single biggest fact that determines the quality of childcare is the workforce. The current childcare workforce includes many capable and dedicated people. However qualification … levels are generally low … if the system is to develop into one that is among the best quality in the world, a step-change is needed in the quality and stability of the workforce. Working with pre-school children should have as much status as a profession as teaching children in schools. (HMT, DfES, DWP and DTI, 2004: 44–5)

This was a period in which the government attempted to rationalize the situation rather than simply add extra layers of reforms. In essence, the 10-year childcare strategy was designed to rationalize, redesign and re-badge existing early years initiatives so that they fitted within the Every Child Matters framework to create a coherent strategy for improving the quality of services. There were seen to be three components to this quality initiative: a better qualified workforce, a single quality framework from birth to 5 (the Early Years Foundation Stage Framework) and a new registration and inspection framework under Ofsted.

This type of rationalization is consistent with the approach of the Every Child Matters agenda. *Every Child Matters: Next Steps* (DfES, 2004b) announced a consultation document on a pay and workforce strategy which would begin to rationalize the situation for the children's workforce as a whole. The document did, however, place a great deal of emphasis on the early years workforce as being key to the Every Child Matters reforms and as being particularly in need of change. A federated sector Skills Council for Social Care, Children and Young People (SSC) was announced, to cover the whole of the UK and all staff working in social care and with children. A Children, Young People and Families Workforce Development Council (CWDC) would represent England on both this UK SSC and on a UK Children's Workforce Network, which would bring together the SSCs for other related sectors such as playwork, health and the school-based workforce. The CWDC has a strong representation from the early years sector, which comprises over half its workforce footprint (see Figure 14.1).

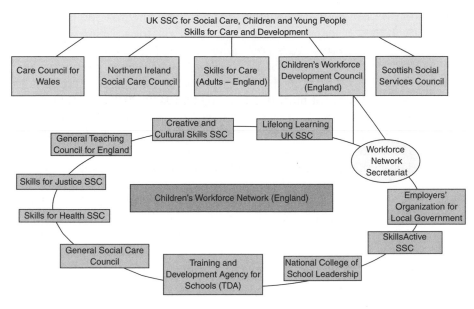

Figure 14.1   Sector Skills Council arrangement, February 2009

This appears to be a complicated structure, but it is designed to deal with a complicated situation. There are numerous agencies representing different workforce and employer interests in different ways in different countries of the UK, and in the short term a structure was needed which would allow all these interests to meet together on a basis of equality and to move, in the long term, towards a more rational and planned approach to the new integrated children's workforce. At the time of writing there are a number of reviews of workforce footprints and organizational remits taking place which arise from the 2020 Workforce Strategy and which could have an impact on the structure. In addition, a new national Partnership for Children and Youth Workforce is being established during 2009.

The consultation on the workforce strategy took place over the spring and summer of 2005 and included a number of face-to-face consultation events with the early years sector as well as written responses. Before the consultation document was published the word 'pay' was quietly dropped from the title of the strategy and Jane Haywood, the chief executive of the CWDC, stressed that improvements in this would have to evolve over time. This has also been the message from government ministers who have stressed the fact that the majority of the workforce is in the voluntary and independent sector and that it is not appropriate or feasible for government to interfere in their pay and conditions. They argue that improved qualifications will, in time, lead to higher status and remuneration.

The government's response to the national consultation emphasized the need for further reform and support for the early years workforce. In particular, the response identified the benefits of developing the role of Early Years Professional (EYP), a status rather than a qualification, for a person who would lead practice in the *Early Years Foundation Stage*. It confirmed the government's aim to have EYPs in each of the planned 3,500 children's centres by 2010 and in every full day care setting by 2015, with two EYPs in full day care settings located in the 30 per cent most disadvantaged areas by 2015. The CWDC was charged with developing professional standards for EYPs with graduate status equivalent to Qualified Teacher Status (QTS); and there are now four different pathways (and two pilot pathways) that aspiring EYPs can follow, depending on their background, experience and ability to commit time to complete the programme and assessment. At the time of writing, 2,500 people have gained the new EYP status and a further 2,400 are on one of the training paths; EYP support networks are being funded and a national campaign is under way to attract the candidates needed to meet the government's targets of 20,000 EYPs by 2015. However, issues of pay and conditions remain unresolved and EYP graduate status is not recognized by the maintained sector as a QTS equivalent. The CWDC's position remains that a new cadre of people will in time 'come together and fight for pay, terms and conditions' in the same way that 'other professions are born' (*Nursery World*, 2008). This view is not widely shared by practitioners and there is serious concern in some quarters that EYP status 'does not become a poor relation' in comparison to that of an early years teacher, leading to a call for a 'national evaluation of the EYP role' to set a benchmark for pay and conditions for EYPs which is 'broadly commensurate' with that of early years teachers.

Since 2005, other government reports, including the update to the *Children's Workforce Strategy* (DfES, 2007), *The Children's Plan* (DCSF, 2007) and *Building Brighter Futures: the next steps* (DCSF, 2008b) set out the direction of children's services reform for the future. The clear aspiration to have a graduate leading practice in every full day care setting, with two graduates in settings in disadvantaged areas, was reinforced in December 2008 through the publication of a report by an expert working group setting out the vision for the whole of the children's workforce (DCSF, 2008c). This was followed up by a more detailed report in 2009 specifically focusing on the childcare and early years workforce, when it is expected that the government will confirm that they will convert 'aspiration' into a requirement and regulate to ensure that all full day care settings will be graduate led by 2015. The government's other main aspiration – that of raising qualification levels to a minimum of level 3, and to provide opportunities for all parts of the early years workforce to achieve this standard – is not so clearly referenced; however, the sector has been invited to contribute their views through a new consultation on these plans.

The new Children and Young People's Workforce Strategy identifies a number of priorities for future work, including that of ensuring that qualifications, training and progression routes are accessible, of high quality, and help people in the workforce to develop their skills and their careers.

The key to achieving all this change will be the successful implementation of the Integrated Qualifications Framework (IQF), due to be operational in 2010. The IQF will be a comprehensive set of approved qualifications that helps people progress and move across the children and young people's workforce.[2] It is being developed by the Children's Workforce Network with the support of all the sector bodies and groups that work with children (see Figure 14.1), and will be relevant for people right across the children and young people's workforce, up to and including degrees and postgraduate qualifications. It will also provide employers with a way of knowing the scale and scope of qualifications so they can be clear about what they really need for a particular role; and it will offer practitioners the clear progression pathways that have for so long been missing from the sector.

The driving force behind these changes is the government's commitment to integrated working, which is leading to changes in working practice, with new roles such as lead professionals and managers of integrated settings being developed. In an effort to underpin the concept of integrated working, in 2005 the government and the CWDC published what is known as the *Common Core of Skills and Knowledge* (DfES, 2005b),[3] which described the six areas of expertise that they believed people working with children and young people must demonstrate in order to be considered competent, that is:

- effective communication and engagement
- child and young person development
- safeguarding and promoting the welfare of the child
- supporting transitions
- multi-agency working
- sharing information.

However, the expert group advising the 2020 Workforce Strategy report raised concerns about the extent to which the *Common Core* really did address issues like integrated working, working in partnership with parents and support for vulnerable children and young people. They also felt that it was not well-embedded in some parts of the workforce, such as health or the police, and as a result of their concerns, the government announced a new consultation led by CWDC to review and refresh the *Common Core*, due by September 2009.

New professionals and leaders

Finally, among these reforms is the important issue of leadership within this new workforce (see also Chapter 15). The 10-year childcare strategy committed to graduate-level leadership for all full day care settings as a first step in a better qualified workforce, and it is undoubtedly true that the leadership of multi-agency teams, together with an understanding of how young children's learning can be supported through all the activities of a childcare setting, is a skilled and demanding job. In 2004 a new National Professional Qualification in Integrated Centre Leadership (NPQICL) was piloted by the National College for School Leadership in partnership with the Pen Green Research, Training and Development Centre. Forty students graduated from this course in October 2005 and it was then opened up for delivery by other universities and colleges around the country. This offered the potential to create a cadre of highly and specifically qualified leaders, drawn from education, social care, early years and health backgrounds, to take forward the vision of the new integrated children's workforce. However, there will need to be effective links between this and the National Professional Qualification for Headship if the early years strand of this workforce is to flourish on a basis of equality with other specialisms.

The most obvious indication that there is a problem with the vision for an integrated and highly qualified workforce is the fact that no steps have been taken to resolve the situation of teachers within the early years sector. The UK has a well established and effective tradition of early education, based on nursery schools and classes, which is linked into the rest of the education system and is staffed by qualified teachers with the same pay, conditions and status as all other teachers. The EPPE study, on which so much of recent government policy has built, indicated that qualified teachers made a positive difference to the learning outcomes of young children when they were employed to work directly with them and to lead the pedagogical practice of others. Despite this the role of teachers in the sector now seems confused as new roles and qualifications are created around them rather than being built on their expertise. It is true that current initial teacher training leaves much to be desired in terms of its fitness for an integrated profession working with children from birth to 6, but this period of reform would have offered a perfect opportunity to review the training of all staff working with young children and build the knowledge and expertise expected of teachers into a system which could be accessed through vocational as well as graduate routes. In response to a question from the *Times Educational Supplement* in July 2008, the Secretary of State for Education, Ed Balls, indicated that he agreed with the aspiration to employ qualified teachers in all early years settings: 'Parents want the same investment in teaching and learning in the early years as they do in primary and secondary years' (Ward and Stewart, 2008: 7). However, capacity and resource constraints meant that he would not say when this would be a reality. This leads to a real concern that local authorities and independent sector managers will be able to use the current lack of clarity over staffing expectations in order to employ the cheapest options and that this will result in teachers gradually disappearing from the early years sector while EYPs and integrated centre leaders would continue to suffer from poor pay, conditions and professional development opportunities. Indeed a significant number of those achieving EYP status are already qualified teachers who have been able to fast-track through the requirements and have been concerned that they should obtain the status in order to ensure their future careers in the early years sector.

Only with raised status, pay and esteem will we be able to recruit and retain workers who can provide the highest standards for young children and their families and, while raised status and esteem are important to early years practitioners, pay and conditions remain the key factor in achieving a transformed early years workforce, which is still predominantly located within the private, voluntary and independent sector. There is no evidence that the government is prepared to intervene in the market to tackle this issue head on, even though as a Day Care Trust report in 2005 pointed out, 'no other country has achieved a well-qualified early years workforce without adopting a tax-based supply subsidy' (Cameron, 2005: 17). Indeed, there is an inherent contradiction in a policy approach which extols the value and necessity of highly skilled practitioners as a prime factor in delivering better outcomes for children while eschewing any action to address low pay. As Cooke and Lawton point out: 'Market failures and gendered conceptions of care work mean that the material reward given to the early years workforce undervalues its economic and social importance' (2008: 6).

However, rather than challenging that framework and acknowledging the economic and social importance of early years work through the policy levers at its disposal, for example, regulation, the government appears to prefer a laissez-faire model which relies on the commitment and enthusiasm of a wholly gendered workforce, while it seeks to find yet more reasons why men are so poorly represented in the statistics.

Low minimum qualification requirements and the absence of a clear progression route will, Cooke and Lawton argue, continue to hold down wages and quality. As described earlier in the chapter, progression routes are being tackled through the introduction of the IQF. However, qualification requirements are still set at too low a level to achieve real change and drive up quality over the long term. Cooke and Lawton's policy proposals to increase baseline targets to a minimum of level 3 through regulation; and to introduce requirements for senior practitioners (level 5) as well as EYPs (level 6) by 2015 would, in their view, 'establish a pathway to expert practitioner status … and put upward pressure on wages' (2003: 8). Cooke and Lawton agree with the recommendations in *Raising the Bar* (Daycare Trust and TUC, 2008) that another important step would be to make the EYP 'graduate' status a reality in terms of pay and conditions, so that there was parity between EYP and QTS, with the effect that EYPs could lead practice in the maintained as well as the private, voluntary and independent sectors. We would argue that this needs to go alongside a fundamental review of the relationship between QTS and EYP in terms of pedagogical practice in order to embed what research tells us makes the most difference to young children's outcomes

Recent reports agree that what is really needed is a 'social partnership' function to establish wage 'floors' which match higher quality with higher pay for early years workers, supported by stronger structures for conveying the voice of practitioners – and, on the face of it, the 2020 Workforce Strategy appears to bow to this request through the establishment of a new National Children and Young

People's Workforce Partnership. However, its remit is to 'support the delivery of the priorities set out in this strategy', with no reference to the issue of pay and conditions (DCSF, 2008c: 20). This is in stark contrast to the new body which was set up in October 2008 to review the pay and conditions of support staff in schools, the Schools Support Staff Negotiating Body (SSNB).

While it must be acknowledged there has been significant progress in training and workforce development in the early years since 1997, including welcome investment in the pay and conditions for the leadership level of the workforce, more radical action and investment will be needed to ensure that in 10 years' time it will not still be the case that early years practitioners, especially those in the private, voluntary and independent sectors, could be earning more in the local supermarket than in their local early years setting. As the authors of *Raising the Bar* contend, the introduction of the *Early Years Foundation Stage* in September 2008, and the requirement that all formal providers must now work to that framework, removes once and for all any historical justification of disparities in pay and conditions in the sector, and paves the way for a more secure and equitable future for all (Daycare Trust and TUC, 2008).

Conclusion: a better future?

Apart from the lack of action on pay and conditions, the new initiatives outlined above promise a better future for the early years workforce and, consequently, a better future for children. Because early years work relies on the development of strong and respectful relationships, this is a profession in which the quality of the outcomes can be directly tied to the quality of the people working within them. The importance of relationships also means that only so much can be effected through changes in structures, it is also vital that we decide what we want for young children in any setting and in any community. It is then possible to support practitioners to reflect on their work and develop relationships based on deep knowledge of the children and families they work with. Getting better at your job should be a way of life, not just the result of a training course.

 Points for discussion

- Should early years continue to be a specialism in its own right within an integrated children's workforce and, if so, how would this work?

- Suggest some mechanisms by which improved pay and conditions could be linked to the qualifications structure for early years practitioners.

- During consultation on the Sector Learning Strategy, respondents strongly endorsed increases in regulation and/or registration for the workforce. Do you think this would help to professionalize early years?

Further reading

Cooke, G. and Lawton, K. (2008) *For Love or Money: Pay, Progression and Professionalisation in the 'Early Years' Workforce*. London: IPPR.

Daycare Trust and TUC (2008) *Raising the Bar: What Next for the Early Childhood Education and Care Workforce?* London: Daycare Trust. It is interesting to see how many of the recommendations in these two reports have been reflected in the update to the 10-year childcare strategy, *Next Steps for Early Learning and Childcare* (published by the government in 2009).

Department for Children, Schools and Families (2008) *Childcare and Early Years Providers Survey 2007*. DCSF-RR047. London: DCSF. Useful to look at the full report as well as the Research Brief (RB), to see what information does *not* get summarized into the more widely accessed RB, for example, average hourly rates for practitioners in the non-maintained sector.

Department for Children, Schools and Families (2008) *2020 Children and Young People's Workforce Strategy*. London: DCSF. This provides a benchmark for the future because, as part of the vision for the Children and Young People's Workforce in 2020 (Box 2.2), the statement notes that as part of being respected and valued as professionals, they will be 'recognised and rewarded for what they do'.

Notes

1 Parliamentary question to Children's Minister by Maria Miller, Shadow Minister for Children, 14 July 2008.
2 www.cwdcouncil.org.uk
3 www.everychildmatters.gov.uk/deliveringservices/commoncore

References

Cameron, C. (2005) *Building an Integrated Workforce for a Long-term Vision of Universal Early Education and Child Care*. London: Daycare Trust.

Cooke, G. and Lawton, K. (2008) *For Love or Money: Pay, Progression and Professionalisation in the 'Early Years' Workforce*. London: IPPR.

Daycare Trust and Trades Union Congress (TUC) (2008) *Raising the Bar: What Next for the Early Childhood Education and Care Workforce?* London: Daycare Trust.

Department for Children, Schools and Families (DCSF) (2007) *The Children's Plan: Building Brighter Futures*. London: DCSF.

Department for Children, Schools and Families (DCSF) (2008a) *Childcare and Early Years Providers Survey 2007*. DCSF-RR047. London: DCSF.

Department for Children, Schools and Families (DCSF) (2008b) *Building Brighter Futures: Next Steps for the Children's Workforce*. London: DCSF.

Department for Children, Schools and Families (DCSF) (2008c) *2020 Children and Young People's Workforce Strategy*. London: DCSF.

Department for Education and Skills (DfES) (2004a) *Every Child Matters: Change for Children*. London: DfES.

Department for Education and Skills (DfES) (2004b) *Every Child Matters: Next Steps*. London: DfES.

Department for Education and Skills (DfES) (2005a) *Children's Workforce Strategy: Consultation Paper*. London: DfES.

Department for Education and Skills (DfES) (2005b) *Common Core of Skills and Knowledge for the Children's Workforce*. Nottingham: DfES.

Department for Education and Skills (DfES) (2006) *Children's Workforce Strategy. Building a World Class Workforce for Children, Young People and Families. The Government Response to Consultation*. London: HMSO.

Department for Education and Skills (DfES) (2007) *Children's Workforce Strategy: Update – Spring 2007*. London: DfES.

Her Majesty's Treasury, Department for Education and Skills, Department for Work and Pensions, Department for Trade and Industry (HMT, DfES, DWP and DTI) (2004) *Choice for Parents, the Best Start for Children: Ten Year Strategy for Childcare*. London: HMT, DfES, DWP and DTI.

Nursery World (2008) *Training Today*, supplement, Summer.

Owen, S. (2005) *Children Come First: The Future of Childminding Networks*. Bromley: National Childminding Association.

Skills for Business and Children's Workforce Development Council (CWDC) (2008) *Sector Learning Strategy*. Leeds: CWDC.

Ward, H. and Stewart, W. (2008) 'Delay formal classes until 6', *Times Educational Supplement*, 4 July.

CHAPTER 15

LEADING AND WORKING IN MULTI-AGENCY TEAMS

Carol Aubrey

Partnership working has become the dominant way to tackle complex social problems of poverty and social exclusion. Key to this has been the requirement of agencies across the sectors of health, welfare and education to work together to improve outcomes for children. To achieve better integration of services and organizations, the Children Act (2004) required local authorities to enter into partnership arrangements with partners who, in turn, carried reciprocal duties to co-operate. This was intended to lead to integration of key services within Children's Trusts through pooling of resources across education, social services, Connexions, some health services and youth teams, but excluding child protection.

Global trends and influences

Partnership as a concept is poorly defined and in practice it is applied to different practices, underpinned by different models and theories. Percy-Smith (2005) noted that partnerships can refer predominantly to organizational forms or structures, decision-making processes or modes of governance, and desired outcomes, or a combination of all three. Partnership may vary in the sectors involved size and scale, purposes, representation and impacts and in the nature of integration and possible relationships.

Engeström (2008: 15) noted that the notion of 'teams' endures and remains a key feature of the 'envisioned cellular, networked, knowledge-creating company': 'The emphasis … is on project teams, internetworked teams, virtual teams and global teams that use information and communication technologies that enable integrated work group computing networks linking design and problem-solving teams across the globe.' Teams are becoming increasingly distributed in space or brought together on a temporary basis for the life of a project. There is no single linear form in which team arrangements are shaped and the term 'team' is used for an increasing variety of forms of collaborative communities. In such communities boundaries are more fluid than has traditionally been the case. The team must adapt to high levels of technical division of labour and diversity of knowledge, allowing authority to rest on knowledge and expertise rather than status. This demands a level of questioning and reflection on established practices and brings values into public discussion. This new type of work generates mutual exchange between users, producers and the product that results in new relationships and configurations, or *co-configurations*. Engeström also identified what he called *negotiated knotworking* as an emergent way of organizing work, where collaboration between partners is of central importance, formed without rigid, predetermined rules or fixed authority.

Challenges to workforce remodelling?

We should not therefore underestimate the many factors that challenge working relations between professionals. Most fundamental is communication. Pietroni (1992) identified that profession-specific languages and discourses reflect attitudes, values and culturally determined meanings. New entrants to a profession are socialized into disciplines, methods and discourses derived from natural science (for medicine, psychology and health-related fields) or social science (for education and social work), reinforced through specific curricula and training, attitudes and behaviours. Exchanges between practitioners from different professions may well be thwarted by organizational policies, bureaucratic procedures and codes of confidentiality. This leaves unexamined the basic trust and mutual goodwill required between professionals in order to share ideas and collaborate.

With workforce reform and the creation of an integrated qualifications framework, the number of early years professionals has grown. As specialisms within the field increase, so too does the need to establish clear and unambiguous intra-professional as well as inter-professional relationships to avoid role confusion and boundary misunderstandings. At a more general level, reform of the workforce can cause tensions, suspicion and a reluctance to cross boundaries. A climate of organizational change, with policies and procedures focused on improved quality and delivering on outcomes to specific targets increases bureaucracy and managerialism. While collaboration is called for, rivalry fed by differences in professional power, status and esteem may exacerbate territorialism and raise concerns about protecting vested interests. Acknowledging existing tensions and imbalances as well as exploring new roles, responsibilities and functions may be prerequisite to workforce reorganization.

Restructuring of children's services requires professionals to work in new ways. Workforce reform creates higher public expectations and higher levels of accountability for work efficiency and delivery on outcomes. It is necessary to take account of additional costs of time investment to create new strategies, common work practices and ethical procedures, exchange of information, collective ownership of child and family problems, joint monitoring and evaluation of services, as well as joint training to understand one another's professional roles.

Perspectives on professional life

Rawson (1994) distinguished between *groups* of professionals and the differing focus of *operations* of work. He suggested different levels of service integration:

- *intra-professional* working, within a professional group
- *inter-professional* working, across different professional groups
- *joined-up* working that can be at policy, strategic, planning or operational level
- *inter-agency* working that involves two or more agencies working together in a planned manner
- *trans- or interdisciplinary* working, with professionals working in an integrated manner with shared goals and service delivery.

Since then, Frost (2005) distinguished processes of:

- *co-operation* between services, while maintaining independence
- *collaboration* between services, who plan together towards common outcomes
- *co-ordination* between services, who work together in a systematic manner towards shared and agreed goals
- *merger/integration* of different services that become one organization to enhance service delivery.

Integrated working may be linked with management and funding arrangements. Øvretveit et al. (1997) identified the need to manage the total team resources related to job descriptions, work and performance appraisal/supervision, normally undertaken by a senior staff member. It may be:

- clinical advice (the supervisee remains accountable)
- clinical supervision (the senior staff member is accountable)
- management monitoring (adherence to agency procedures), or
- full management (the manager assumes responsibility for both clinical and organizational components).

This leads to different types of management and supervision structure for multi-disciplinary teams:

- *profession-managed* (the professional leader manages and supervises)
- *single manager* (the team manager manages and supervises)
- *joint manager* (management and supervision are shared)
- *team manager-contracted* (professionals are supervised by the professional leader)
- *hybrid* (based on the other four models).

This illustrates the potential lack of clarity in roles and responsibilities that might ensue. The Sure Start national evaluation revealed that the nature of staff contracts did not facilitate the smooth running of the programmes (Belsky et al., 2007). These included short-term attachments, temporary transfer of an employee from one agency to another in a secondment and recruitment of staff, including parents and other community members to train them to work as befrienders, managed by a professional member of staff. The challenge of getting skills right was complicated by workforce shortages and finite finances, so local workers were developed and employment of expensive specialists took place only when essential. Loss of good staff in search of better salaries and employment conditions created higher workloads for remaining staff that lowered job satisfaction and raised staff turnover.

Multi-agency teams

Percy-Smith (2005) noted that developing and sustaining a partnership is not easy and partnerships may also have to confront and overcome barriers during the development phase that are:

- structural (fragmentation of responsibilities across agency boundaries)
- procedural (differences in organizational arrangements, for example, information sharing or accountability)
- financial (differences in budgetary cycles, accounting and funding mechanisms)
- professional/cultural (differences in professional ideology and value)
- status and legitimacy (organizational interests and autonomy)
- inter-organizational dissensus (lack of agreement about organizational responsibilities).

To demonstrate the challenges to multi-agency work at both the 'set-up' and implementation stage two case studies undertaken by the writer and colleagues are presented.

 ## Case study 15.1: working in multi-agency teams

The goal of the first case study (Aubrey et al., 2005) was to capture the development phase of multi-agency working in four local Sure Start five-year programmes at a time when they were gathering together teams of midwives, health visitors and speech therapists, teachers and community development workers, librarians, and care and welfare workers. A goal was to enhance the life chances of young children and their families by improving services in areas of high deprivation. Set up between 1999 and 2003, they were experimental in having freedom to try different ways of working with deprived communities where provision had been poor.

An initial survey of staff and partnership board members and follow-up interviews with representatives of particular agencies, their lead professionals and parents, explored facilitating factors in and barriers to setting up and implementing multi-agency working. We then followed up this work with case studies of joint-agency working: with the speech and language therapy team representing health; an early years worker, educational psychologist and outreach worker representing a special educational needs team; and a social worker representing social care and welfare.

Those who took part also included representatives from the accountable body, in this case the primary care trust (PCT) responsible for resources (budget allocation from central government, human resources and legal arrangements) and the lead agency or local council with strategic management and broader governance responsibilities involving development of the individual programme's vision and mission into a comprehensive strategy owned by stakeholders. The lead agency also provided line management of programme managers to ensure that they worked collaboratively with one another and their own multi-agency teams. Programme managers provided strategic leadership for multi-agency teams and chaired local partnership boards. They were active in holding the programme together through organization and planning, communication and facilitation of teamwork.

Questions that we asked were:

- How much do we really know about effective multi-agency working?
- What are the key factors for their success and what kinds of challenges are raised?

Questionnaires were designed with a series of relevant fixed-choice questions and opportunities for respondents to elaborate in a more open-ended way. The semi-structured interview schedule was designed to probe ambivalent and conflicting responses identified by the survey, using open-ended questions. A total of 79 questionnaires were returned from 159 staff and partnership board members, with four responses from the leading agencies. This gave a 50 per cent response rate.

Regarding local authority structures and boundaries, views on whether these constituted a facilitating factor or hindrance were mixed. Factors thought to facilitate multi-agency working related to being able to exploit systems and people already in place.

Working relationships within teams, with parent agencies, and other voluntary and statutory agencies, were seen as both facilitative and a force for development. The need to understand the roles and responsibilities of others was emphasized by the majority. Several described adopting roles within Sure Start programmes as 'blurring the edges of your role to take on new responsibilities and work in a new way'. Practical factors thought to hinder multi-agency working were different terms and conditions, holiday allowance, pay scales, policies and procedures. Respondents' views on the effect of professional and agency culture on Sure Start practice were mixed, with nearly two-thirds feeling that specific policy and practice differences hindered shared practice. Different data management systems affected information-sharing and impacted on shared practice.

The majority thought resources in the form of staffing arrangements and time investment were facilitative of multi-agency working. Staff had high expectations of working as a multi-agency team, though the development towards a fully integrated team had been slower than desired. This was due to several factors, such as staff not being clear about their roles within the team. Concern was expressed about staff who remained managed and supervised by the parent agency and the tensions that this caused. 'The development of multi-agency working has been slow. "Baggage" brought by the local programme members and, in some cases, with professional management being maintained within statutory agencies needed to be overcome.'

Aims and objectives of local programmes were regarded by the vast majority as facilitative of multi-agency working. 'A number of agencies in the area would not get together formally if it were not for the Sure Start programme.'

Respondents were less certain of whether or not aims of specific agencies competed with local Sure Start programme aims. This they attributed to agencies' working to different government targets and different emphases in the workplace of different professionals, some working on the basis of crisis intervention, others on preventative work. Others felt that targets of different agencies should be seen as complementary and not in competition. Still others felt that such tensions arose from existing work cultures. Several respondents expressed the view that the ethos of all agencies was changing and becoming much more prevention-focused. 'There is a general move towards preventative work which places Sure Start at the heart of the Government's agenda and which all agencies are beginning to recognise.'

Views concerning confidentiality and information-sharing strategies between various agencies were again mixed, with the need expressed for common systems and protocols to reduce the amount of time wasted on this matter. The accountable body was highlighted as a hindrance. 'Lack of information-sharing has ground to a halt several very positive procedures we have tried to put in place, mostly on behalf of the accountable body.'

The need to develop a common language across professional groups was felt by the overwhelming majority and there was a strong sense that language used should be accessible to parents. The majority also felt that poor communication within and between agencies created problems for those working at different levels within agencies. Successful multi-agency work could also be undermined by poor communication between different local authority departments. Several respondents highlighted that despite problems at strategic level, the local programme teams were delivering services in a multi-agency manner.

Views regarding the challenge that budgets and financial arrangements posed to multi-agency working were again mixed. Problems specifically between the lead agency and accountable body and their respective responsibilities were highlighted. Establishing 'good agreements' between the two, in order to reduce possible conflicts of interest, was emphasized. The majority of respondents also felt that non-financial resources created a challenge. Areas highlighted were, allocation of time, provision of staff and physical space in which to work effectively. This resulted in a less effective delivery of services than otherwise might be the case.

By contrast, the majority of respondents felt that the leadership or drive of individual Sure Start programme managers demonstrated clear strategic direction, and tenacity to overcome obstacles to progress and bring together the Sure Start team to effect change. Respondents were very positive about leadership of the programmes. In terms of management strategy, the vast majority felt that multi-agency working was strongly supported and promoted at programme-management level to remain credible at delivery level. A majority felt that Sure Start programme management strategy encouraged 'like-minded individuals who sought new ways of working in order to meet shared goals and work across existing management structures'.

Key themes were then explored in interviews with 34 respondents: representatives of the leading agencies, partnership board representatives and, finally, with team members.

In terms of knowledge of local authority structures, representatives of leading agencies acknowledged a 'lack of capacity' and hence delay in prioritizing support for Sure Start at the strategic level. This resulted in the finance team being employed on temporary contracts. Understanding of and acquaintance with leading agencies by partnership board representatives varied and their views on their effect on multi-agency working were very mixed. Team members' views were similarly mixed and while they acknowledged strategic commitment of leading agencies, it was felt that once they developed more effective ways of working, things could be achieved 'more quickly and efficiently'.

In respect of roles and responsibilities, representatives of leading agencies identified their priorities at strategic and operational levels, but realized that having two leading agencies 'added complexity' and hence challenge to multi-agency working. The accountable body was described as having a less than positive effect on local programmes in terms of time taken to make decisions: 'operational issues of one leading agency created particular challenges'. Partnership board members' views on the roles of leading agencies were again mixed with some uncertainty as to whether Sure Start programme services duplicated or complemented those of their parent agency. Team participants shared the same ambivalent views about the complementary nature of aims of partner agencies and Sure Start programmes.

Regarding staffing, resources and workspace, representatives of leading agencies acknowledged challenges posed by placing staff on temporary contracts and lack of office space. Partnership board representatives and team participants both highlighted recruitment issues and problems of locating staff while suitable premises were being secured.

Data protection and information sharing were acknowledged to be a challenge by all three groups. Reluctance of different agencies to share information was highlighted and lack of data procedures and protocols for data storage and information exchange. It was acknowledged that the strategy for sharing confidential information was being reviewed.

Finally, with respect to communication, multiple channels were advocated by all groups of respondents, with improved IT networks, regular team meetings, direct telephone contact between locations, daily transfer of internal post, as well as informal chats and social events. Challenges were posed at the strategic level in the local authority, and lack of leadership was shown by Sure Start national office with regard to constantly changing policies.

Despite the real enthusiasm of the Sure Start programme survey respondents, effective multi-agency working had not been easy to achieve. What emerged was the impact of leading agencies' line management of programme managers, who had overall control of strategic management, financial arrangements and 'contracting-in' the services of different professionals. Staff with different backgrounds and skills strove towards common goals and shared values, despite barriers to effectiveness and efficiency in the form of constantly shifting policies, local authority structures, lack of space and split sites, and challenges to data storing, information sharing and communication. Though staff clearly had an appetite for the new and 'hybrid' professional being thrown up, challenges related to their joint management by Sure Start programme managers yet remaining employed by a parent agency, who provided both professional leadership and supervision. Navigating local authority structures and constraints, and shifting internal organizational changes as they 'formed and reformed' multi-agency teams in response to changing requirements in a shifting outside environment, may well be described as Engeström's 'knotworking'.

Professionals' experience of multi-agency working

To gain the perspective of agencies, case studies of social work, communication, speech and language therapy services and special educational needs (SEN) support were carried out.

Regarding professional training and socialization, social workers, speech therapists and educational psychologists all hold postgraduate qualifications. But different professionals carry different beliefs about knowledge and their relationship to it, how to investigate it, what to measure and assess, and how to judge claims that result from an investigation, creating practices based upon those beliefs. While value differences between professions cannot be attributed entirely to professional training and experience, it is beyond the scope of this chapter to debate status differences or the relative strength and prestige of their professional associations.

All three professional groups were 'contracted out' part-time to work in Sure Start local programmes, with clear job specifications and service-level agreements. All three were jointly managed by Sure Start programme managers and their own professional leaders, who were also responsible for their clinical supervision. None of them had a defined caseload so were free to pursue preventative approaches to avoid the need for more specialist and targeted services. All subscribed to multi-agency co-operation and multidisciplinary teams as key features of quality and effective service delivery.

In practice, the social worker and psychologist saw few children and families and made few home visits. Their role outside the statutory process of child protection or SEN assessment and statementing was seen as 'supporting' generalist team development through staff development, though this did not appear to be clearly defined in terms of the professional knowledge involved. Neither was it altogether clear how this aspect of their work was monitored and evaluated or its impact judged. At the same time, both of their professional leaders expressed the view that their respective services were neither staffed nor resourced to provide indirect service delivery at the pre-school level.

By contrast, all members of the local programme speech and language therapy team worked to achieve agreed targets to increase the proportion of children having normal levels of communication, language and literacy at the end of the Foundation Stage (at 5 years and at the end of reception year at school) and to increase the proportion of young children with satisfactory language development at age 2. To achieve these targets, they worked in local nurseries providing advice for staff on individual children and working with identified children to help them develop communication, individually and in a group. They provided training for nurseries, parents and professionals, took part in local programme activities with other team members, carried out joint assessment sessions and followed up requests for contact from other personnel, making home visits and working with individual parents. Audits of speech and language skills of 3-year-old children in programme nurseries took place in 2003 and 2006, and annual data collection for a sample of children continued. In terms of effectiveness, speech therapists were keen to secure evidence for benefits of indirect service delivery, gathering case data over a three-year period on early intervention with children who had avoided formal referral to the mainstream speech and language service. Their practice was marked by the clear articulation of a communicable knowledge base. This comprised core clinical activities and training responsibilities that distributed the knowledge base as widely as possible to other professionals and parents, thus working at the preventative level for the majority, yet recognizing the need for more specialized intervention for a small number with longer term additional needs.

Case study 15.2: leading multi-agency teams

Our second case study (Aubrey, 2007) was stimulated by a seminar that brought us together with 25 early childhood leaders and middle leaders. They were asked what leadership meant in their setting, about factors that facilitated and hindered its effectiveness, staff training needs and how capacity could be built in the field. Focus groups stressed that the central goal was valuing learning and having a commitment to ongoing professional development was important to this aspiration. Fundamental was the recognition of its multidisciplinary nature. They felt that commitment to continual professional development and support of staff contributed to successful leadership. Lack of knowledge was characteristic at all levels in the local authority and lack of training was a hindrance. New knowledge, skills and capacity should be brought into the field, through trainers who knew the field, and setting up networks and mentoring systems across the sector was also recommended.

The first stage was to survey the perspectives on early childhood leadership. Asked to rank aspects of the leadership role, again there was broad agreement that the most important aspect of the role was to deliver a quality service and there was a correlation between the quality service delivery and professional development. A principal components analysis of a rating of personal characteristics of effective leaders revealed that leadership meant different things to practitioners with different qualifications and heritages. Those with postgraduate qualifications favoured what we called *leaders as guides*, being warm and knowledgeable and providing coaching, mentoring and guiding. Those with 'other' qualifications, for instance from community development, health, library services or social work, favoured *leaders as strategists.* Those with NVQs favoured *leaders as motivators*, empowering and motivating. Those with postgraduate qualifications also favoured economic competitiveness, business awareness and risk-taking, characteristics of those we called *leaders as entrepreneurial and business oriented.* Practitioners with differential initial qualifications and following different routes into the early childhood sector held different views about early childhood leadership and different attitudes towards this role. Overall, the survey confirmed a unanimity in response regarding the fundamental importance of valuing learning and quality provision. It also uncovered ambivalent attitudes towards entrepreneurial and business skills.

In the second stage, conversations with leaders and staff pursued in more depth key themes that emerged from the survey. Common themes in leadership continued to emphasize raising children's achievements, focusing on personal and social development, enjoyment and well-being and staff performance in the provision of quality care. Understanding the local community (knowledge of children, families and other provision) was another common theme. Mixed and ambivalent responses towards business and entrepreneurial skills again surfaced. According to one, there was a 'fine line to be drawn between making it a business and making it a place for children'. Another said, 'I came here from the private sector because I did not like the idea of making a profit … exploiting those on low wages'. In terms of decision-making, it was felt that their organizations were 'hierarchical at the strategic level and collaborative at the operational level'. Top-down decision-making, reflecting local authority line management of the leaders, was contrasted with collaborative decision-making at team level. Finally, in terms of training, staff had had no experience of leadership training mentioning 'role models and nuggets … what people say about leadership'. Books, studying and first-hand experience were also mentioned. Leaders talked about formal qualifications, short courses, internal training, conferences and meetings. They also stressed contact with other professionals, talking to people and reading but thought that 'experience was more useful than theory'.

The third stage was to follow a variety of leaders into a diverse range of settings. Leaders of multi-agency Sure Start children's centres reported and demonstrated a rich and varied range of activities, that included meetings, paperwork, telephone calls, staff interactions, communication with parents and children, training and visiting other establishments, some events being planned, others unplanned. Meetings played a large part. There were differences between those multi-agency leaders who were working indirectly, through those at the 'front line' with children and families, and those who were more tightly 'coupled' to children's learning, development and care by close 'mentoring' of staff; for instance, they coached staff in assessment and record-keeping, in one case, and in curriculum design and development for the nursery, in another. What distinguished children's centre leaders' activities was their observed co-ordinating of multiple tasks, staff teams and projects, and sharing of decisions related to operating matters or delegating decision-making to project leaders.

The multiple domains of their activity demanded multiple leadership functions. Moreover, integrated children's centre leaders who were located within a wider local authority organization were observed to have their own decisions about staffing, finance and equipment overturned. As one leader mused – who leads the leader? The traditional, 'vertical' and hierarchical decision-making of the local authority contrasted with the more flexible decision-making that took place in close contact with children, parents, community and other stakeholders. This called for a more 'distributed' model of leadership among individuals, groups and networks.

The challenge of change and growth was ever present, with major new building work being planned and carried out. There were meetings with builders, visits to building sites, discussion of plans with colleagues and architects, disputes about pathways and visits to neighbouring centres to get ideas about fitments and furnishings. They found themselves taking on major operational tasks, with a demand for financial management and technical expertise, for which they had no training and hence had to learn 'on the job'. Crucial to this process was the capacity of leaders and staff to accommodate to change:

- *creating a climate for change*, when collaboration was established
- *engaging and enabling the whole organization*, through the development of a culture of collaboration, trust and flexibility
- *sustaining change* (Kotter, 1995) through distributing leadership.

The need for new skills and understanding and, hence training reform across the sector was another feature of the video highlights. Celebration of new NVQs, welcoming trainees on work placements as well as new entrants to the profession, also marked the new pathways into early childhood work.

When the leaders met to share their successes and challenges and compared their video highlights, they commented on the pace of work, their observed tiredness under the weight of job and task overload, but showed a willingness to consider their own discomforts and uncertainties as a source for learning rather than as a weakness. This reflected the culture of trust and openness that they had established as well as the intensification of work associated with multiple innovations and imposed policy change. They marvelled at their capacity to respond to the new national childcare strategy in the local context. They experienced changed local authority structures in terms of increased bureaucracy and felt that the local authority was not moving as fast as leaders in children's centres to create new dynamic patterns in relationships between individuals, teams and partners to create 'collaborative advantage' (Kanter, 1994) or the ability to create and sustain fruitful collaborations and more productive relationships.

Finally, they reflected on their own journeys into leadership, the paths that they had taken and the roles that they had fulfilled. Of note was their recollected lack of support and the perceived attractiveness of receiving support from a more experienced colleague. The position of the early childhood leader in a multi-agency context has reached a critical state of development.

Ways forward?

This chapter has outlined key changes to multi-agency working framed by the Children Act (2004) that have been taken place to raise the skill level of the early years workforce and practitioners' responses to these. It has raised important questions about leadership for this workforce. Significantly, a new National Professional Qualification in Integrated Centre Leadership (NPQICL) was piloted in 2004 by the National College of School Leadership in partnership with Pen Green Research, Training and Development Centre, before being rolled out nationally for children's centre leaders and their deputies. It is the first national programme to address specifically the needs of leaders in multi-agency, early years settings. It is recognized as a qualification in working in multi-agency and multidisciplinary contexts across education, health and social services and as an opportunity to collaborate across the community to provide joined-up high quality services for babies, children and families. National Standards for leaders of children's centres (DfES, 2007) have now been introduced to assess the leadership capacity of NPQICL participants completing their course. The NPQICL is designated an equivalent qualification to the National Professional Qualification for Head teachers (NPQH) and its core purpose is to ensure the centre makes a difference to the lives of the children and families they serve.

Our early childhood leaders are in a very real sense pioneers in delivering the new national childcare strategy and among the first to provide a joined-up service. As noted by Ann Nelson (2006: 5) 'our youngest children deserve the best leaders to prepare them for the challenges they will face as they move forward into adulthood'.

Points for discussion

- Evidence for the effectiveness of multi-agency working processes and outcomes of such work has been difficult to demonstrate. Why do you think that this should be the case?

- At the moment, only children's centre leaders and their deputies are eligible for the NPQICL. Do you think that there is a need to extend this training to other groups?

- What type of joint training would be useful to further multi-agency work?

- Does coaching and mentoring have a role to play?

 Further reading

Anning, A., Cottrell, D., Frost, N., Green J. and Robinson, M. (2006) *Developing Multiprofessional Teamwork for Integrated Children's Services. Research, Policy and Practice*. Maidenhead: Open University Press.

Aubrey, C. (2007) *Leading and Managing in the Early Years*. London: Sage Publications.

Frost, N. (2005) *Professionalism, Partnership and Joined-up Thinking. A Research Review of Front-Line Working with Children and Families*. Dartington: Research in Practice. www.rip.org.uk

Øvretveit, J., Mathias, P. and Thompson, T. (1997) *Interprofessional Working for Health and Social Care*. London: Macmillan.

Percy-Smith, J. (2005) *What Works in Strategic Partnerships for Children*. Ilford: Barnarado's.

References

Aubrey, C. (2007) *Leading and Managing in the Early Years*. London: Sage Publications.

Aubrey, C., Dahl, S. and Clarke, L. (2005) *Multi-agency Working in Sure Start Projects: Successes and Challenges*. Coventry: The University of Warwick.

Belsky, J., Barnes, J. and Melhuish, E. (eds) (2007) *The National Evaluation of Sure Start. Does Area-Based Early Intervention Work?* Bristol: Policy Press.

Department for Education and Skills (DfES) (2004) *Children Act*. London: DfES.

Department of Education and Skills (DfES) (2007) *National Standards for Leaders of Sure Start Children's Centres*. London: DfES.

Engeström, Y. (2008) *From Teams to Knots: Activity-Theoretical Studies of Collaboration and Learning at Work*. Cambridge: Cambridge University Press.

Frost, N. (2005) *Professionalism, Partnership and Joined-up Thinking. A Research Review of Front-Line Working with Children and Families*. Dartington: Research in Practice. www.rip.org.uk

Kanter, R.M. (1994) 'The art of alliances: collaborative advantage', *Harvard Business Review*, July–August: 7–17.

Kinder, K. (2001) *Multi-agency Working*. Slough: NFER.

Kotter, J. (1995) 'Leading change – why transformation efforts fail', *Harvard Business Review*, 73: 59–68.

Nelson, A. (2006) 'Foreword', in C. Aubrey *Reflecting on Early Childhood Leadership. A Research-based Resource Pack to Support Leadership Training for Local, Regional and National Needs*. Coventry: University of Warwick.

Øvretveit, J., Mathias, P. and Thompson, T. (1997) *Interprofessional Working for Health and Social Care*. London: Macmillan.

Percy-Smith, J. (2005) *What Works in Strategic Partnerships for Children*. Ilford: Barnarado's.

Pietroni, P.C. (1992) 'Towards reflective practice – languages of health and social care', *Journal of Interprofessional Care*, 6(1): 7–16.

Rawson, D. (1994) 'Models of inter-professional working: likely theories and possibilities', in A. Leathard (ed.), *Going Interprofessional: Working Together for Health and Welfare*. London: Routledge.

INDEX

Added to a page number 'f' denotes a figure and 't' denotes a table.